W0091622

Advance Praise

If you want to learn the lessons of Nobel Prize winning economists such as Markowitz, Fama, Kahneman, Thaler and Shiller on investing in the stock market, then Abhishek's book is your best bet. The book will not only teach you the scientific and behavioural theories which are essential to creating a robust portfolio, but it will also take you to a real-world tour of Dalal Street and show how you can bypass most of the financial predators to come out as a real winner.

Ram Kumar Kakani, *Professor of Finance, IIM Kozhikode*

With *Index Investing*, Abhishek has made a bold attempt to bring out the ugly truth of the Dalal Street. A truth that has been gloriously guarded by the financial intermediaries such as stockbrokers, fund managers and marketers. Like Yin and Yang, Abhishek has meticulously balanced his book to be simple and straightforward for common investors as well as thorough enough to be featured in the bookshelves of the academicians.

Pulkit Srivastava, *Co-founder, GeekyWorks*

Index Investing is an eye-opener for both the common and self-proclaimed sophisticated investors on why investing in the equity market is not what they have been made to believe and why their money doesn't grow as advertised by the industry. The book takes a scientific approach with references from academia including the works of Nobel laureates and clearly shows how the financial system works and who is the end beneficiary. If you want to avoid the investment traps and work towards your own financial well-being, you must read this book.

Ankit Singh, *Senior Associate, Morgan Stanley*

If you are an investor and didn't know about the inherent conflict of interest between those who invest their hard-earned monies and the people who manage those investments, then you will do a great benefit to yourself by reading this book. *Index Investing* which is a low-cost, low-risk and tax-efficient approach to stock market investing is one solution for which your kids and grandkids will ever be thankful to you.

Suman Saurabh, *Assistant Professor of Finance, IIT Kanpur*

Be it the unguided common investors or misguided experts, walking through the labyrinth of the equity market is always full of conceptual and emotional challenges. Abhishek takes readers on an eye-opening journey of this mysterious world busting many myths with lucid concepts, sound reasoning and practical analogies. Readers will love the intellect of the book and will thank him for its easy practical solution.

Somesh Srivastava, *M&A Consultant, PricewaterhouseCoopers*

Indian mutual fund industry has been up and running for over 30 years and it is for the first time that a book has been written which brings out its real picture. No sales pitch, no promotion and no false promise. Only the reality which has been kept hidden till now by the gatekeepers of the fund industry.

Abhinav Anand, *Associate Vice President,*
Mortgage Industry Advisory Corporation

As with every business, the investment management business is not a story of golds and glories. At the bottom of this industry, there is a truth that is ugly and brutal. The genius of Abhishek is that he has brought out this truth in a spectacular fashion and great detail. More importantly, he has backed all his inferences with empirical evidence and researches done by noted academicians. If you want to avoid the snares that lurk in money management, and save yourself lots of money, you must read this book.

Jugal Rasilay, *Associate Vice President, ICICI Lombard*

INDEX
investing

INDEX
investing

A LOW-COST, LOW-RISK STRATEGY TO INVESTMENT SUCCESS

Abhishek Kumar

SAGE | Response Business Books

Los Angeles | London | New Delhi
Singapore | Washington DC | Melbourne

First published in 2020 by

SAGE Publications India Pvt. Ltd
B1/I-1 Mohan Cooperative Industrial Area
Mathura Road, New Delhi 110 044, India
www.sagepub.in

SAGE Publications Inc
2455 Teller Road
Thousand Oaks, California 91320, USA

SAGE Publications Ltd
1 Oliver's Yard, 55 City Road
London EC1Y 1SP, United Kingdom

SAGE Publications Asia-Pacific Pte Ltd
18 Cross Street #10-10/11/12
China Square Central
Singapore 048423

Published by Vivek Mehra for SAGE Publications India Pvt. Ltd. Typeset in 11/14 pt Arno Pro by Fidus Design Pvt. Ltd, Chandigarh.

Library of Congress Control Number: 2020933006

ISBN: 978-93-5388-325-6 (PB)

SAGE Team: Namarita Kathait, Madhurima Thapa, Ankit Verma and Anupama Krishnan

Disclaimer

The ideas, concepts and the principles discussed in the book are of the author's alone and are in no way associated with any of the institutes/organization that the author has been part of/affiliated with in the past or present.

Further, these ideas and principles are designed to provide information that the author believes to be accurate based on his research and experience. The publication is sold with the understanding that neither the author nor the publisher is offering individualized advice tailored to any specific portfolio or to any individual's particular needs. If legal advice or other expert assistance is required, the service of a competent professional should be sought.

While the author and the publisher have used their best efforts in preparing this book, they make no representations or warranties with respect to the accuracy or completeness of the information contained herein, and both the author and the publisher specifically disclaim any responsibility for any liability, loss, or risk, personal or otherwise, which might be incurred as a consequence, directly or indirectly of the use and application of any of the contents of this book.

Dedicated

To
my loving parents

Thank you for choosing a SAGE product!
If you have any comment, observation or feedback,
I would like to personally hear from you.

Please write to me at **contactceo@sagepub.in**

Vivek Mehra, Managing Director and CEO, SAGE India.

Contents

Preface

If there is one place where misconceptions, myths and misinformation rule over knowledge, truths and facts, then it has to be stock market where the big market players, namely mutual fund houses, brokerage firms, investment banks and media outlets have played a major role in keeping the masses and end investors ignorant of some simple facts and practical knowledge. This mass ignorance about some of the fundamental principles of investment has resulted into three major consequences, namely a low participation of the investors in the Indian equity market, a below par investment return for those invested in the market and a huge income for the mutual fund houses and brokerage firms in the form of fat fees and commissions.

So what are these misconceptions and misinformation which have plagued the Indian equity market? Well, we can answer this question by simply analysing the profile of the end investors about what they think of the market and, most importantly, what they think of themselves. Presently, there are four different types of people when it comes to investing in the equity market as detailed further.

- The first set thinks that the equity market is like a gamble where one can win only if luck is on their side. Result: they stay away from the market and, thus, lose a lot of their money by missing the ride of the growth of Indian economy.

- The second set thinks that one can make easy money in the equity market by carefully analysing and studying stocks. They believe studying the trends, reading books on security analysis and value investing, and taking such courses will enable them to pick just the right stocks and will help them make millionaires. Result: they invest on their own by carefully cherry-picking the stocks and get beaten by the big players, namely institutional investors who systematically milk them till such individuals don't have much to offer and are forced to exit the market. Again, a big loss for such individual investors.

- The third set thinks that they can't pick stocks on their own so they hand over their money to the mutual funds thinking that they would get the benefits of the expertise of security analysts and fund managers. They feel that their mutual funds will help them earn a market beating returns for a very nominal fees and they can relax while their funds keep on buying good stocks on their behalf. Result: they invest with the 'hot' mutual funds, pay huge fees and commissions, earn a suboptimal return and finally get dejected.

- The fourth set of investors thinks that it is very difficult, if not impossible, to earn a market beating return and are happy with the return the overall market delivers to them. Result: they invest in index fund and let the market do its job.

Now there have been numerous academic researches on the beliefs of all these sets of investors, and the consensus of most of these researches is that only one set of investors is 'more' right than the others. The other three beliefs are misconceptions and a wrong understanding of the equity market spread by the mutual funds, stockbrokers and media houses.

The purpose of this book is to dispel those misconceptions, myths and misinformation which are being spoon-fed to the common masses by these financial croupiers and to bring equity in the equity market. Further, the book will show which set of investors is 'more' right and how they can change their approach to investing by being a more informed and better investor.

Now as you start reading this book, let me help you with its broad outline so that you know beforehand what to expect in each section. The book has been divided into four parts covering the four essential parts of the investment process: the Theory of Investing, the Psychology of Investing, the Business of Investing and the Solution for the investors.

The Theory of Investing brings out the scientific approach of investing developed by the finest of the academicians and researchers as it surveys some of the important theories and data relevant to everyday investing. Just like before cooking a meal, it is imperative to know and understand its recipe; the same is the case with the investments. Without understanding the basic theories and the factors influencing the stock market and the return, you are bound to make mistakes—mistakes which might cost you too much. This part of the book is the recipe you need to know if you want to cook a good meal.

The Psychology of Investing talks about the relatively new field of behavioural finance and shows how human mind functions when they take their everyday decisions and why many a times such choices may not be the most rational and optimal for them. This part of the book brings out the various human biases, especially those relevant to investment in the equity market and shows how those biases act as an impediment to the growth of the investor's wealth.

The Business of Investing presents the real picture of today's investment world and shows how the major players, namely security analysts, fund managers, stockbrokers and financial journalists work. It also throws light on the challenges faced by these players—both structural and behavioural—and how these challenges handicap them from doing their duty. This part of the book is your opportunity to grab the lens and see the real world of Dalal Street.

The Solution, as the name suggests, presents the practical solution to all the investment woes of the end investors and guides them how to build a robust portfolio which will not only survive in market lows and highs but will also provide the investors the necessary support when they would need them the most.

I hope this book serves its purpose of dispelling myths and ignorance, and, at the same time, help its readers understand the realities of the equity market. Additionally, you will learn the true working of the investment industry—the working which has been till now kept hidden from the outside world by its gatekeepers, namely the investment managers, stockbrokers and media houses.

Wishing you a great reading experience and may this book become a companion of yours which would guide you into this mysterious world of equity market, which isn't mysterious at all.

Acknowledgements

I started writing this book when I was studying at the University of California, Los Angeles. Now as I was about to graduate, I was faced with a dilemma whether I should start searching for the job and join the corporate workforce or should I take a break, continue my research and complete the book which I had been writing with all my passion. I wanted to finish it off because I knew once I resume my corporate job, I wouldn't be able to do justice to my writing. Also, I didn't want to wait much because I knew I have learnt something useful which will benefit the common investors. But at the same time, I understood that it was too risky a proposition because it's usually hard to get back to the corporate world once you take a break. And yes, we had our share of financial liabilities which we needed to take care of.

So it was at this time of uncertainty that my wife Rakshmi backed me and said to continue writing while she would carry on shouldering the financial burden of the family. And once I had her support, I took the plunge, immersed myself completely into my research and writing, and didn't stop till the entire manuscript was ready. Rakshmi, a big thanks to you. You have always been my rock and I feel blessed to have you.

Writing a book in all your solitude, though may feel appealing, is not an easy task. You got to keep your focus intact so as not to lose any content and at the same time keep yourself rejuvenated and refreshed so as to keep yourself creative in presenting those contents. With my wife in her office all through the day, my three-year-old daughter Arshika kept me engaged and lively as I continued penning down my thoughts. Thanks to you my sweetheart. I know you are young to read it but your contribution to the book is something non-descriptive.

To my friends Ateet Omer and Pulkit Srivastava for reviewing the book and providing feedback which helped me make it more useful for the readers. It was Ateet who read the very first draft of the book and suggested to make the book more readable for the common investors by putting the name of the professors and researchers in the references rather than keeping them as part of the main body of the text.

I would also like to express my sincere thanks to the editorial team at SAGE Publications India Pvt. Ltd. Special mention to Namarita Kathait, Ankit Verma and Madhurima Thapa who played the key role as we worked through the book's development, editing and publication.

Finally, I would like to thank all my teachers and professors without whose lessons I wouldn't have been able to be in a position to write something on a subject which is not only critical but essential to one's wellbeing.

PART

1

THE THEORY OF INVESTING

Do Your Homework!
Know the Rules of the Game before Playing the Game

In 1671, the growing and powerful Mughal Empire which had already established its base and supremacy in the mainland of Indian subcontinent led an expedition under the command of Kachwaha King to extend its empire into the Kingdom of Ahom—the present-day Assam. The Ahoms were led by its then commander Lachit Borphukan and the battle was fought on the Brahmaputra River at Saraighat, now in Guwahati.

The Mughal army, which was much big and powerful, possessed only rudimentary maps and had almost no knowledge of the climate or the terrain of the Brahmaputra basin. It came as a no surprise that the invasion was a disaster. Although much weaker, the Ahom army defeated the bold and powerful Mughal army by brilliant use of the terrain, clever diplomatic negotiations to buy time, guerrilla tactics, psychological warfare, military intelligence and by exploiting the sole weakness of the Mughal forces—its navy.

The Battle of Saraighat draws a parallel between the approach taken by the Mughal army and that of the present-day investors. Most of the investors muster the same degree of planning and understanding in their investing as did the Mughals for the Battle of Saraighat. Without an understanding of the history of the stock market, the relationship between return and risk, the cost of investing, the inter-play between the various players involved in the game and the mechanics of well-designed portfolio, these investors are doomed to failure, much like the Mughal Army. And that is what is happening to most of the investors. People are losing their money in the equity market, not because it's a tough game to play but because people have not taken out time to understand the rules of the game and how to play it smartly.

But you would say that investing is not a battle and probably we wouldn't need that much planning and preparation before we invest. After all, we have the professionals' help in the form of financial advisors, stockbrokers and fund managers at our disposal. Wrong!

The reality is that the professionals whom you consider as your allies are not your friends. Your financial progress and prosperity are at stake in the hands of the very people whom you consider your allies and to claim your financial freedom, you have to win against them.

In my discussion with the average Indian investors who are responsible family people and who invest regularly and diligently to create a better future for their family, I have realized that they tend to be touchingly naïve about stockbrokers, mutual fund companies and financial advisors. The truth is that the interests of all these financial players are highly divergent from those of yours and you are engaged in a continuous battle with the entities and players of the investment industry. Further, losing that battle would put you at an increased risk of running out of wealth far sooner than you'd like. As you will see later in the book, you will realize how the modern financial services industry is designed solely to serve itself and how it exists almost entirely for one purpose: the extraction of fees and commissions from investing people like you and me. William Bernstein, the noted neurosurgeon turned financial author in his book *The Investors Manifesto*, says:

> *Investors should always be wary of the investment industry. People do not seek employment in investment banks, brokerage houses, and mutual fund companies with the same motivations*

as those who choose to work in fire departments or elementary schools. Whether investors know it or not, they are engaged in an ongoing zero-sum, life-and-death struggle with piranhas, and if rigorous precautions are not taken, the financial services industry will strip investors of their wealth faster than they can say 'Bernie Madoff'.[1,2]

So how do you—the average retail investors—who are not fully armoured with the knowledge and technical sophistication of security analysis, factor investing, greeks and the supercomputers running the complex algorithm of picking stocks can compete with the professionals who claim to possess such knowledge and resources?

The answer lies in the simplicity and common sense. With the understanding of the stock market and factors affecting the stock returns, you will do as well as the professionals—perhaps even better as you would not be bowed down by the structural hindrances[3] most of the professional face in their job. And it is because of these constraints that they fail to deliver what they claim to promise and that is the reason why you as the retail investors can use their weakness to your competitive advantage and do much better than what these professionals do.

Now, let's get going with an open and blank mind and see how we can fine-tune our understanding to get the best result for ourselves.

---

[1] Bernie Madoff is an American investment advisor and market maker who has been convicted of running the largest Ponzi scheme in world history.

[2] William Bernstein, *The Investor's Manifesto: Preparing for Prosperity, Armageddon, and Everything in Between* (Hoboken, NJ: Wiley, 2009).

[3] Most of the professional money managers are handicapped not because they are unintelligent but because of the economic environment and the industry structure under which they operate. Details are present in Parts II and III of the book.

2 The Act of Faith
Without Trust, There Is No Investment

In a discussion with some of my friends, who were MBA from top Indian business schools and either worked in investment banks (I-Bank) or asset management companies (AMC), we realized that we did not share a common view on *investments*. During that conversation, I was asked to state my definition of 'investment'.

I would have easily vomited the definition of 'investment' listed in a typical finance book had this question come from someone else. But since the question was coming from a friend who worked as an investment banker, I knew I had to be very accurate in my reply. Thinking of no better answer at that time, I told him I would get back to him sometime soon.

The truth is that the MBAs from top business schools working in I-Banks and AMCs don't agree on one proper definition of investment. Then what can be the common understanding of investment for people who may not be so much financially literate?

WHAT IS AN INVESTMENT?

In his classic book *Common Sense on Mutual Funds*, John Bogle, who is the founder of Vanguard, the world's second biggest AMC says, 'Investing is an act of faith'.

Think over it for some time. When you purchase certain shares of a particular company or a mutual fund, you entrust your capital to the corporate stewards—CEOs, CFOs and the fund managers—with the hope that their efforts will generate high rate of return on your invested money and you would receive back your money along with the dividends and capital appreciation of your desire. And when you invest in an index fund mimicking a benchmark or the entire Indian stock market, you basically profess your faith that the long-term future of the India Inc. and the country's economy will be bright and better.

However, just to say that 'investing is an act of faith' wouldn't seem good enough for some of the people. So let me add some technicalities to it to make it more complete. First of all, investment is the deferral of your present consumption for future consumption. Whenever you invest in something, you forgo your present consumption (which you could have bought with the money invested) for a more desirable future consumption.

Second, it is an act of purchasing assets to gain profit in the form of reasonably *predictable* income in the form of dividends, interest and/or capital appreciation over the *long term*. The keywords here are 'predictable' and 'long term', and it is these two words which differentiate *investment* from *speculation*. A speculator is the one who buys or shorts[1] stocks in an attempt to earn some short-term gain over the next few days, weeks or probably months. An investor, on the other hand, buys (and usually never shorts) stocks or funds which are likely to produce a dependable future stream of cash returns in the form of dividends and capital gains when measured over years or probably decades.

However, most of the people in today's world who claim to be an investor rarely put their money into some stocks or funds thinking 10 years or 20 years down the line. What most of them do is see the

---

[1] Shorting stock which is also known as short selling involves selling of stocks which is not owned by the seller. Usually, when a person thinks that the stock is overvalued and is likely to decline in value in near future, he/she borrows those stocks (mostly from his stockbroker) and sells them in the market at the present price. And when the stock declines in value in line with his/her prediction, then he/she buys that stocks at the lower value and returns it to the lender (stockbroker) from whom he/she had borrowed initially, thereby making the profit by selling high and buying low. Shorting stocks is usually considered a risky proposition as it involves leverage (borrowing) and there are chances that he/she may lose a lot of money during 'short squeeze'.

past two–three years performance of a particular stock or fund, listen to the claims and opinions of the self-appointed market experts coming on TV shows and business magazines, discuss with the stock market enthusiast friends and colleagues, and then put their money into the zeroed-down stock or fund hoping to earn better than average return. A wrong approach for a sensible investment, I would say.

Now you would say what is wrong with this approach. The problem with this approach is twofold. First, past performance of any stock or fund is in no way an indication of its future return. The equity market is simply unpredictable on any short-term month-to-month or year-to-year basis. We should not and cannot expect it to be predictable, nor should we base our investment decisions on impulses inspired by the conventional wisdom of the day. If there was any easy method of harnessing prediction (only if there exists such methods), then all of us would be millionaires and billionaires in our own league.

Second, the opinion of anyone including the self-appointed experts on the future prediction of the stock market is as good as the as the prediction of the man sitting on the railway platform with a parrot who tells you about your future based on the card picked up by his parrot. Now you would say that the experts would have done some analysis and their prediction must hold some value. Well, as you will see in later chapters, the analysis (if any) carried out by these experts are done with an agenda and hold no value for the common investors like you and me.

Further, to impress the common people with their so-called market acumen, these experts and their firms also come out with investment newsletters with the notion that the investor who would subscribe to and read these newsletters can indeed time the market. The reality is not what they want you to believe. These newsletters are filled with reports on the overall economy, sector and individual companies and do you no good other than increasing your general awareness which can be used for gossiping on a coffee table or a beer bar. And if you thought that you could use this knowledge to reap extraordinary rewards from your investment, then you have got it wrong. In fact, some of the studies and researches have concluded that you would benefit if you would pick the worst newsletter and do the opposite of what they recommend.[2]

During one of my classes at UCLA Anderson School of Management, one of my professors shared how people form opinion of the stock market and of mutual funds. He said that people these days are always on the lookout for seeking some information which will help them pick some hot stock or fund so that they are able to edge out the investing crowd. Guess what? Almost all the investors share this trait of finding information and marching past their neighbour silently. And whenever there is a demand, there is a supply and so we have an army of experts doling out opinions and views of the market, thereby making money by increasing the TRP of their respective TV channels. And what are these opinions and views? Well, open a business news channel and you will hear one 'blah' from one expert. Switch to another and you would hear a different 'blah'. Switch to third and there is a third 'blah' and the process continues. At the end of the day, the normal investor would have formed his opinion of the market. And what is his/her opinion. Well, it is nothing but the average of all the 'blahs' that he/she listened to all through the day.

So how should you as a rational investor form an opinion of the stock market and choose your pick from the platter of stocks and funds?

The answer is that you don't need to form an opinion. Second, you need to read the story of 'Chance: The Gardener' from the book *Being There* by Jerzy Kosinski.

---

[2] Graham R. John, and Harvey R. Campbell, 'Grading the Performance of Market Timing Newsletters', *Financial Analysts Journal* 53, no. 6 (1997 Nov–Dec).

CHANCE: THE GARDENER

Chance is a middle-aged man who lived all alone in a rich man's mansion. He had kept himself reserved to the extent that he never thought of moving outside the mansion to see the life out there in the world. He was happy, for all his needs were met in the mansion and he was content with his solitude and tending to the needs of his master. He, however, had two interests: watching television and looking after the garden outside his home.

So one fine day, the mansion's owner dies, and *Chance* is forced to move out of the mansion. On his first foray into the outside world, he is hit by the limousine of a powerful industrialist who happened to be an advisor to the president. He is carried to the industrialist's home by his wife. During the drive, he identifies himself as 'Chance: The Gardener'. However, the lady confuses it to be 'Chauncey Gardiner'.

When the president visits the industrialist, Chauncey Gardiner happens to be in the meeting room where the president and the industrialist talk about the slowdown of the American economy, crashing of the stock market and how all the big companies are under stress. Unexpectedly, the president addresses our 'Chance: The Gardener' and asks, 'And you, Mr Gardiner? What do you think about the bad season on The Street?'

Chance shrank. He felt that the roots of his thoughts had been suddenly yanked out of their wet earth and thrust, tangled, into the unfriendly air. He stared at the carpet. Finally, he spoke: 'In a garden', he said, 'growth has its season. There are spring and summer, but there are also fall and winter. And then spring and summer again. As long as the roots are not severed, all is well, and all will be well'.

He raised his eyes and sees that the President was quite pleased by his response.

> *'I must admit, Mr Gardiner', the President said, 'that what you've just said is one of the most refreshing and optimistic statements I've heard in a very, very long time'. He rose and stood erect, with his back to the fireplace. 'Many of us forget that nature and society are one! Yes, though we have tried to cut ourselves off from nature, we are still part of it. Like nature, our economic system remains, in the long run, stable and rational, and that's why we must not fear to be at its mercy.'.... 'We welcome the inevitable seasons of nature, yet we are upset by the seasons of our economy! How foolish of us!'[3]*

The lesson which the president learnt from our simple and polite Chance is worth remembering. As long as the roots are not severed, all is well, and all will be well. And this is the approach which you as a rational investor should undertake in your investment journey if you truly want to benefit anything out of the equity market and growth of our India Inc. The reality is that you don't need to form an opinion on the short-term movement of the equity market, and you don't need to hear the opinions of someone blabbering *blahs* on TV shows, but you do need to have a trust in the long-term growth of India Inc. And in case you can't trust the long-term growth of India Inc., then your money in the bank deposits and real estate won't be as valuable as you would like them to be.

So worry not and get prepared for a ride which will change your entire perspective of equity market. And when you would have the complete knowledge of the market and an understanding of how our human biases play a role in our investment decision, you will be better equipped to take a more informed and objective call. And that is the purpose of this book—to help you become a better and informed investor.

---

[3] Jerzy Kosinki, *Being There* (New York, NY: Harcourt Brace Jovanovich, 1970).

3

No Pain No Gain
Only by Shouldering Risk, One Can Expect to Earn a Return

Over the past few years since I developed a curious desire to understand the subject of personal finance and investments and at the same time disseminate my learnings through my books to people, I have talked to many people on this topic. And whenever I have talked about the factors one should consider while investing, I have got to hear only two of them—return and time—with the former being the prime consideration.

Why do we get such response from the investing public? It is because of the compound interest formula that we studied in our high school where our return is raised to the power of time and the resulting value is multiplied with the principal amount of invested capital to get the total amount that we would receive at maturity.

It is true that return and time are important factors to be considered when one is putting his/her hard-earned money into the hands of corporate stewards. But these two factors don't complete the picture. And that is the reason why people get suboptimal return on their investment and blame the equity market. To invest in equity market with an incomplete knowledge is not only injurious to your wealth but may also leave you with some permanent scar on your psyche that you would never return to the stock market again. And that is what I have seen happening to many people who started out with all the energy and enthusiasm when they took part in the stock market but are now settled with earning a mediocre return on their fixed deposits.

Here are some additional factors that should be considered when one starts investing and how these factors interact among themselves.

THE FOUR DIMENSIONS OF INVESTMENT

Whenever you invest your money in the hope of earning return over your investment period, you automatically do two more things, that is, you carry a risk and you incur a cost during this investment process. And these two additional factors complete the four dimensions of investment.

The process is something like this—when you *invest* in the equity market either directly or through the mutual fund route, you incur a *cost* as you would have to pay fees and commissions to your stockbroker/fund manager, and you take a *risk*. The risk here is that you may not get the return as per your expectation or that you may lose your money either partially or, in some cases, a great bulk of it. Then, over a period of *time*, you earn some *return* (positive in

Figure 3.1. The Four Dimensions of Investment

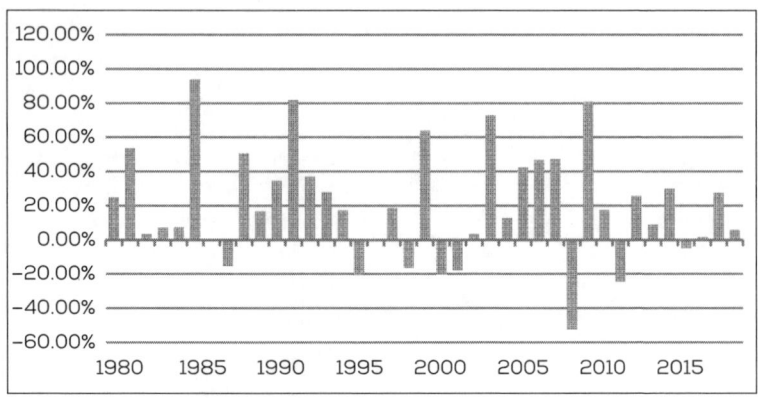

Figure 3.2. BSE Sensex Returns, 1980–2018
Source: BSE.

the base value of 100 as on 1 April 1979. Figure 3.2 is of the annual return with a holding period of one year generated by the BSE Sensex.

As you would see in Figure 3.2, there have been periods when the investors didn't earn any considerable return. Also, there have been periods when the investors kept on losing their money— the case being the dot-com bubble crash of the early 2000s and the 2008 Financial Crisis—and the investors started moving away from the equity market. However, most people forgot what our 'Chance—The Gardner' had told that just like there are natural seasons, there are seasons in our investments also and as long as the roots of the tree is not completely severed; all is well, and all will be well. The same happened to the Indian stock market when after the declines of 1998, early 2000s and 2008; the market bounced back in 1999, 2003 and 2009 by delivering a handsome return of 64 per cent, 73 per cent and 81 per cent, respectively.

Now you may be wondering that why did I present the historical data to you when it is said that past performance doesn't indicate or guarantee any future return. It is because to make you understand and appreciate that stocks can behave badly for years at a time. They can keep on going down and down and will test your patience and capability to hold on to your investments even when you are losing your money. However, there is one peculiar characteristic of stock returns—they are *mean reverting*, that is, a series of bad years is likely to be followed by a series of good ones, repairing some of the damage and, in many instances, will make up for all the bad returns the investors had to bear during those bad years. Unfortunately, this is a two-edged sword, as a series of very good years is likely to be followed by bad ones. The history confirms it and the future will be no different. However, when the pattern will repeat and after how much time will it repeat, nobody knows and that is the real beauty of stock market.

Once, Charles Munger, who is the renowned investor and partner of Warren Buffett at Berkshire Hathaway, was asked what an individual should do to become a better investor. His response was, 'Read History, Read History, Read History'. Understanding history is not only critical in the financial market but also in other fields as well. For instance, airline pilots are made to undergo a rigorous training before they are allowed to fly an actual flight. They spend countless hours in flight simulators flying through simulated storms, rains and other unusual crises so that they are accustomed to being calm, composed and rational during such stressful events and know exactly what to do when faced with such situation. Similarly, the more you study history of the stock market and understand how they have behaved in the past, the better you would be equipped to act rationally when faced with stressful situations that you would encounter in your investment journey.

My purpose of presenting the historical data of Indian stock market was the same—to help you understand what you can expect from the stock market. When you invest in the stock market, you should always remember that during your investment journey you will continue to experience seasons of decline, but you can be confident that they will be succeeded by the reappearance of the long-term pattern of growth. And that is why it is said that if you want to invest with success, you must be a long-term investor.

So how do we measure the risk of our investment and how do we quantify it? Are there any specific metric that we should look at or just go with our hunch or trust on the words of our stockbrokers.

Well, we don't need to do all these as this problem was solved by a gentleman called Harry Markowitz nearly 70 years ago.[2] A grocer's son from northwest Chicago, Markowitz sped through a special two-year undergraduate program at the University of Chicago. And while he was pursuing his PhD—working and understanding the stock market—he wanted to develop a scientific approach with which common investors could invest in the equity market. And, thus, he found the metric with which the common investors could gauge the riskiness of a stock which was nothing, but the old statistical measure called *standard deviation*.[3]

Now if you are from a non-maths or non-engineering background, don't get bogged down by this term. Standard deviation is nothing, but another name given to the *variability of a data*. If a particular datum varies a lot, meaning if it can have a wide *range of values*, then it will have a higher *standard deviation*. For example, consider two classrooms full of students. In the first classroom, we have students from Grade 1 to Grade 10 and in the second classroom we have students only from Grade 4. Suppose we are interested in measuring the height of the students. Definitely, the heights of students from the first classroom will vary a lot than those from the second classroom. So we can say that the standard deviation of heights of students from the first classroom will be higher than that of the second classroom.

Similarly, if your investment return over a given period of time varies a lot then it will have a high standard deviation and if your investment return varies little then it will have a small standard deviation. And if the investment return doesn't vary at all (a perfectly

---

[2] It's sad that our stockbrokers haven't learnt this lesson yet as they get more training on selling than on understanding the nuances of finance.
[3] Harry Markowitz was one of the pioneers to apply mathematics and statistics to the analysis of stock market and developed multiple theories and models for creating optimal portfolio. He won the Nobel Prize in economics in 1990.

safe investment), then its standard deviation will be zero. So, in the earlier example of two investment alternatives, while alternative one had the standard deviation of zero, alternative two had the standard deviation of 19 per cent. Thus, we can very easily conclude that *an investment return with a high standard deviation is riskier than the one with a low standard deviation.* Put differently, an investment with return having a wide range of values is riskier than the one with a narrow range of values because for the one with a wide range of values the uncertainty about our future expected return increases.

Now, if you would observe the Sensex returns that were presented in Figure 3.2, you would notice that the returns vary a lot. In fact, it ranged from a positive return of 94 per cent in 1985 to a negative return of 52 per cent in 2008. So we can very easily say that the stock market return has a high standard deviation and it is risky as there is a good chance of earning a very high return and an equally good chance of losing a lot of your money.

Now let us see the returns generated by a bond. In Figure 3.3, I have plotted the returns of 10-year sovereign bonds. You would notice that the range of bond returns is very small as compared to the range of stock returns. In fact, this bond has delivered a maximum return of 31 per cent and a minimum return of negative

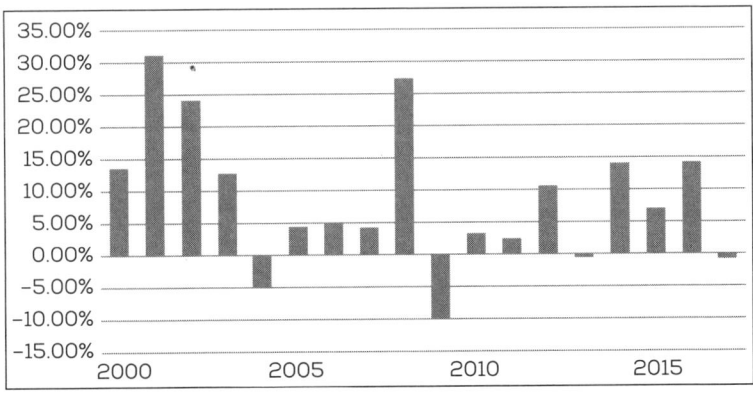

Figure 3.3. 10-Year Sovereign Bond Returns, 2000–2017
Source: BSE.

Think of this in another way. If there is a risky investment proposition where there is a good chance of making some money and an equally good chance of losing your money, then you wouldn't part with your money so easily. You would demand a higher return from the investment because you fear that you might lose some part of your invested money. So to compensate for the higher risk, you ask for a higher return. However, if there is some safe investment opportunity, you wouldn't ask for a higher return as there would be many investors ready to invest in it and the expected return from that investment would decline. So, distilled to its essence, *investing is all about earning a return in exchange for shouldering risk.*[7]

So if you want to earn high returns, you will need to put your money into some risky assets and prepare yourself to suffer grievous losses from time to time. And if you want perfect safety, resign yourself to low return (case in point being fixed deposit where you are certain to get your return but that is much less than what you usually desire). In fact, the best way to spot investment fraud is the promise of safety and very high returns. If someone offers you this, then turn 180° and do not walk—run. Run away from that person and run away from the investment opportunity he/she was discussing and offering you to put your money into because that was not an investment opportunity; it was a *Ponzi* scheme.

Now, this fundamental law of the investment is so important that I'm going to repeat it:

High investment returns cannot be earned without taking substantial risk. Safe investments produce low returns.

---

[7] The underlying assumption of the above explanation is that most of the investors are risk-averse, meaning that people usually don't like to take unnecessary risk.

MANAGING THE RISK–MODERN PORTFOLIO THEORY

Having understood what risk is and how it affects the return of our investments, let's dive a little deeper and see if there is any way in which we can increase our return and/or reduce risk at the same time and, thus, get a higher return for the same risk or the same return with a lower risk. The answer is yes, and the solution was provided by Markowitz again.

When Markowitz was analysing the risk and return in the stock market and the trade-off between the two, he realized that the riskiness of a portfolio of securities had to do not only with the riskiness of the individual securities therein but also to the extent that they moved up and down together. He also discovered that portfolio of risky stocks might be put together in such a way that the portfolio as a whole could be less risky than the individual stocks in it.[8] And, thus, was born the modern portfolio theory (MPT) which is now the most widely used portfolio selection strategy for most of the professional investment manager on Dalal Street.

Yes, this is the essence of MPT, that is, the combined risk of two stocks[9] put together is usually less than the risk of individual stocks separately. This theory which emerged out of Markowitz's doctoral dissertation and which was subsequently published as a book titled *Portfolio Selection: Efficient Diversification of Investments* in 1959 tells the common investors how to combine stocks in their portfolios to give them the least risk possible, consistent with the return they desire. And yes, it gave birth to the most popular maxim of investment: *diversify your portfolio* or in the layman's terms *don't put all your eggs in the same basket.*

---

[8] Harry Markowitz, 'Portfolio Selection', *The Journal of Finance* 7, no. 1 (1952).
[9] This works as long as the two stocks don't always move in tandem, that is, as long as there is some lack of parallelism in the fortunes of the individual companies in the economy, diversification can reduce risk.

So how an individual investor can avoid the stock group risk and individual stock risk which doesn't give any reward? The answer is *diversification*. Let's see how it works and why you should always diversify your equity portfolio.

As we saw earlier that when we have invested in only TCS stocks, we carried all the three risks. Now let us add the stocks of Wipro, Infosys, HCL and Tech Mahindra into our portfolio. And by doing this, we have eliminated the individual stock risk because the behaviour of our portfolio is no more determined by the stock of TCS only but by the collective movement of all the five stocks. Assume Bank of America had floated an IT contract worth several million dollars and TCS was the front runner to get this contract. Suppose for some reason the deal didn't materialize and TCS didn't bag that contract. What would happen to the TCS stock price? It will fall down immediately because the market was expecting it to get that contract. Now if you had only TCS stock, then your portfolio value would fall sharply. However, if you had the stocks of Wipro, Infosys, HCL and Tech Mahindra in addition to the TCS, then your portfolio value wouldn't decline. Why? It is because if TCS didn't bag that contract, then chances are that its other competitors such as Wipro or Infosys would have bagged it and their stock price would have increased, thereby making good for the loss incurred with the TCS stock.

However, our portfolio is still impacted by the risk pertaining to the IT sector. What if a part of the contracts coming to Indian IT companies starts shifting to IT companies based out of Indonesia or the Philippines? The entire Indian IT sector would get impacted. So, to eliminate this stock group risk, we can add stocks from different sectors. Say, in addition to the five IT stocks that we have in our existing portfolio, we added stocks of HDFC Bank, ITC, Asian Paints, Bajaj Auto, Reliance Industries, ONGC, Hindustan Unilever and the likes so that we are no more exposed to only IT sector and, thus, the second level of risk, that is, the stock group risk has been eliminated and what remains is the market risk. And this is the maximum risk you should carry in your portfolio until and unless you like gambling with your money.

Now you may be wondering up to what level should an individual investor should diversify so as to completely eliminate the unsystematic risks (individual stock risk and stock group risk). While there is no exact answer for this, it has been found that when you have invested in over 50 equal sized and well-diversified stocks belonging to different sectors, you can very easily assume that you have almost eliminated the unsystematic risks and what remains is the market risk. Figure 3.5 demonstrates how unsystematic risk decreases with an increase in the number of securities in the portfolio. And since the investors are usually not rewarded for these unsystematic risks, the job of you as a rational investor should be to diversify these risks to the oblivion. Why to carry unnecessary risk which doesn't pay anything?

Remember, you can eliminate the unsystematic risks, but you must manage the overall market risk. Further, this market risk can be increased by selecting volatile securities or by using leverage, and it can be decreased by selecting securities with low volatility or by keeping part of the portfolio in cash. So once you take a particular

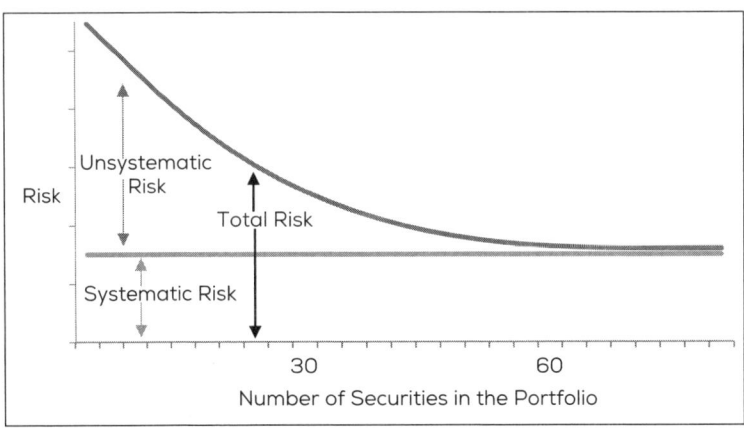

Figure 3.5. Reduction in Risk by Diversification: Risk of Portfolio
(Standard Deviation of Portfolio Return)

Now you may be thinking what this cost of investing is and how does it reduce the return that your portfolio generates. To answer that, let us first understand the simple case of investing in a bank's fixed deposit. Whenever you put your money in a bank's fixed deposit, you usually don't pay any fees. You put ₹1 lakh in the fixed deposit for, say, 1 year and assuming the rate of interest for 1 year to be 8 per cent, you get back ₹108,000 when you fixed deposit matures. Here, the cost of investing is nil (though you may be paying taxes on the interest earned on your fixed deposit depending on your overall income slab).

Let us now suppose you want to invest ₹1 lakh to buy shares of Reliance Industries Limited. So how do you invest? Definitely, you don't give your money to Reliance Industries directly. Neither you call Mr Ambani and say, 'Hey, I want to invest ₹1 lakh in your company. Can you please give me your company account details so that I can send the money?' You buy the shares of Reliance Industries through a registered stockbroker (either online or offline). And these stockbrokers charge fees—also called brokerage commission—when you place an order to buy stocks for their service. Similarly, you pay brokerage commission when you sell the stocks to get back your money. So in your total investment round trip of putting money (buying stocks) and getting back your money (selling stocks), you pay the brokerage commission to your stockbroker twice. Additionally, there is a bid-ask spread[11] which you need to pay to the market maker for the aforementioned round-trip transaction.

And if you invest in a mutual fund, then your cost of investing increases as you pay to the mutual fund companies (which invests in a pool of stocks on your behalf) for their expertise and management of your money in addition to the fees paid to the stockbroker and market maker. On an average, a common stock mutual fund, managed by a professional money manager who buys and sells securities in an effort to outperform the market, incurs annual

---

[11] Details of various costs involved in buying and selling stocks are covered in Chapter 15: Death by a Thousand Cuts.

operating expenses equal to about 1 per cent (known as expense ratio). Then with portfolio transaction costs (including the brokerage commission) estimated at around 1 to 1.5 per cent and other costs[12] estimated at another 0.5 per cent, total costs reduce the gross return of the portfolio by nearly 2.5 percentage points each year.

So the actual return that you get is not what your portfolio delivers. The actual return that you as an investor get to keep in your pocket is net of all these costs. And if you have invested in a typical mutual fund which actively buys and sells securities in an attempt to outperform the return delivered by the overall market, you can very easily subtract 2.5 percentage points from your gross portfolio return. So no matter if your portfolio delivered a return of 20 per cent or 5 per cent or negative 10 per cent, you would have to pay the mutual fund companies their fees; the stockbrokers their commission; the market makers their spreads and your real return would come down to 17.5 per cent, 2.5 per cent and negative 12.5 per cent, respectively. Yes, you pay to your fund managers and brokers even if your portfolio earned a negative gross return.

Now you may be thinking why cost of investing is important and how you can benefit from its understanding. The reason I discussed the cost of investing is because it is not something you always have to pay. You can reduce your cost of investments, thereby increasing your actual return. And how do we do it? Well, we will see that in the Part IV of the book. For the time being, just hold on and try to appreciate the fact that costs are an inherent part of investments and they reduce your overall return. Further, there are ways in which you can bring down your costs considerably.

Remember, the return in the stock market is uncertain. But your costs are always certain. You have to pay to your stockbroker and/or mutual fund companies no matter what. And that is why an investor who pays the least cost has the greatest opportunity to earn most of the real return provided by the stock market.

---

[12] We will discuss about the costs involved in investing in a mutual fund in detail in Chapter 15: Death by a Thousand Cuts.

TIME PERIOD OF INVESTMENT

Time is interesting than other three factors of investment in the sense that it not only interacts with the return but also with risks and costs. Let us see how time interacts with other factors and why it is important for a rational investor to take time by his side and become a long-term investor.

TIME AND RETURN

We all know the powerful link between time and reward (return) as the 'magic of compounding'. The longer the time horizon, the greater the power of compounding investment returns in transforming an initial outright investment, or a series of modest annual investments, into a truly breathtaking terminal value.

In Figure 3.6, I have presented the growth of two investments. This is a typical mutual fund industry format for comparing the result of an initial investment of ₹10,000/- in stocks, held for a working lifetime of 40 years, earning a high return of 15 per cent annually (average return of Sensex since 1980 has been 15.5%) with a fixed deposit alternative that is earning the much lower annual return of 8 per cent.

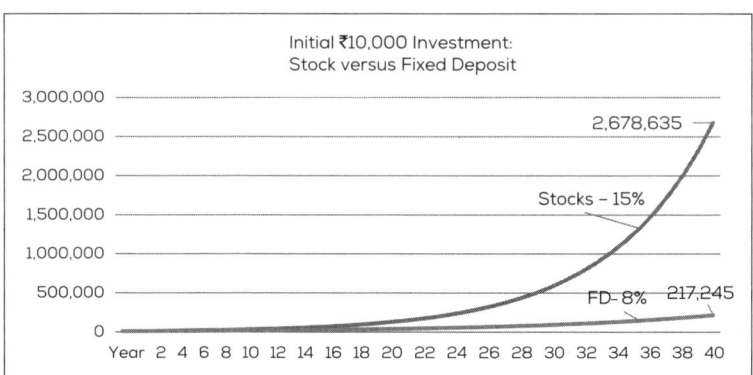

Figure 3.6. The Magic of Compounding (Time and Return)

The investment in stocks builds its reward over the fixed deposits year after year. Figure 3.6 shows how this edge in reward grows over the decades. The returns on stocks produce a final reward of ₹26.78 lakh, while the returns on fixed deposits produce a final reward of just ₹2.17 lakh. So, over a period of 40 years (investment horizon of a typical investor who starts his/her investment journey at the age of 25 and continues to do so till he/she is 65), an investment in stocks is worth nearly 12 times the investment in fixed deposits.

Definitely, the growth of capital when invested in equity market will not be as smooth as shown in the graph because, in some years, the return will be less than 15 per cent and in some it will be much more than 15 per cent. However, over the period of 40 years where the average return on the stock is 15 per cent, the final value at the end of the investment horizon would be pretty close to ₹26.78 lakh.

Also, an interesting point to note from Figure 3.6 is that the difference in the growth of capital in stocks vis-à-vis that in fixed deposits is not visible clearly till the 15 years of investment. However, post 15 years, this difference starts to explode and at the end of 40 years the results are worth to look at—investments in stocks have grown more than 12 times the investments in fixed deposits.

Now since most of us are short-sighted and since stocks carry a higher risk (fixed deposits virtually carry almost no risk), we feel that we are paying too much price by investing in stocks as the results are not something great and there were instances when we lost our money too. But what most people forget is that stock returns are mean reverting—a series of bad years will be followed by a series of good ones often more than compensating for the losses in early years. Also, the higher return as delivered by the stocks will have a substantial impact on your invested capital only when considerable time has elapsed. And this is the essence of relationship between time and reward. To reap true rewards of investing in equity market, you need to give time to your invested capital. Remember, *equity market is not a casino where you can become rich overnight. It's more like a forest of bamboo trees where there is no visible progress in the initial period but once a substantial amount of time has passed, it explodes like anything.*

TIME AND RISK

While it is easier for most of us to appreciate the magic of compounding and how time helps in growth of our investment, very few of us would know how time plays a crucial role in decreasing the risk in our equity investment. In fact, it is this relationship between time and risk that you will love the most and will help you understand why it is beneficial to be a long-term investor in the stock market.

There is a common wisdom shared by many academicians and noted practitioners about the stock market. They say that *the stock market is fascinating and quite volatile in the short run. However, over the very long run, the market can be almost boringly reliable and predictable.*[13] As we will see in the next few chapters, the stock returns behave differently over a short period of time vis-à-vis over a long period of time. In the short term, it is the investors' sentiments which largely determine the stock return. Accordingly, the daily stock return varies a lot as the mood of the investors keep on changing every day depending on the change in market-specific, sector-specific or company-specific factors.

However, over a longer period, the mood swings of investors usually cancel out and the return that the investors get is nothing, but the fundamental return of the stock. So, over a longer period, there is less variation of stock returns and consequently the stocks become less risky.

In Figure 3.7, I have presented the range of returns delivered by the Sensex (consisting of top 30 companies listed on BSE) over different holding period. As can be seen in Figure 3.7, the range of

---

[13] Charles D. Ellis, *Winning the Loser's Game: Timeless Strategies for Successful Investing* (New York, NY: McGraw Hill, 2002).

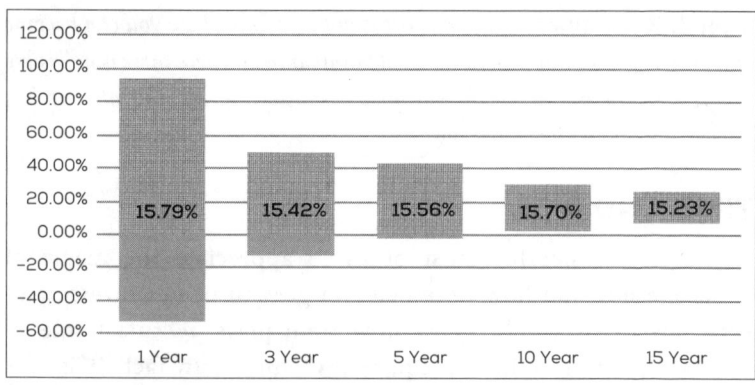

Figure 3.7. Time and Risk—Risk Decreases as Holding Period Increases

returns decreases considerably when we increase our holding period from 1 year to 15 years. For example, merely extending your time horizon from 1 year to 5 years reduces the absolute range of stock returns from +94 per cent to –52 per cent all the way down to a range of +43 per cent to –2 per cent. So if your holding period was 1 year, that is, you held the stock only for one year, then the maximum loss that you would have suffered was –52 per cent. However, increasing your time horizon to 5 years reduces your maximum loss to just –2 per cent. And if you were wise enough to increase your time horizon to 15 years, then the minimum return that you would have got was 7.3 per cent (which is what the maximum interest rate most of the banks offer on its fixed deposits). Isn't it a good proposition? The minimum return that you got from the stocks (if you held them for 15 years and more) is more than the maximum return that you can get from your fixed deposits.

And by the same token, the normal measure of risk as computed by the standard deviation decreases from 32 per cent to 12 per cent when you increase your investment holding from 1 year to 5 years. Extending your time horizon to 15 years reduces the risk (standard deviation) to the level of just 4 per cent. This explains why over a longer time horizon your investment in the stock market becomes less risky.

	1 Year (%)	3 Years (%)	5 Years (%)	10 Years (%)	15 Years (%)
Mean return	15.79	15.42	15.56	15.70	15.23
Std. dev. (risk)	32.12	15.66	12.34	7.17	4.03
Upper range	93.98	49.76	43.13	30.61	26.27
Lower range	−52.45	−12.29	−1.80	2.59	7.31

Figure 3.7 shows how risk diminishes with the passage of time (it's worth remembering that lesser the range of values, lesser the risk and wider the range of values, more the risk). Remember, as your time horizon increases, the variability of stock market returns declines and, consequently, the risk of your investment decreases. *As the years roll on, compounding not only increases your invested capital, it decreases the market risk as well.*

The second important lesson from Figure 3.7 worth remembering is that while the longer time horizon decreases your risk considerably, it hardly has any material impact on the average (expected) return of your portfolio. The average actual rate of return is almost the same in all cases. Why? It is because the data shown are all samples from the same continuous stream of investment experience. Another reason why you should always be a long-term investor. Your average return doesn't change but the risk comes down considerably when you are a long-term investor.

On observing the pattern of stock returns for different holding period, Jeremy Siegal in his book *Stocks for the Long Run* said it aptly. He says:

> *When I look at stocks in the very short run, they seem so risky that I wonder why anyone holds them. But over the long run, the superior performance of equities is so overwhelming, I wonder why anyone doesn't hold stocks![14]*

---

[14] Jeremy J. Siegel, *Stocks for the Long Run* (New York, NY: McGraw Hill, 1998).

TIME AND COST

As we discussed earlier in Figure 3.6 how the mutual fund industry shows the magic of compounding over the years and how investing in equities help generate much more wealth than what could be created by investing in fixed deposits. But fund investors do not earn the full stock market returns. As a group, they cannot possibly do so, because fund investors incur costs, and costs are subtracted directly from the gross returns the fund earns. Only the net returns are passed along to the end investors.

However, the mutual fund industry almost never shows the relationship between time and cost. If shown, the chart would be a rather disturbing one and chances are that you wouldn't buy the mutual fund which the mutual fund relationship manager was trying to sell you. They would always present the same time period, the same stock market return of 15 per cent and the same ₹26.78 lakh end result. But if we add a second line assuming a 13 per cent mutual fund return, the market return reduced by estimated all-in annual mutual fund expense of 2 per cent, and we will get to see what will actually come into our pocket. So when we draw a line at 13 per cent growth, we see the investment still grows, the line still rises exponentially, nicely sweeping upward as the years pass, but

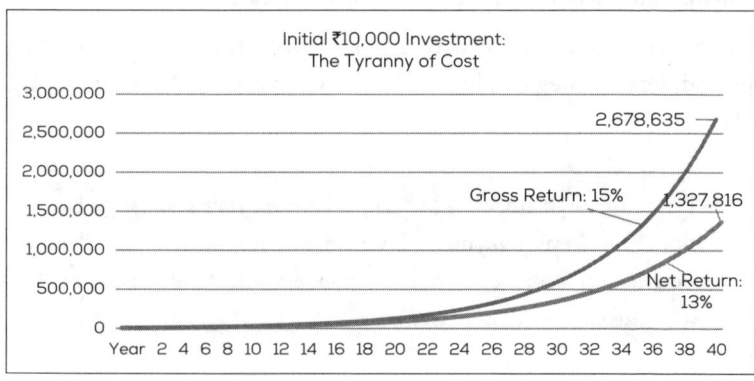

Figure 3.8. Time and Cost

to a 40-year total of only ₹13.27 lakh—less than half of the value generated by the stock market's return. Over the full 40-year period, the mutual fund cost of 2 per cent per annum have confiscated fully ₹13.50 lakh. And where did this money of ₹13.50 lakh go? It went to the pockets of your mutual fund company, its fund manager and the stockbrokers.

This relationship of time and cost is so important that it would be better if we repeat what we just learnt. With our one-time invested money of ₹10,000, the stock market helped it grow to a whopping amount of ₹26.78 lakh over a period of 40 years. However, this amount is divided into two parts: the smaller part of ₹13.27 lakh comes to us and the bigger part of ₹13.50 lakh goes to our mutual fund companies and brokerage house. Put another way, more than half the market's returns has been consumed by the financial intermediaries and the end investors settle with less than the half of the total returns.

This evidence, brutal but factual, reflects the tyranny of cost and depicts the relationship between time and cost. Most importantly, it also says what I said in the very first chapter that the typical mutual fund companies are not standing on your side of the battle, they are standing on the opposite side always looking out how to fleece you by way of multiple fees and commissions. Needless to say, an investor who minimizes his/her cost of investing settles with more money than the one who pays handsomely to his/her stockbroker, financial advisor and mutual fund manager.

LESSONS FOR THE INVESTORS

- Reward and risk go hand in hand. By increasing your risk, you can earn more return. However, with an increased risk, chances of you losing your money also increases. Don't expect high returns without high risk and don't expect safety without correspondingly low returns.

- Diversifying your portfolio reduces your overall risk to a great extent. And it is important to diversify because the risks that get eliminated via diversification are usually not rewarded by the market.

- Cost has a significant impact on your reward. By decreasing your cost of investment process, you increase your net return by the corresponding amount. While the year-on-year return is not certain, your costs are certain, fixed and you must pay them no matter if you made money or lost it. And that is why you should never ignore your costs and work towards minimizing it.

- By increasing your investment horizon, you decrease the risk associated with your investment in the equity market, that is, the longer a risky asset is held, the less the chance of loss.

4 Measuring the Beast
Worth of a Stock

Having understood the basic premise of investment and its four dimensions, let us now see how stock derives its value and how we can measure the return from a stock or a portfolio of stocks.

THE BEAST: PREDICTING THE RETURN

For centuries, economists and finance professors have struggled to come up with some magic formula which would help them model the movement of stock price and, in turn, predict its return. But you would say how one can predict the return when it lies in the future. True. No one can predict the future. But when there lies the money, people tend to do all sort of things to gain control over it. And since all investment returns are dependent on some future events, people have been working tirelessly to get a peep into the future.

So it was in this attempt to foresee the future that led to the origination of *intrinsic value theory*, and it is this theory based on which the entire mutual fund industry works.

THE INTRINSIC VALUE THEORY

In the history of modern-day investing, one economist towers above all other in influencing the way we examine stocks and bonds. He was a distinguished professor of economics at Yale University and often considered as the greatest economist the

USA has ever produced. In 1930, he published a seminal treatise on investment value titled *The Theory of Interest* in which he scientifically attempted to answer the age-old question of *'What is a thing worth?'* His name was Irving Fisher.

It was Fisher who saw that the economic value is not only a function of the *thing* owned but also of the moment in time at which it is purchased with money. He postulated that a thing available now has a different value than the same thing available at a future date. Yes, a rupee today is much more valuable than a rupee tomorrow.

Then, in 1938, another classic was published by John Burr Williams. After graduating from Harvard Business School in 1923, Williams worked as a security analyst where he realized 'how to estimate the fair value was a puzzle indeed and to be a good investment analyst one needs to be an expert economist too'.[1] So, in 1932, he enrolled at Harvard for a PhD in economics and it was his PhD thesis based on which he published his 1938 classic, *The Theory of Investment Value*, fleshing out the mathematics in much greater detail than what Fisher had earlier attempted to do.

So in *The Theory of Investment Value*, Williams talked about *intrinsic value* of a stock which is nothing but the true value of the stocks of a company. This intrinsic value depends on the fundamental nature of the company, its business, its operation, its earnings and its growth. More importantly, this intrinsic value is not dependent on what the public and investors feel about this company. Rather it's what the company truly is worth. And, thus, the intrinsic value theory was born.

Now the interesting question is: what this intrinsic value theory is and how it can be used to value a stock?

Well, the basic premise of the intrinsic value theory is that every stock has an intrinsic value which can be computed using a simple

---

[1] Available at http://www.numeraire.com/theory.htm (accessed on 30 December 2019).

mathematical formula. So whenever the market price of the stock falls below its intrinsic value, then buy that stock because this deviation of stock price from its true value will eventually be corrected, and the stock price will return to its intrinsic value. Similarly, when the market price is above the intrinsic value, sell that stock because the market will correct this overvaluation and price of the stock would dip.

So how well this intrinsic value worked and how Williams calculated the intrinsic value of the stock?

The answer lies in understanding that *human beings prefer present consumption to future consumption.* Think about it for some time. What would you like: a chocolate brownie today or the same brownie one year down the line? You would say why to wait for one year when you are getting the same brownie today. And this is what the basic premise of Fisher's theory was, that is, a rupee today is worth much more than a rupee tomorrow and if we need to find the value of a rupee that we would be receiving in a months' time then we need to *discount* that rupee to today's *present value.* So Williams worked out an actual mathematical formula where he discounted the future dividend income of a stock to its present value and argued that the *intrinsic value of a stock was equal to the present (discounted) value of all its future dividends.*

Do pay attention to the aforementioned idea *that the value of a stock is simply the present value of all its future income stream.* It is this basic idea which differentiates an investment from speculation. Remember an investment is centred on the central idea of future income stream in the form of cash inflows. When you invest in a stock, you receive dividends and capital appreciation and when you invest in bond (or a fixed deposit) you receive interest income. Similarly, when you invest in a real estate, you receive rental income. So when we put Williams' theory to your real estate investment, then it simply states that the true value of an apartment would be the present (discounted) value of all its rental income earned throughout the lifetime of the apartment.

Now how do we discount the future income stream (dividends in case of stocks) to its present value to find its intrinsic value? Are there any mathematical formulae to it?

Well, there was one gentleman called Myron Gordon who after studying Williams' book put out a very simple formula in 1956[2] along with his colleague Eli Shapiro at MIT to evaluate the intrinsic value of a stock and made its reference in a paper in 1959.[3] And the formula is so simple that once you see it you can't forget it. The formula for the intrinsic value of a stock at present (P_0) is:

$$P_0 = \frac{D_1}{K_e - g}$$

D_1 = Expected dividend for year 1

g = Growth rate

K_e = Discount rate

This formula is now popularly called dividend discount model (DDM) or Gordon Growth Model.

While the expected dividend for each company is more or less known to the general public, the same can't be said about the growth rate and discount rate. The major part of this simple equation is how do we determine discount rate[4] (also called the interest rate) and the growth rate of that particular company. The entire army of security analysts working 14 hours a day on Dalal Street has this one job of determining the discount rate and the growth rate of each company so that the intrinsic value of the stock can be determined. And if the market price is below the

---

[2] M. J. Gordon, and Eli Shapiro, 'Capital Equipment Analysis: The Required Rate of Profit', *Management Science* 3, no. 1 (1956). Reprinted in *Management of Corporate Capital* (Glencoe, IL: Free Press of Glencoe, 1959).

[3] Myron Gordon, 'Dividends, Earnings, and Stock Prices', *The Review of Economics and Statistics* (1959).

[4] Discount rate is simply the rate of return we expect from holding that particular stock taking all its risk into consideration. The greater the risk in owning a stock, greater is the discount rate. And that is why the big and stable companies usually have low discount rate and small companies tend to have high discount rate.

calculated fair intrinsic value, buy that stock and if the market price is above the fair value, sell.

Mind you, this is no easy task. In fact, as we will see in subsequent chapters, it's almost an impossible task to determine the true intrinsic value of a company. Very frequently, we come across promising companies doing very well with large expected future dividend streams stumble and fall. Similarly, we do come across companies which the market pundits have professed to be dead suddenly recover and provide shareholders with huge amount of future income.

THE REAL BENEFITS OF DDM

Now you would be thinking why we spent so much time and effort on DDM when it is so difficult to use it to accurately price a stock. Well, there are some good reasons why DDM is such a good thing.

First and foremost, DDM provides an intuitive way to think about the value of a stock. A stock is not an abstract piece of paper that has some random fluctuating value; it is a claim on the real future income and assets of that company.

Second, it enables us to test the growth and return assumption of a stock. For example, assume a stock's average historical return over the past 10 years is 15 per cent and its dividend growth is around 5 per cent. Assume the expected dividend to be ₹20. Now, with DDM, the intrinsic value of the stock comes to ₹200. And if the present stock price of this particular company is, say, ₹500, then you can very safely assume one of the following:

- The company has developed some pathbreaking product or has discovered some mine or oil well which will increase its earning and consequently dividend growth from present 5 per cent to 11 per cent.

- The public is showing too much trust in this company (a case of overvaluation) and its expected return is very likely to come down from 15 per cent to 9 per cent, that is, at this present price of ₹500 the stock won't be delivering a 15 per cent return which it had been doing on an average for the last 10 years, but it will deliver a lower return of 9 per cent.

So while the DDM may not be able to give us the true value of a stock price as it depends on various assumptions (including discount rate and growth rate), it does give us with a handy tool to analyse whether the stock is highly overvalued or undervalued.[5] Additionally, it provides us with one of the fundamental laws of finance which most of the people find it difficult to accept and appreciate. And what is this law? Well there is no specific name for this law. I call it the *law of price and return*.

Look at the previous example where the stock price has increased from ₹200 to ₹500 (remember this stock has historically delivered an average return of 15% over the past 10 years). If this increase of ₹200 to ₹500 happens in the real world, then most of the people would flock to this stock in anticipation of a better return. And if there has not been any pathbreaking product development, then the expected return from this stock will fall from 15 per cent to 9 per cent. Why? It is because the price of the stock has increased too much, and delivering even the average historical return of 15 per cent would mean that the stock price has to increase from ₹500 to ₹575 which may not be so easy for the company.

On an intellectual level, most investors have no trouble under-standing the notion that high past returns lead to high prices. What they have trouble in understanding is that *high prices usually lead to lower future returns*. Why is it so? It is because with past returns, we multiply those returns to the past price to arrive at the present price. However, when we are calculating the future return,

---

[5] To determine whether the stock is slightly overvalued or undervalued is an extremely difficult task and even most of the professionals fail to arrive at such conclusion. But to determine whether it is highly overvalued or highly undervalued is not so difficult.

we divide the future earnings by the present price today (just rearrange the DDM equation). And higher the present price today, lower will be the future return from the stock.

While there is a direct relationship between past return and present price, there is an inverse relationship between the present price and future return (read it again to fully grasp it). If you understand this simple concept, then it will help you manage your investment portfolio in a much better way than what most professional can claim to do. Further, understanding this simple concept will help you appreciate the fact that why a stock or a mutual fund which has increased considerably in its value usually delivers a much lower return in future. And many a times since this increased value is nothing but mass hysteria which may burst anytime soon, the return can be negative as well. Put simply, this law of price and return can be stated as follows:

A higher price (that you pay to purchase stock/fund) will usually deliver a lower return in the future and a lower price is likely to deliver a higher return.

Charles Ellis expressed the same principle when he said:[6]

> *A falling stock market is the necessary first step to buying low.... Just as we buy cows for their milk and hens for their eggs, we buy stocks for their current and future earnings and dividends. If you ran a dairy, wouldn't you prefer to have cow prices low when you were buying so that you could get more gallons of milk for your investment in cows?*

In the world of investments, don't get swayed by your emotions and always rely on the maths. And the maths says that the lower the price of the shares when we buy, the more shares we will get for every ₹100 and greater the amount of money we will receive in future dividends. So don't get disheartened when the market

---

[6] Charles D. Ellis, *Winning the Loser's Game.*

tanks. It's a time to celebrate as you get to buy stocks at cheaper price and since mean reversion is always at work, your portfolio value will increase in value as the market rebounds.

Third and most importantly, the real beauty of DDM is that it can be rearranged to calculate the expected return of a particular stock, giving us an equation, which is simple and yet elegant.

Discount rate (expected stock return) =
Dividend yield + dividend growth

The aforementioned formula, which is known as the 'Gordon Equation', provides an accurate way to predict *long-term* stock market return. The dividend yield is the regular cash flow (in the form of dividends) that you get when you own a stock and the dividend growth is what helps in generating the capital appreciation from that stock.

But you would say that there are companies who don't pay any dividends, then how we can calculate its long-term return. Well, for such companies, the dividend yield is zero and the amount by which its dividend yield gets reduced; its growth rate increases by the corresponding amount and there is not much impact on the expected stock return.

Now coming back to the Gordon equation, one point that is to be remembered is that this equation is useful only in the long term—it tells us nothing about day-to-day or even year-to-year returns. In the short run, no mathematical formula can help you accurately predict return as the short-term return is not governed by any fundamentals but by the investors' madness (some people prefer it to call as sentiments) and till date we have not devised any tool to measure the madness of a crowd.

But if you are a long-term investor, you would rarely care for the short-term fluctuations. Think about it, which would you rather know: the market return for the next 2 weeks or for the next 20 years? I can't say much about you, but I would rather know the latter. And within a reasonable margin of error, you too can by using the DDM. However, you can't sell newspaper, magazines and prime-time shows talking about the 20-year return.

To conclude on this intrinsic value theory, I would say that this theory is scientific, but it relies on some tricky forecasts of discount rate and the extent and duration of company's future growth. Accordingly, the foundation of intrinsic value and DDM may not be as dependable as claimed by the industry practitioners to predict the short-term return of the stocks.

LESSONS FOR THE INVESTORS

- A stock is worth only the future income stream it produces. This income stream must be reduced in value, or discounted to the present, to reflect the fact that it is worth less the incomes that would be accrued in the future.

- The discount rate is the same as the expected return from that asset and is determined by the asset's perceived risk. The higher the risk, the higher the discount rate (expected return) and lower the present value (price) of the asset.

- In the long term, the expected return is approximately the sum of the dividend yield and the growth rate. The current high price and low dividend yield of stocks suggest that they will have much lower returns in the future than they have had in the past.

- Further, the earlier considerations pertain only to long-term returns (15–20 years). Over shorter periods, future returns are primarily determined by the speculative factors and cannot be predicted with precision.

- In the short term, no scientific formulae work as in the short term the stock market is nearly random and is driven by the sentiments of the masses.

The Drunkard's Tale

Too Much Random and yet so Efficient

5

Imagine you are walking alone in a lonely night back to your home. Just when you turn around a corner, you see a drunk man walking towards you. The lane that you were walking on is rather a narrow lane and you try to gauge the movement of that drunkard so that you can avoid the path he is likely to follow. However, to your surprise, you find that he is not following any pattern and his next step is almost unpredictable having no relationship to the steps he just took. You again try to focus on his steps so that you can avoid the embarrassing collision you might end up. But again, you were unable to find any predictable pattern. So what do you do? You just step aside to one side of the lane and pray that the drunkard doesn't fall upon you. And after you safely cross him, you say to yourself, 'what a random walk it was'.

Now you must be thinking why I discussed a drunkard's walk when I am supposed to be talking about stock price and returns. Well, I not only discussed a drunkard's path, what I actually referred to was about the price movement of a typical stock. Yes, you read it correctly. Replace that drunkard with a stock price and the path followed by the drunkard is the typical path followed by the price of a stock—not exactly rational but not predictable either.

Further, there is one more similarity between the drunkard's walk and that of a stock price. Just like the drunkard is very much likely to reach his home (until and unless he is completely out), though we are not sure what path he would take to reach there, the stock prices on an average are likely to reach to the level as determined by their respective fundamentals over the long term, though we are not sure what would be its level during a particular short-term period. Further, just there is a good chance of seeing that drunk man in the gutter the next morning, we do come across instances of stocks piled up in the gutter.

THE RANDOM WALK

The idea that the price of a stock follows a kind of random walk has been shared by academicians for over a century and the first to make this connection was Frederick McCauley, who is now popularly known for introducing the concept of *bond duration*. Being an observant of the stock market and with a PhD in economics from Columbia, he was invited to a statistician's club in New York in 1925 where he observed that there was a striking similarity between the fluctuations of the stock market and those of a chance curve which may be obtained by throwing dice. He said, 'everyone will agree that the course of such a purely chance curve cannot be predicted'.[1]

While McCauley's observation drew attention, it didn't gain much traction as the USA went through the Great Depression during the early 1930s and later got involved in the Second World War where most of the statisticians were assigned the task of tracking the missiles and submarines rather than the stock prices.

However, during the early 1950s, when the world became a little peaceful, there was a statistics professor in England who was putting the computers to good use in analysing time series data of stock prices. Maurice Kendall from the London School of Economics upon analysing the stock price movement realized that he couldn't find any predictable pattern in the stock prices.[2]

---

[1] *Journal of the American Statistical Association* 20 (1925): 248. Comments made at the Aldine Club in New York on 17 April 1925.
[2] Maurice Kendall, 'The Analysis of Economic Time Series, Part I: Prices', *Journal of the Royal Statistical Society* 96 (1953).

The prices seemed to evolve randomly implying that they were as likely to go up as they were likely to go down on any particular day, regardless of the past performance. The historical data of the stock prices provided no way to predict price movements in the future. Kendall said, 'almost as if once a week the Demon of Chance drew a random number... and added it to the current price to determine the next week's price'.[3]

And as Kendall was taking the help of computer in analysing stock prices, another statistician called Harry Roberts from University of Chicago was busy in flipping coins. Roberts simulated movements in the market by plotting price changes that resulted from completely random events, such as flips of a coin. And to his amazement, he found that these simulations (chart formed by tossing of coins) looked like the charts of actual stock prices. Now, since the next period's price change was, by construction, a completely random event (you don't know whether the next flip will be a head or a tail), such patterns could not logically have any predictive content.[4]

And finally, there was one young economist during the early 1960s—who is now widely considered as the 'Father of Modern Finance'—by the name Eugene Fama. So before he became one of the most influential economists of all time and went on to receive Nobel Prize in 2013, he had worked for a finance professor who used to publish stock market newsletter. Fama's job was to analyse market trading rules. In other words, he had to come up with strategies that would produce market beating returns.

Looking at historical data, Fama found plenty such strategies that worked in the past. But something funnier happened during his analysis. Each time he identified a strategy that had done

[3] Justin Fox, *The Myth of the Rational Market—A History of Risk, Reward and Delusion on Wall Street* (New York, NY: Harper Business, 2009).
[4] Jeremy J. Siegel, *Stocks for the Long Run.*

beautifully in the past, it fell flat on its face in the future. Slowly and steadily, he realized that *although it is easy to uncover successful past stock picking and market-timing strategies, none of them worked going forward.*[5]

Now you would be wondering what importance these early researches on the stock price movement holds for common investors like us. And do we really need to care if the stock prices followed a random path in the short term?

Well, understanding the basic nature of the stock price movement is crucial to help you avoid some of the mistakes that you might be doing now or would commit in future if you don't spend time now understanding them. There are far too many investors who would look at the past record to predict the near future movement so that they can buy/sell the stocks just at the right time. However, few can claim to have really benefitted from such strategies because as evidenced by the earlier researches, *the short-run changes in stock prices are nearly random and, hence, unpredictable.* Burton Malkiel adds up to this and says, 'Taking the concept of random-walk to its logical extreme, it would mean that a blindfolded monkey throwing darts at the stock listing could select a portfolio that would do just as well as one selected by the experts'.

Let us now see why stock price follows nearly a random walk in the short term and what implication it has on you as an investor.

THE EFFICIENT MARKET HYPOTHESIS

Imagine for the time being that instead of finding that stock prices follow a random path in the short term, Kendall had discovered that stock prices are predictable, that is, you could predict the future movement of the stock prices by looking at its historical chart. And if investors could use Kendall's forecasting equation to

---

[5] William Bernstein, *The Four Pillars of Investing* (New York, NY: McGraw Hill, 2002).

predict stock prices, they would reap limitless profits simply by purchasing stocks that the computer told were about to increase in value and by selling those stocks which the computer predicted to fall.

If you think for some time you would realize that such a situation couldn't persist for long. For example, suppose there exists a company called Abhishek Inc. whose current stock price is ₹100. Assume our stock price model predicts with a great confidence that the price of Abhishek Inc. would increase from ₹100 to ₹120 in the next 2 days. Now, what would all the investors who had such a formula do today? Obviously, they would place a great wave of immediate *buy order* to cash in on the prospective increase in the stock price of Abhishek Inc. Further, no one holding that stock would be willing to sell. The net effect of this sudden jump in buy and almost nil sell orders would increase the stock price of Abhishek Inc. to ₹120. The forecast of a future price increase will lead instead to an immediate price increase. In other words, the stock price will immediately reflect the 'good news' implicit in the model's forecast.

This simple example tells why predicting stock price movement is likely to fail. Any forecast about favourable future performance will instead lead to a favourable current performance as all the investors are likely to get into action before the price jump. More generally, it could be easily said that any information that could be used to predict stock performance should already be reflected in the current stock prices. As soon as there is any information indicating that a stock is underpriced, and it offers a great profit opportunity, investors will flock to buy the stock and immediately bid up its price to a fair level, where only *return commensurate with the risk inherent in that stock* could be earned from that stock. This human nature to cash in any possible profits immediately was captured by Benjamin Graham very well when he said:

> *A moment's thought will show that there can be no such thing as a scientific prediction of economic events under human control. The very 'dependability' of such a prediction will cause human actions which will invalidate it.*[6]

Thus, if we are to assume that the market is efficient, then stock prices will change only when new, unanticipated information about the stock is released to the market. And as soon as there is some positive information about the company (say, the company got a new contract worth ₹1,000 crore), its stock price will jump immediately to its fair level. This new price would have taken this new information (signing of contract) into account and just because you knew about this deal wouldn't help you reap any extraordinary profit because the price of the stock has already risen. Similarly, as soon as there is some negative news about the company (say, a biotech company didn't get requisite approval for bringing its new drug to the market), its stock price will fall immediately to its fair level and you can't simply benefit from this because the price would have already dipped by the time you got the information and acted upon it.

To validate this hypothesis of stock price change happening quickly upon release of new information, two economists from Stanford University conducted a study on the effect of corporate dividend and earnings announcement on the stock prices and they found that most of the stock price response to corporate dividend or earnings announcements occurs within 10 minutes of announcement.[7]

And since new information—the news, by definition—must be unpredictable, the stock price movement has to be unpredictable. If the news was predictable, then it wouldn't be news at all. Moreover,

---

[6] Benjamin Graham, and David Dodd, *Security Analysis: Principles and Techniques* (New York, NY: McGraw Hill, 1934). Reprinted in 1996.
[7] James M. Patell, and Mark A. Wolfson, 'The Intraday Speed of Adjustment of Stock Prices to Earnings and Dividend Announcements', *Journal of Financial Economics* 13, no. 2 (1984).

that predictable news would already have been exploited by the investors to increase or decrease the stock price to its fair level.

Eugene Fama who is said to propose this efficient market hypothesis (EMH) argued that since there are many intelligent and well-informed analysts, traders and speculators working competitively and effortlessly, their very existence would 'insure that actual market prices are, on the basis of all available information, best estimates of intrinsic value'.

This is the essence of the argument that stock prices should follow a *random walk*, that is, the stock price changes should be random and unpredictable in the short term. Further, this belief that current stock prices reflect all the available information related to that particular stock is referred to as the EMH.[8]

Now there are few people who say that market is not efficient because if that would be the case, then all the stocks would be trading at their fair price (intrinsic value) and there would not be any chance of mispricing. Well, they have got it wrong.

Eugene Fama who coined the term 'efficient market' never said that in an efficient market the price of the stock will always be correct and close to its intrinsic value. What he basically said that a market in which prices always 'fully reflect' available information is called 'efficient' and the current market price is the *best estimate* of the intrinsic value of the stock.[9]

In fact, Nobel Prizewinning professor Robert Schiller gave ample evidences that the price is not always right,[10] which basically meant that prices can stay away from their fair value and that too for a quite long period of time.[11] If the hypothesis that prices are 'right'

---

[8] Actually, there are three levels of EMH: weak form, semi-strong form and strong form. Readers are encouraged to read them on their own (easily available online).

[9] Eugene F. Fama, 'Efficient Capital Markets: A Review of Theory and Empirical Work', *Journal of Finance* (1970).

[10] Robert J. Shiller, 'Do Stock Prices Move Too Much to Be Justified by Subsequent Changes in Dividends?' *American Economic Review* (1981).

[11] In 1996, Robert Shiller had warned Federal Reserve Board that the prices seemed very high. If he was right, then the market should have fallen in some near future. However, the market fell only in 2000 meaning he was wrong for a long time before he was right. This lack of precision means that even though you believed that the price is not right, you cannot make money so easily. Always remember that the market can remain irrational longer than you can remain solvent.

was true, then there can never be bubbles and recessions because during these extreme times prices are definitely not right and they sooner or later revert closer to their fair value once the bubble burst and recession subsides.

Remember, an efficient market does not mean that stocks will always sell at the 'right' price. What it essentially means is that the price of the stock has already incorporated all the information available about the company. So given the prevailing sentiments, the market can be rational or irrational. However, it will still be very efficient at incorporating into market prices any available information about companies. *And that makes it very difficult to find any mispriced stock before the market corrects it.*

Remember, the heart of the efficient market is that you cannot earn outsize returns without taking on additional systematic risk until and unless you are in possession of some exclusive information which you can use to your advantage before that information reaches to the market.

IMPLICATIONS OF MARKET EFFICIENCY

Now comes the important question. What implications do market efficiency have for the average investors and what lessons they can learn about their investments in the stock market?

To answer that question, we would need to appreciate the fact that if the markets are efficient then the stock returns are not predictable at short horizons, which essentially means that stock prices follow a random walk. So it becomes extremely difficult to earn superior returns though earning the return delivered by the entire stock market is rather easy.

Thus, the first implication of stock market efficiency is that simple trading rules should not work, that is, you cannot predict the short-term future return on the basis of observing the past prices.

The second implication of market efficiency is that the fundamental analysis performed by security analysts employed by I-Banks and brokerage house has no power to pick stocks, and professional money managers should do no better than monkeys with darts at picking stock portfolio.

Most of the investors get it wrong thinking that by doing deep research and comprehensive analysis they can cherry-pick stocks which will outperform the market but what they don't know is that it is not the analysis but the exclusive material information about particular stocks which has the potential to earn excess return above the market. No doubt, most of the time of the fund managers is spent not in analysing stocks but building deep networks with the 'right' people so that they are the first in line to get any material information which would help them leverage upon that and earn superior return. Meir Statman, the noted economist and often considered one of the founding fathers of *behavioural finance* in his book *Finance for Normal People: How Investors and Market Behave,* said:

> *Hard-to-beat markets are not impossible to beat. Investors with exclusively available information find it easy to beat the market, and investors with narrowly available information find it hard but not impossible to beat the market. Yet, on average, investors with nothing more than widely available information find it impossible to beat the market. Such investors are beaten by the market more often than they beat it. Indeed, investors with exclusively available and narrowly available information gain their market beating returns by emptying the pockets of investors who attempt to beat the market with widely available information alone.[12]*

IS STOCK MARKET REALLY EFFICIENT?

There has been a long debate on whether the stock market is really efficient. The rationalists have put forth their research and paper

---

[12] Meir Statman, *Finance for Normal People: How Investors and Market Behave* (Oxford: Oxford University Press, 2017).

citing efficiency in the market, and the behaviouralists have shown evidence of inefficiency in the market and many a times most of them don't agree to each other's view. So what is the final verdict and what we as an investor have got to do with whether the market is efficient or inefficient?

To say that the stock market is completely efficient is to say that we live in a utopian society where everything is perfect and ideal as they should be. Definitely, such a society doesn't exist and most importantly a 100 per cent efficient stock market also doesn't exist. There has been ample number of evidences to show that market inefficiency does exist.

So what could be the possible causes for inefficiency in the market given that in theory it looks so convincing?

One of the reasons for market inefficiency is that, many a times, investors overreact to a particular news, thereby magnifying the impact of news on the stock price change. Say, our Abhishek Inc. just developed a new product which would increase its earning and accordingly the stock price should increase by another ₹20 per share. However, the investors who are not so good at discounting the future dividends overreact to such good news and everybody jumps to buy the stock. Result, the stock price of Abhishek Inc. increases by ₹30 per share, while in the rational world it should have increased by only ₹20 per share.

The Nobel Prize winning professor Richard Thaler along with his colleague Werner De Bondt conducted a comprehensive analysis on this overreaction nature of investors and found that most people overreact to unexpected and dramatic news events.[13]

Another reason is that investors react slowly to the news and, thereby, it takes time for the market to adjust the stock price to its fair value.

---

[13] Werner F. M. DeBondt, and Richard H. Thaler, 'Does the Stock Market Overreact?' *Journal of Finance* 40, no. 3 (1985).

One more reason for market inefficiency is the presence of transactional cost. Suppose you find a good information about a stock and wish to take advantage. But buying that stock involves cost as you would need to pay to your stockbroker to buy the stock and then there would be a *bid-ask spread* too. On close scrutiny, you find that it doesn't make much sense for you to purchase that stock because after incurring those costs you wouldn't make any profit. So what do you do? You don't buy that stock and the information that is now available to you doesn't get incorporated into the stock price.

Thus, we can easily say that market is not entirely efficient; however, the notion that anyone could easily exploit this inefficiency to his/her benefit should be taken with many grains of salt. *The stock market may not be entirely efficient but is competitive enough that only differentially superior information or insight will earn money; the easy pickings have already been picked.*

EFFICIENT OR INEFFICIENT: DOES IT MATTER?

Imagine for the time being that the stock market is inefficient which essentially means that there is some information about a particular stock which is yet to be incorporated into its price and, hence, it's possible to earn superior return on this information.

Assume you are one of the top-notch security analysts and you have been able to find some information about stocks of XYZ Ltd which will increase its current price from ₹100 to ₹150. So what do you do? You buy as much of the stock as you can get your hands on (you can't buy all the stocks of XYZ as not all shares of XYZ would be free-float and I am assuming that you won't have that much capital to buy the entire company with your own money; further, the stock exchange limits the number of shares that you can purchase of a company in a single day). So you keep buying the shares of XYZ Ltd every day and this starts pushing the share price of XYZ towards ₹150. The whole process is expected to take a few days' time[14] and is accomplished in great secrecy as you don't want to share your profit with someone else.

Now as the price of XYZ starts increasing, it won't go unnoticed. As other analysts who are equally smart and intelligent notice the stock's price and volume increase, they take a closer look at the stock, do their research and find the same information which you had. So they too jump in, and the price which should have taken at least 3–4 days to rise to the level of ₹150 reaches immediately as more and more analysts jump in. And with this your chance of making money decreases substantially.

Jason Zweig who is a senior writer at *Money* magazine and who has written about Investing since 1987 says:

> *The problem with the stock market today is not that so many financial analysts are idiots, but rather that so many of them are so smart. As more and more smart people search the market for bargains, that very act of searching makes those bargains rarer—and, in a cruel paradox makes the analysts look as if they lack the intelligence to justify the search.*

The simple fact that there are so many talented security analysts examining stocks and with so much money being poured in to identify undervalued stocks guarantees that none of them will have any kind of advantage over other, since the stock price will nearly instantaneously reflect their collective judgement.

And by now it would be very much apparent to you that a casual effort to pick stocks are not likely to pay off. Any individual investor who tries to pick stocks on his/her own is very much likely to fail. He/she will fail not because he/she would be unintelligent or

---

[14] You may argue that while in the earlier example I said the stock price jumps immediately, here I am saying that it would take a couple of days. The difference is because in the earlier example the information about the prediction of stock price to increase is known to all the investors and here it is assumed that only you know that information. The moment information becomes public, the increase in price is abrupt and it will hardly take a few minutes for the share price to reach to its fair value.

stupid but because no matter how deep he/she would have studied the stock market and how much he/she would have read books on security analysis he/she cannot win against the collective judgement of the entire stock market participants.

And who are these market participants? Well, they are all the smart and intelligent investors looking to outsmart other investors and, most importantly, they are all the big players such as mutual funds, I-Banks and hedge funds which have been in the stock market for nearly five decades or probably a century and have the collective intelligence of its thousands of analysts and fund managers accumulated over this long period of their operation. More importantly, they have money, resources and latest computing technologies which they use to their advantage. They have Bloomberg and all the other sophisticated information services at their disposal. Their professionals meet regularly with the companies' CEOs and CFOs. They all have teams of in-house analysts and portfolio managers with best of the degrees and with an average of 15 years of investing experience—all working their contacts and networks to get the best information all the time. You get the picture. These institutions have all the advantage that any average individual can't even dream of. Do you think that with your intelligence and market experience of 10 years or 20 years you can beat Goldman which has the intelligence of thousands of professional analysts and market experience of over 100 years? If yes, then go ahead and pick stocks on your own. If not, follow the advice presented in Part IV of the book.

And yes, there is not one Goldman Sachs. We also have the likes of Morgan Stanley, Citibank, ICICI Prudential, HDFC Mutual Fund, BlackRock, Kotak Mahindra Asset Management among others who are always on the lookout for finding the undervalued stocks with all their sophisticated research techniques and an army of stock analysts. Even if the market is not efficient and there are stocks which would be undervalued or overvalued, then it wouldn't come to your notice first; it will first be identified by these giants and since they have loads of money and resources at their disposal, they will immediately buy all those stocks available and raise their price and by the time you identify and buy those stocks it would have already risen to a much higher level.

THE SHARK–SEAL THEORY[15]

Let us consider our equity market to be an ocean where the market participants are the fishes of all kinds swimming across the length and breadth of the ocean. So individual investors are the dogfish shark (length 3 feet) and the I-Banks, hedge funds and mutual funds are the great white sharks (length 20 feet). While they can live happily eating other sea animals and small fishes, they love eating seals (market inefficiency) and are always in the lookout for it. And the moment they find such seals, they eat it immediately, thus, cleaning the ocean of the seals.

Now in an ideal world, where the market should be completely efficient, we would never have any seals in the ocean. But we know that market is not entirely efficient and so we do get to see seals sometime swimming in the ocean. But the fact that there are seals available doesn't mean that dogfish shark (individual investors) can enjoy and relish it. Any seals, if available, are very much likely to be eaten by the great white sharks as dogfish shark stand no chance in front of them. And yes, if the dogfish shark tries to tease their bigger friend then they are very much likely to get eaten by them too.

So this is the first lesson from EMH. It doesn't matter whether you believe in such an efficient market or not and it really doesn't matter how intelligent you are (you may be the best chartered accountant, or a gold medallist from IIM Ahmedabad or Harvard), you have almost no chance to pick the undervalued stocks on your

---

[15] The shark–seal theory analogy of stock market is entirely my creativity, and I find it really useful in explaining the real world of equity market to common investors.

own to reap extraordinary profit. In case you happen to pick one such undervalued stock, then it would be mostly by chance or luck.

Now you must be thinking: 'Okay boss, I agree. I cannot beat the market on my own. So what shall I do? Shall I hand over my money to the professionals so that they can beat the market and provide me with excess return?'

Well as you will see in Part III of the book, even the professional investment managers have their own challenges and it is not easy for them to beat the market consistently. Second, as we just saw, there is not one professional out there in the market but many and all of them are equally smart and intelligent. Further, all of them are vying to earn the extra profit from the same pie. So it is this cut-throat competition among them that not one of them can claim to beat others all the time. One year, ICICI Prudential and BlackRock will win, and others would earn less than market return. And the next year, it would be the chance of HDFC Mutual Fund and Citibank to take the crown, while ICICI Prudential and BlackRock would be biting the dust. Third, beating the market and earning excess return entails cost, and this cost reduces the extra return (if any) substantially. Fourth, no matter whether the professionals win or lose (against the market), they will always charge you fees and commission for their service (yes, they charge you fees for their underperformance as well) and this really brings down your net return over your holding period.

Now you must be really depressed. You cannot pick stocks on your own and you cannot trust the professional investment manager to give you good return. So what is the solution? The solution lies in the Part IV of this book.[16]

---

[16] More information is available about picking stocks in the book *Master Your Money, Master Your Life* by Abhishek Kumar.

LESSONS FOR THE INVESTORS

- In the short run, stock prices follow nearly a random walk and it is extremely difficult to predict future returns in the short term by looking at the past prices.

- The real armour in earning superior return is not in the ability to analyse companies and crunching numbers but in getting hands on some exclusive information about the companies. The moment this information is dissipated to the public, it loses its magical power in delivering market beating results. Hence, any information that investors get from newspapers, business magazines, TV channels, stockbrokers and the likes are worthless as far as earning any superior return is concerned. And if investor acts on such information, it is very much likely that their very act will go against their well-being.

- Any individual investor who tries to pick stocks on his/her own is very much likely to get beaten by the market.

- While the stock market may not be entirely efficient, it is competitive enough to ensure that no one reaps extra profit on a continuous basis.

Floored by the Factors
Investment Managers 'Factor' Their Portfolio

Most of the mutual fund companies today invest using the concepts of intrinsic value theory. However, with the advent of advanced computational technologies, many of them have now resorted to 'smart beta' strategies also known as factor investing. Now don't get confused thinking that this 'smart beta' is the old 'beta' with the added feature of the Internet. It's just a fancy nomenclature to lure millions of investors to bring in with them their money to the investment house which uses this strategy. But you would say: to heck with the name, tell me what exactly this strategy is. Well, the strategy is rather straightforward, and it can be explained as follows:

> *'Smart Beta' is the strategy of picking stocks not by analysing each and every stock individually but to sort stocks based on particular factors (such as size and value) and then to create portfolio of stocks which exhibits such factors. Say, you sort the stocks based on their size and once you have arranged them, you buy small-sized stocks and sell big-sized stocks.*[1]

In the present investing world, three of such factors are very popular—size, value and momentum. Now let us see how these

---

[1] The strategy is slightly complicated. But, in essence, it boils down to the one as explained earlier.

factors help in creating portfolios and why an understanding of this is important for you.

SIZE: IT DOES MATTER

Now don't get me wrong when you read the heading for this section. What I really was referring to is the size of the company in terms of its market capitalization and nothing else. So coming back to our discussion, the companies listed on any stock exchange can be easily sorted and arranged based on their size—their market capitalization. For example, at the time of writing, TCS is the biggest company in the Indian stock market by market capitalization which is followed by Reliance Industries Ltd and then HDFC Bank.

So what is the importance of size and why does it matter?

Size of the company is important because it has been observed and found out that *the stock returns over a long period of time was higher for small company stocks than the returns delivered by large company stocks.*

In one of their studies, our genius economist Eugene Fama along with his brilliant collaborator Kenneth French from MIT divided the stocks of US companies into 10 groups called deciles on the basis of their market capitalization. For example, if such study was conducted on Indian stock market, then TCS, Reliance Industries, HDFC Bank, HUL, etc., would be in decile 10 and smaller stocks such as MRF, Colgate, Berger Paints would be in decile 1 (if we were to sort top 100 companies based on their market cap).

So what did Fama and French found in their study? They found that decile 1, with stocks having the smallest size, produced the highest rates of return, whereas decile 10, the largest capitalization stocks, produced the lowest rate of return. Figure 6.1 shows the results of the study of Fama and French.

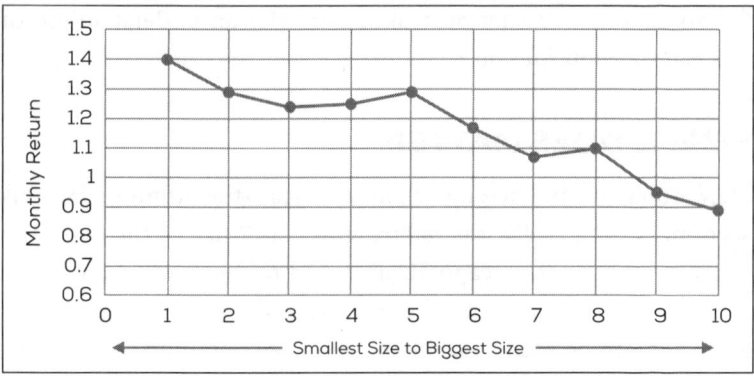

Figure 6.1. Average Monthly Returns versus Size for US Stocks: 1963–1990[2]

Now you may be thinking: it's such a great finding, 'I can increase my return by investing in smaller companies'. But there's a catch here. Smaller companies are usually considered to be more risky than larger companies and, hence, they need to give a higher rate of return to the investors.

But you might think why smaller companies are riskier. It is because smaller firms (with lesser money) usually have more difficulty sustaining themselves during recessionary periods and, thus, they may have more systematic risk relative to fluctuations in the overall economy.

Another explanation for smaller firms delivering higher return is because of something called survivorship bias.[3] The today's list of companies includes only those small firms that have survived—not the small firms that later went bankrupt. And if we were to include such firms, then the extra return as earned by small firms may not be as prominent as was shown in the study.

Thus, we can easily say that the higher return is nothing but the risk premium which the smaller companies have to pay to its

---

[2] *Source*: Eugene Fama, and Kenneth French, 'The Cross-Section of Expected Stock Returns', *Journal of Finance* (June 1992).
[3] Burton Malkiel, *A Random Walk Down Wall Street* (New York, NY: W. W. Norton, 2016).

investors for taking greater risk. So do remember that buying a portfolio of small firms is not a sure shot technique of earning abnormally higher return. Chances are that you may be able to get better return but there is a good chance that you may also lose a chunk of your money if you happen to withdraw your money at some 'wrong' point of time.

VALUE: THE DARK HORSE

In 1934, there were two professors from Columbia Business School who wrote and published a manifesto for general investors which has attracted strong followers, including the legendary Warren Buffet. The two professors were Benjamin Graham and David Dodd, and the book they authored was *Security Analysis*.[4] This book laid the intellectual foundation of what would later be called *value investing* and they argued that *value* wins over time.

To those who may not be very familiar with this concept or have found it a little confusing, let me help you with what is value investing and why value wins over time. Usually, the companies listed on any exchange can be classified into two categories: growth stocks or value stocks. And in common parlance, *the shares of good companies are called 'growth stocks' and those of bad companies are called 'value stocks'*. Now let us see what these stocks are and how value stocks (bad companies) deliver a higher return to its investors than the growth stocks (good companies).

Growth stocks, as the name suggests, appear to have a high growth *potential* in the eyes of investors.[5] Do pay attention to the word potential. It is not that the company had a good growth in the past; it is more about the future growth prospect of the company.

---

[4] Later, Benjamin Graham supplemented this book with a less technical one which he named *The Intelligent Investor* and which has become all the more popular among the general masses.
[5] It's the belief of the investors as a group about a particular stock which drives its price in the market and this belief may not be exactly the same what the company actually is.

And what does an investor like more than anything else? They like growth because only when a company has a good growth potential, it can grow the money which people would invest with them. So any company which shows some signs of growth potential in future becomes the darling of investors and everyone loves to have those stocks in their portfolio. They are the most famous and fashionable stocks and media loves to talk about them all the time. Think of Bajaj Finance, Asian Paints, Bharti Airtel, HUL, Sun Pharma and you will get the feel. And since everyone flocks to buy that stock, its price increases to such a level that its future return decreases. The company may still grow as per the initial expectation of the investors but since you purchased that stock at a very high price, your future return from the stock decreases.

It is not that you invested in a wrong company, you invested in a wrong stock because the price of the stock was way too high to give you any better return. Further, what if the growth that you had predicted didn't materialize? You get the double whammy. First, you paid too much for the stock. Second, since the company didn't meet its expectation, its prices fell, and your portfolio value decreased further.

And how do you identify such growth stocks? Well, such stocks have a high price–earning (P/E) ratio meaning they are selling at premium. Yes, good companies (and not stocks) always sell at premium.

Value stocks, on the other hand, are those companies which don't show any obvious sign of growth potential and so investors are usually reluctant to buy those stocks. As I stated earlier, they are bad companies having not so great financial results in the recent past and not showing any obvious sign of recovery (if the signals of recovery and consequent growth were obvious, then this company would fall into the category of growth stocks). These companies may not have a good management and, in fact, they can be so bad that they could be on the verge of bankruptcy. Further, the price the stock of these companies' command is based on current realities rather than on future projections of growth (since there are no obvious signs of growth to be considered).

And how do you identify such value stocks? Well, such stocks have a low P/E ratio and low prices relative to book value, meaning they are selling at discount. Yes, bad things always sell at discount.

Now take the example of Kotak Mahindra Bank and Karnataka Bank. The former is financially healthy and universally admired, with a great management team and presence across the country and a steady growing stream of assets and earnings. The latter is a relatively laggard and not so great company with limited presence across the country. Kotak Mahindra Bank is definitely a good (growth) company and Karnataka Bank a bad (value) company.

More importantly, Kotak Mahindra, aside from being the better company is also the safer company. Because of its steadily growing earnings and assets, even the hardest of economic times would not put it out of business. On the other hand, Karnataka Bank's finances are not so healthy and if there was any economic recession, then chances of it going out of business are much higher.

Now we arrive at one of the most counter-intuitive points in all of finance. It is so counter-intuitive that even the professional investors have trouble understanding it. Here is a twist: since Karnataka Bank is a much riskier company than Kotak Mahindra, investors expect a higher return from Karnataka Bank than they do from Kotak Mahindra. Think about it. If Karnataka Bank had the same expected return as Kotak Mahindra, no one would buy it. So its price must fall to the point where its *expected* return exceeds Kotak Mahindra's by a wide margin so that investors are finally induced to buy its shares. The keyword here is *expected*, as opposed to *guaranteed*. Karnataka Bank has a higher expected return than Kotak Mahindra Bank, but this is because there is a great risk that this may not happen. Remember, the risk of owning stock in a single shaky company is very high. But in a portfolio of many such losers, a few might reasonably be expected to pull off, providing the investor with a handsome return.[6] Thus, the logic of market is:

Good companies are generally bad stocks, and bad companies are generally good stocks.[7]

Now it may be difficult for you to appreciate that good companies are bad stocks. But the reality is that it's the fact. There have been a large number of studies of the growth-versus-value question in many nations over long period of time. They all show the same thing: *unglamorous, unsafe value stocks with poor earnings have higher returns than glamorous growth stocks with good earnings.*

Another explanation why value (cheap) stocks perform better than growth (expensive) stocks is that investors overreact to the recent past, that is, they give too much emphasis to the company's most recent performance. So if a company's last two quarter results were excellent, then investors extrapolate its superb performance into future and push its price high. Similarly, if a company has been underperforming lately then it starts selling at discount and is stereotyped by the investors as a 'bad' company. But the reality is that a 'bad' company is not as bad as it looks, and, on average, is likely to do surprisingly well in the future.

Further is the chart (Figure 6.2) from the same study[8] conducted by Fama and French, and the results speak for themselves. Value stocks characterized by low P/E ratio deliver a higher return and growth stocks which are characterized by high P/E ratio yield lower return.

---

[6] Venture capitalists (VC) funding the start-ups follow the same strategy. Investing in start-ups is a risky proposition, and we have already seen so many start-ups failing. The VCs understand this and that is why they invest in a wide number of start-ups. And even if 8 out of 10 start-ups fail, the 2 who succeed do so good that VCs are able to make a good amount of money from their investment in all the 10 start-ups they invested in.

[7] William Bernstein, *The Four Pillars of Investing.*

[8] In their study, Fama and French didn't actually sort the stocks based on P/E ratio but on their book equity (BE) to market equity (ME). This ratio of BE/ME is inversely related to P/E ratio and, hence, to avoid any confusion, I have shown the x-axis as P/E.

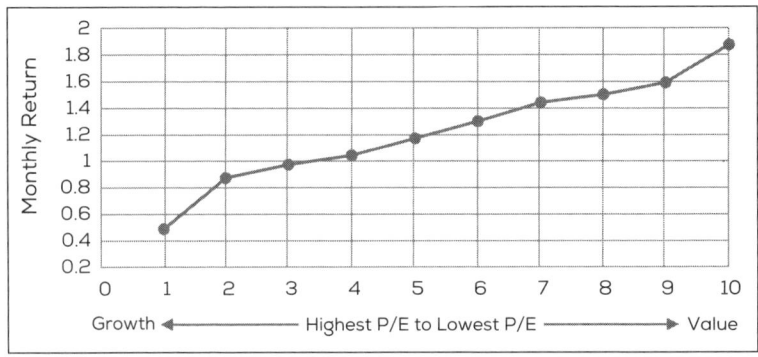

Figure 6.2. Average Monthly Returns for Value versus Growth for US Stocks: 1963–1990[9]

Again, these results would not have surprised our old value investors, Graham and Dodd, who, in their classic 1934 book, *Security Analysis,* stated the following:

> *Hence, we may submit, as a corollary of no small practical importance, that people who habitually purchase common stocks at more than about 16 times their average earnings are likely to lose considerable money in the long run.*[10]

DOES VALUE ALWAYS DELIVER?

Now don't get excited if you thought that you have found the magic wand of earning higher return by investing in undervalued stocks as denoted by their low P/E ratio. The thing is that low P/E multiple can reflect the risk factors that are already priced into the market. As we already saw earlier that value stocks with low P/E ratio is a bad company with more risk. So *if you are investing in value stocks in an attempt to earn a higher return, then do remember that you are carrying a higher risk.*

---

[9] *Source*: Eugene Fama, and Kenneth French, 'The Cross-Section of Expected Stock Returns'.
[10] Benjamin Graham, and David Dodd, *Security Analysis.*

Now there is another explanation why value stocks on an average give higher return, and that is because these cheap stocks are unpopular or out of favour and, hence, sell at discount, while growth stocks are fashionable and, hence, expensive. And by being a contrarian, Graham argued that you could beat the market, although not all the time. In his book *The Intelligent Investor*, he cautioned that 'Undervaluation caused by neglect or prejudice may persist for an inconveniently long time, and the same applies to inflated prices caused by overenthusiasm or artificial simulants'.

This particular advice of Graham was worth heeding during the dot-com bubble of the late 1990s when all the so-called value investors saw their portfolio perform badly as the most expensive stocks—the Internet darlings—kept increasing in price, leaving those boring value stocks behind.

Yes, buying a stock that the market does not fully appreciate today is fine, as long as the rest of the market comes around to your point of view sooner rather than later. And what happens when the market doesn't accept your view? Your portfolio value doesn't increase in the way you would have liked them to, which basically means that you made a bad bargain.

MOMENTUM: SWIM WITH THE FLOW

This is by far the most popular factor in the world of *smart beta* strategies and is often the most followed one. However, unlike the first two factors of *size* and *value*, this factor is not based on any rational logic or on some mathematical numbers and ratios but on the investor's psychology.[11]

Economists have been studying and trying to find pattern in stock price movement. They love to do so. And in a number of studies, it was found that over short holding periods, there is some evidence

---

[11] Many academicians argue that even the size and value factors are not rational and risk factors but are more related to behavioural biases of investors.

of momentum in the stock market which essentially meant that increase in stock prices are slightly more likely to be followed by further increases than by price declines and decrease in stock prices are more likely to be followed by further decrease.

For longer period, however, *mean reversion* of the stock returns come into action. So if a stock has had experienced a large price increase over a period of months or few years, then it is very much likely to decrease and vice versa.

So investors believing and following in the momentum strategy buy stocks that have recently risen in price and sell stocks that have recently fallen, expecting that the stock price will, for a time, continue to move in the same direction. While this may seem at odds with the old maxim of 'buy low–sell high', there is substantial research to support this 'buy high–sell higher' strategy. In 1993, two economists found that stocks with the highest returns over the past six months outperformed stocks with the lowest returns by about 1 per cent per month over the next six months.[12]

Now you would be thinking what the possible causes of such momentum can be to let it persist over short period of time. Well, three possible explanations have been offered by the academicians: the first is based on behavioural considerations; the second, on slow response of the investors to the new information and, third, on the unequal access to the fundamental information about the company.

Robert Shiller, the Noble Prizewinning professor from Yale University, in his book *Irrational Exuberance* says that the individuals see stock prices rising and are drawn into the market in a kind of 'bandwagon effect'. So when your friend says that 'stock price of XYZ has been increasing and I have invested in it', what do you do? You buy the stock of XYZ, thereby further increasing its stock

---

[12] Narasimhan Jegadeesh, and Sheridan Titman, 'Returns to Buying Winners and Selling Losers: Implications for Stock Market Efficiency', *Journal of Finance* 48, no. 1 (1993).

price and when you see that a particular stock is falling, you sell it fearing that it would decrease further and, thus, make it fall further. It's kind of self-fulfilling prophecy.

The second explanation is based on the argument that investors are slow to accept and digest the new information. It is said that people do not adjust their expectations immediately when new information arises—especially news of company earnings that exceeded (or fell short of) anticipated value (yes, the market is not completely efficient).

Third possible explanation for the momentum in the stock prices is because of unequal access to the fundamental information about a company. Assume there is some positive development in a company, so the first set of people who would get to know this information is the executives working in that company. Hence, it is often alleged that the first persons to act on such information are the insiders.[13] So they buy the stocks causing its price to rise. Then the insiders often tip this information to their near and dear ones who act next. Soon, the news reaches to the professional investors and they put big blocks of money increasing the price nearly to its level congruent to the new information. And then media (magazines, newspaper and TV channels) makes this information public and the individual investors thinking that they have got some exclusive information buy causing the price to increase a little further. This whole process makes the increase in the price of the stock a bit gradual when the information is positive. The same happens with the decrease in the price of the stock with the negative information.

Now you must understand that the momentum strategy works only in the short term and should not be part of your long-term strategy. In the same study, it was found that over half of the excess

---

[13] Insider trading is illegal in many countries including India. But it doesn't stop people from indulging in such activities. And yes, we Indians are good at finding loopholes in the system to exploit them. Bottom line is that making something illegal doesn't make it impossible.

returns generated in the first 12 months were lost over the following 2 years. Thus, over the longer periods, the advantage of buying 'winning' stocks is completely eliminated. In fact, in an earlier study,[14] it was found that stocks that performed poorly over the previous 3- to 5-year period significantly outperformed those stocks that had done well, over the next 3–5 years, implying a *reversion* to *mean reversion* of longer run stock returns.

LESSONS FOR THE INVESTORS

- Small-sized companies tend to produce higher returns than the large-sized companies over an extended period of time.

- Value stocks on an average perform better than the growth stocks.

- Over short holding period, there is an evidence of momentum observed in the stock market.

- To the extent that 'smart beta' funds generate excess returns, it is very much likely because of extra risks these funds carry. The moment the funds deviate from their overall market portfolio, they become less diversified and, hence, are exposed to more risks.

- 'Smart beta' funds require periodic rebalancing. For example, if you follow the value investing strategy then you need to keep changing your portfolio every time your value stocks become a growth stock, or a growth stock becomes a value stock. As such, there is a cost associated with such rebalancing and such costs tend to reduce the extra net return generated by such funds.

---

[14] Werner F. M. DeBondt, and Richard H. Thaler, 'Does the Stock Market Overreact?'

PART
2

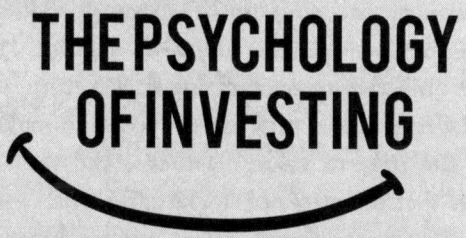

THE PSYCHOLOGY
OF INVESTING

7

Do You Blink or Think?
A Sneak Peek into Human's Mind

Whatever we have read, appreciated and probably assimilated into our blood till now about the theories pertaining to the stock market and its return is based on one single premise that *investors are rational and will always behave in their own self-interest. Further, they take decisions with the objective of maximizing their wealth and are constrained only by their tolerance for bearing risk.* There's only one problem with this assumption. And the problem is that it isn't true.

The MPT, EMH, the random walk and the relationship between risk and return, all are built on the premise that investors are rational, and they would take judicious call with their money with the sole objective of maximizing their return and minimizing their risk. As a whole, they are supposed to make reasonable estimates of the present value of stocks, and their buying and selling ensures that the prices of stocks fairly represent their future prospects. But since the investors are not machines which were programmed by their creator to always act in their self-interest, they act many a times in such a way that if a rational spectator was put away from the arena of stock market and was asked to watch the investors playing the game, he/she would say, 'these people (investors) lack the common sense and are unnecessarily harming themselves'.

So before we proceed to see why we act in ways which are not always rational and optimal for our well-being, let us understand the two moods of our mind.

THE TWO SYSTEMS OF OUR MIND

In his bestselling book *Thinking Fast and Slow*, Daniel Kahneman says that we human beings have two modes of thinking and, in any instance, it is either of the two modes which is at work. He refers the two systems in the mind as System 1 and System 2 and he defines the two systems as:

> *System 1 operates automatically and quickly, with little or no effort and no sense of voluntary control.*
>
> *System 2 allocates attention to the effortful mental activities that demand it, including complex computations. The operations of System 2 are often associated with the subjective experience of agency, choice and concentration.*[1]

Think of the aforementioned two systems as follows.[2] System 1 is the intuitive 'blink' system—automatic, fast and effortless—whereas System 2 is the reflective 'think' system—controlled, slow and effortful.

So what exactly are these two systems of our mind and why it is important for us to understand it?

Imagine you are in cricket field where multiple teams are playing their respective games in their own pitches (a common sight in most of the towns and semi-urban centres in India). You are standing at one spot as a fielder looking towards the batsman (from your own game). Suddenly a group of people shouts at you and asks you to save yourself as the batsman from some other game has hit the ball towards you. Now you hear the sound and the immediate action that you take is that you raise both your hands up, shield your head with the hands and duck down. You didn't move to see from which direction the ball is coming. Neither you tried to run

---

[1] Daniel Kahneman, *Thinking Fast and Slow* (New York, NY: Farrar, Straus and Giroux, 2011).
[2] As discussed by another behavioural economist, Meir Statman, who is a professor of finance at Santa Clara University.

away from your spot because you didn't have time. You simply shielded your head. Why? It is because you have been evolved to do so as this was your best effort to save yourself from not being heavily injured or probably killed. John Mauldin, who is a renowned financial expert and author, says:

> Much of our decision-making process is hard wired into our brains, developed for survival on the African savannahs some 100,000 years ago. We adapted to movement, learning to make decisions quickly, because there was quite a difference, literally life and death, between dodging dangerous lions and chasing succulent antelope. And while those survival instincts are quite useful in general, when translated into a modern world, and especially a modern investment world they make us prone to all sorts of errors.[3]

System 2, on the other hand, is not something natural but comes into action when we use our brain and logic to find what we should do or say which would be in our best interest. Consider yourself where you are interviewing for a job which you had wanted for long. The interviewer asks you a tricky question. So what do you do? You don't reply him/her with whatever thoughts flashed in your mind at that instant. Instead, you listen to your interviewer carefully, think about the possible replies in your mind, weigh their pros and cons, and then speak out the answer which you thought would be best suited for you to get the job.

If you would observe carefully, you would realize that System 1 is actually our default option, so all information goes first to the System 1 for processing. It is instantaneous, automatic and effortless. The judgements made by our System 1 are generally based on aspects such as similarity, familiarity and proximity, and allow shortcuts to deal with large amounts of information simultaneously.

---

[3] James Montier, *The Little Book of Behavioural Investing* (Hoboken, NJ: Wiley, 2015).

James Montier, who is a noted finance author, says, 'our System 1 is a quick and dirty "satisfying" system, which tries to give answers that are approximately (rather than precisely) correct'. However, System 2 follows a deductive, logical approach to solve a problem, and it requires a deliberate effort to actually engage this system (remember, System 1 is your default mode). Only when System 1 runs into difficulty, it calls on System 2 to support more detailed and specific processing that may solve the problem of the moment. However, the only problem with System 2 is that it can handle only one step at a time, so it is a slow and serial way of dealing with information.

DO YOU BLINK OR THINK?

Now if someone asks us whether we are a System 1 or System 2 person, most of us would like to identify ourselves with System 2 because it appears to give a better impression of ourselves to others. But what we don't understand is that no matter what we say about ourselves to others, it is our System 1 which does most of our decision-making and it is only because of System 1 that we as a human species have evolved to this stage and it is only because of our System 1 that we have survived so long to be writing (me) and reading (you) this book at this point of time.

Consider one example which James Montier has discussed in his book *The Little Book of Behavioural Investing*. Imagine there is a glass box containing a large live snake on the table in front of you. And you are asked to lean forward and concentrate on the snake. So when you are focusing on the snake, it rears up and your immediate action would be to jump backwards.

Now why did you move backwards? It was because your System 1 was in action to keep you safe. In fact, the moment your eyes saw the snake's movement, it sent a signal to your brain and since System 1 is always at work (unless we consciously suppress it by bringing System 2 in action), it reacted and made you move back.

However, a fraction of second later when all the information regarding the set-up and surrounding is reached and processed by your System 2, you realize that your moving back was not necessary as the snake was inside the glass box and could do no harm to you. But you had already reacted by this time. From a survival point of view, a false positive is a better response than a false negative.

Now imagine if you always used your System 2 in all your decision-making and there was no glass shield between you and the snake. By the time your System 2 takes the decision to move back (since in this case there is no glass box and moving back is the only solution if you want to be safe and live another day), the snake would have already bitten you.

So next time someone asks the aforementioned question, I don't know what you would like to say but my answer would be, 'I am a *Blink* person who also *Think* when situation demands'.

THE ROLE OF THE TWO SYSTEMS IN YOUR INVESTMENT DECISION

When we are investing, we take decisions about what we should do with our money. And the kind of decisions in the investment process ranges from—where to invest, when to invest, what would be our asset allocation, which stocks or funds we should invest, for how long we should invest and the likes. And as we discussed earlier that since our System 1 is always at work (it cannot be turned off, though it can be overridden sometimes by System 2) and is the default mode of our thinking, we invariably take our investment decisions using System 1. And while System 1 is generally very good at what it does, it suffers from one big draw-back and that is System 1 is emotional, has biases and has little understanding of logic and statistics.

Also, our biases of System 1 cannot always be avoided because many a times even our System 2 would have no clue about it. And in case there would be some hints for System 2 to find the likely error in our judgement, we don't always involve System 2 because it is tiring, painful and requires an effort. Also, constantly questioning our own thinking would be impossibly tedious as System 2 is very slow and inefficient to serve as a substitute for System 1 in making our routine decisions.

Now, some of you may not agree to this. You would say, 'I know other people make financial mistakes by bringing in their emotions and biases, but I always act rationally and logically when it comes to my investment decisions'. Guess what, even our Nobel Prizewinning economist Harry Markowitz who proposed the MPT and taught the world how they should allocate their portfolio rationally and efficiently couldn't do it when it came to his own investment decisions. When asked how he invested his own money, he said:

> *I should have computed the historical co-variances of the asset classes and drawn an efficient frontier. Instead, I visualized my grief if the stock market went way up and I wasn't in it—or if it went way down and I was completely in it. My intention was to minimize my future regret. So, I split my contributions 50/50 between bonds and equities.*[4]

Seeing that even noble laureates were prone to making mistakes, Daniel Kahneman said, 'the best we can do is a compromise: learn to recognize situations in which mistakes are likely and try harder to avoid significant mistakes when the stakes are high'.

And this is what I would be discussing in next few chapters about our biases in our judgements and the situations in which they are likely to occur during our investment process. Then our job as a rational investor would be to recognize those biases—not as our weakness but as a part of our thought process—and then take

---

[4] Jason Zweig, *Your Money and Your Brain: How the New Science of Neuroeconomics Can Help Make You Rich* (2007; repr., New York, NY: Simon & Schuster, 2008).

appropriate action by recognizing the fact that we are humans and not machines and we are very much susceptible to making mistakes caused by our emotions, pride, fear and ego.

LESSONS FOR THE INVESTORS

- We all have two modes of thinking and taking decision: System 1 and System 2.

- System 1 is a quick fix to solve our daily routine jobs. It is also essential for our survival, and it protects us from some grave fatalities. System 2 is a slow and painful mechanism to find out the most optimum decisions for our well-being.

- System 1 is the default mode of our operation. Unfortunately, it doesn't deliver the best result when it comes to investment decisions.

Oozing with Overconfidence
Everyone Cannot Be above Average

Given further are 10 questions and I would like you to give a high and low estimate for each question. In case you are sure that you know the answer correctly, then you may give the same figure for both the high and low values. The only constraint to your answers is that you must be 90 per cent certain the correct answer will fall within these limits.

(The answers are at the end of this chapter.)

	90% Confidence Range	
	Lower value	Upper value
Rajendra Prasad's age when he became the president		
Length of Narmada River (in km)		
Total run scored by Kapil Dev in ODI		
Year of birth of Lata Mangeshkar		
Diameter of the earth (in km)		
Number of cars sold by Maruti Suzuki in 2017–2018		
Number of India post offices		
Number of national parks in India		
Air distance from Indore to Imphal (in km)		
Height of the highest dam in India (in m)		

Now if you are like most of the people, you may have gotten four to seven of your answers wrong and if you got more answers right then chances are that you love playing quizzes. Two professors ran a similar test over a thousand participants and less than 1 per cent got nine or more correct answers, with most respondents missing four to seven questions.[1]

Why do we get our estimates wrong? In other words, why did we set our confidence interval so small?

The simple reason is that we are generally far too confident in our abilities. Psychologists who have studied human emotions and biases say that the most pervasive of our biases is the tendency to be overconfident about one's beliefs and abilities, and overoptimistic about assessment of the future. And that is the reason we set overly narrow confidence intervals around our forecasts and tend to overweight our own forecasts, relative to those of others.

For example, when we drive cars, say for over a year or two, we naturally become confident in our driving ability. Hence, it came as a no surprise when a survey issued by Allstate Insurance Company found that 64 per cent of drivers in the USA considered themselves either 'very good' or 'excellent' drivers.[2] So all these very good and excellent drivers in an ideal scenario should not have violated any traffic rule (because they are good drivers). But among this pool of excellent drivers who rated themselves as the best, 53 per cent had received a speeding ticket, while 44 per cent have been tagged with three or more traffic tickets.

Another instance where this trait of overconfidence was exemplified is from the book *In Search of Excellence*, where the authors report that a random sample of male adults were asked to rank themselves in terms of their ability to get along with others. And 100 per cent of the respondents ranked themselves in the top half of the population. Further, 25 per cent believed that they were in the top 1 per cent of

[1] Edward Russo, and Paul Schoemaker, Decision *Traps: Ten Barriers to Brilliant Decision Making and How to Overcome Them* (New York, NY: Simon & Schuster, 1989).
[2] Available at http://www.breslinandbreslin.com/blog/2011/09/study-most-drivers-are-overconfident-in-their-driving-skills.shtml (accessed on 31 December 2019).

the population.[3] Statistically, this sounds absurd because everybody cannot be above average, and 25 per cent can't be in top 1 per cent. Mathematically and practically, only 1 per cent of the population can be in top 1 per cent and not 25 per cent of them.

Further, Daniel Kahneman has argued that this tendency of being overconfident is particularly strong among investors. More than most other groups, investors tend to exaggerate their own skill and deny the role of chance. Also, almost all the investors overestimate their own knowledge, underestimate the risks involved and exaggerate their ability to control events.

For example, in the summer of 1998, there was a sharp decline in the US stock market.[4] The Gallup organization polled investors in both June and September of that year—before and after the market decline—on what they thought their own portfolio returns, and that of the overall market, would be.[5] And the results are tabulated further.

Expected Returns for Next 12 Months	June 1998 (%)	Sep 1998 (%)
Own portfolio	15.20	12.90
Overall market	13.40	10.50

From the earlier table, we observe two things very clearly. The first is that the average investors think that he/she will do better than the overall market by nearly 2 percentage points. The second is that since the market has fallen by nearly 15–20 per cent (from June 1998 to Sep 1998), the stock market returns expected by the investors have decreased post the market decline.

[3] Thomas Peters, and Robert Waterman, *In Search of Excellence: Lessons from America's Best-Run Companies* (New York, NY: Harper Business, 2006).

[4] In August 1998, one of the biggest hedge funds of that time, Long-Term Capital Management (LTCM), founded by Nobel prizewinning economists, had blew up following the Russian debt crisis, and the US market and other major economies of the world were greatly impacted. The US market had fallen at the rate of approximately 15 per cent causing great panic among the investors. This case of LTCM is so interesting that many case studies and books have been written just to show how geniuses (the Nobel prizewinners) can fail.

[5] Greg Ip, 'The Bull Market May Be on the Ropes, But the Bull Mentality Acts Like a Chimp', the *Wall Street Journal* (14 Sep 1998).

Now both the investors' expectation is not only wrong but is detrimental to their own portfolio growth. Let us see how.

The first observation that a typical investor thinks his/her portfolio can beat the market by nearly 2 percentage points is mathematically impossible. While it is possible that some of the investors would do better than the overall market next year, it is impossible for everyone to do so. After all, everyone can't be above average. In fact, a typical investor must obtain the market return less the expenses and transaction cost. Even a cursory glance on the earlier table would reveal one simple fact that people tend to be overconfident on their abilities and their choice of stock pick and they are too optimist about the return they expect from their portfolio.

The second observation that investors reduce their expectation from the stock market after a fall in the stock market is rather more surprising. Consider an example. On 1 January, you buy a gold coin for ₹30,000. In the next one month, the price of the gold decreases and your colleague buys the similar coin for ₹25,000. Then on 31 December, both of you sell the coin at the prevailing price at that time. Now who do you think has earned the higher interest? If you do your maths correctly taking all the possible scenarios of gold coin price on 31 December, you will realize that your colleague would have earned a higher return. Why? It is because he/she purchased the same thing at the lower price. So no matter what the gold coin price was as on 31 December, your colleague would have earned ₹5,000 more than you because he/she paid less by the same amount.

Viewed in this context, it is astonishing that any rational investor would impute lower expected returns from falling stock prices. *A falling stock price is rather an indication for a higher future stock return.* However, since we tend to overweight more recent data and underweight older data, we usually lower our expectation about the stock return from the stock market once the market starts to fall. No wonder, many people sell their entire portfolio and exit the market during the bearish period incurring heavy losses and carrying remorse of investing in the stock market.

ILL EFFECTS OF OVERCONFIDENCE

Now come to the crucial part. You would say 'Okay. Understood that people tend to be overconfident in whatever they say or do. Also take your point that when it comes to investing, there again people are overconfident. But how does it impact me as an investor?' Well this bug of overconfidence impacts you in not one but three ways. Let us see them one by one.

ILLUSION OF STOCK PICKING ABILITY

The first way your overconfidence impacts you is to give you an illusion that you can successfully pick stocks by following a few simple (or probably some complicated) set of rules by reading books claiming to teach stock picking skills or by listening to self-proclaimed stock market experts or by subscribing to an advisory service (either online or offline). I have seen people discussing and sharing their invest-ment and trading strategies on how they identify the next big hot stock and/or fund and how they are certain about their stock/fund selection criteria.

Right now, if I wanted to, with a few keystrokes, I could screen a database of all the nearly 5,000 listed companies on BSE and/or National Stock Exchange (NSE). Further, I can arrange these stocks on various criteria such as P/E ratios, dividend yields, profitability and earnings growth. And to help me in this endeavour, there are many inexpensive commercially available tools and software which can easily do it in few seconds. Also, there are free Internet portals where you can arrange stocks based on multiple criteria. You just have to filter the stocks based on your criteria and there you have a neatly arranged list of stocks inviting you a flashing tag line 'Buy me; Hold me; Invest in me'. And then what do you do? You invest in overpriced stocks with a high probability of lower future return.

The thing is that this bug of 'overconfidence' has bitten not only you but millions of other investors who are equally eager and busy in scanning the market to find the undervalued stocks which would quadruple in the next six months or one year. Additionally, there are big boys out there—not with the free or inexpensive tools and software—but with the most sophisticated machines and servers being run by the best of software engineers, quantitative analysts and ably supported by the best of MBAs and PhDs who not only know the ins and outs of the market but also the who's who of the companies whose stocks you are trying to pick. Do you really think that you have any chance to beat them? If you really think so, then I wish you luck. Both history and data show that you are going to need it badly.

ILLUSION OF BEATING THE MARKET

The second way your overconfidence impacts you is that it mistakenly convinces you that you can beat the market. As a result, you speculate more than you should and end up trading too much and earn less than what you should have ideally earned.

But wait! You would say that 'the only reason I trade is because I want to earn more so how come trading stocks make me earn less'. Well, there is a reason for that. So let me help you understand this with one simple fact which is overlooked by most of the investors or rather traders. And the fact is that 'the more you trade, the less you earn'.

However, you wouldn't be convinced yet just because I told you not to trade. So here is the maths for you. If you want to earn more by trading stocks, then, on an average, when you sell one stock and buy another stock, you want the stock that you bought to do better than the stock that you sold by enough margin so that it exceeds your total trading cost. Suppose you sold stock A and bought stock B and this transaction of selling A and buying B costs you ₹100. Now, and here is the catch, the only way you could profit from this trade is that when stock B outperforms stock A by more than ₹100.

Stock B's performance – Stock A's performance > 100

The moment the earlier equation fails, you lose. It doesn't matter whether stock B (which you bought) delivered a good performance. What matters is whether it did better than yours earlier holding of stock A. Moreover, did it yield better than stock A by more than ₹100? If yes, then you made a profit. If no, you lost. And if you thought that results would be in your favour, then probably you might be on for some rude shocks.

Terrance Odean, a noted finance professor at the University of California, Berkley, and a former student of Daniel Kahneman, has spent his entire career studying a very specific type of investor: the one who is overconfident, short-sighted and brings in his/her emotional biases in every investment decision. Odean's specialty, in other words, is the average investor like you and me.

So Odean along with his colleague Brad Barber conducted a number of studies analysing the behaviour of individual investors and how different decisions of these investors impacted their wealth. In one such study, Odean analysed the trading records of 10,000 investors and found that stocks bought by individual investors underperformed the stocks sold by nearly 3 percentage points in the next 12 months after the transaction had happened.[6] And this underperformance by the stocks which were bought was excluding the trading cost. If those trading costs were included, the underperformance would be much higher.

But you would argue that in a trade there has to be a buyer and a seller and if everybody lost their money in the buy side of the trade then somebody would have made money at the sell side of the trade. So how come all the stocks bought by individuals underperformed the stocks sold? It is because when an individual is trading, he/she isn't trading with another individual. Odds are that he/she is trading with the big boys (institutional investors, I-Banks, mutual funds) of the Dalal Street. So the loss incurred by

---

[6] Terrance Odean, 'Do Investors Trade Too Much?' *American Economic Review* (1999).

the individuals during a trade is not a gain of another individual, rather it's a gain of one of the big boys. Remember, every time you decide to get in the market (or get out), the investors you buy from (or sell to) are the best of the big professionals. Of course, they're not always right, but how confident are you that you will be 'more right' more often than they will be?

Almost all the people who trade in stocks believe that they can easily beat other investors by buying cheap from them and selling at high price to them. They may be correct, but they are mostly unaware of one important aspect—that in trading you only make money when you know more than those on the other side of the trades. And the problem is that you almost never know who those people are. If you could, you would find out that they have the names such as Goldman Sachs, Morgan Stanley, Motilal Oswal, Citibank and ICICI Securities. William Bernstein, in his book *The Four Pillars of Investing* says, 'trading is like a game of tennis in which players on the other side of the net are invisible. The bad news is that most of the time, it's the Williams sisters'.

Further, in a similar study which Odean conducted along with his colleague Brad Barber, they looked at 66,465 household accounts at a large discount broker during 1991–1996. And they found that those accounts that trade most earn an annual return of 11.4 per cent during the period, while the buy-and-hold investors (who traded the least) earned a return of 18.5 per cent net of costs.[7] This difference in returns of 7 per cent is too high, and such difference came mainly from the cost of trading incurred by the two set of investors. Definitely, trading is hazardous to your wealth.

So when professors Odean and Barber were asked why people trade when it's so much evident that trading reduces the net return of the investors, they said that it is primarily because people are overconfident in their abilities to beat the others. And it is in

---

[7] Terrance Odean, and Brad Barber, 'Trading Is Hazardous to Your Wealth: The Common Stocks Investment Performance of Individual Investors', *Journal of Finance* 55 (2000).

this optimism and their overconfidence that they speculate and gamble with their money. Result: they lose their money. And who makes the money? It is the stockbrokers, market makers and the institutional investors.

Now another interesting aspect of this bug of overconfidence is that it doesn't bite the two genders equally. In various studies, it has been found that men tend to be more overconfident than women.[8] And men typically display far more overconfidence than women, when it comes anything related to cars and money. So, in a study aptly titled, 'Boys Will Be Boys', Odean and Barber studied over 35,000 household accounts from 1991–1997 and they found that men trade 45 per cent more than women. And, on average, the men's investment returns were lower than women's returns by nearly 1 per cent point per year.[9] Yes, women make better investors than men.

Seeing the implications of trading on individual investors' wealth, Charles Ellis, who is a noted investor and professor, once said in an interview:

Watch a pro football game, and it's obvious the guys on the field are far faster, stronger and more willing to bear and inflict pain than you are. Surely you would say, 'I don't want to play against those guys!' Well, 90% of stock market volume is done by institutions, and half of that is done by the world's 50 largest investment firms, deeply committed, vastly well prepared—the smartest sons of bitches in the world working their tails off all day long. You know what? I don't want to play against those guys either.[10]

---

[8] K. Deaux, and E. Farris, 'Attributing Causes for One's Own Performance: The Effects of Sex, Norms, and Outcome', *Journal of Research in Personality* 11 (1977): 59–72.
[9] Terrance Odean, and Brad Barber, 'Boys Will Be Boys: Gender, Overconfidence, and Common Stock Investment', *Quarterly Journal of Economics* (2001).
[10] Jason Zweig, 'Wall Street's Wisest Man', *Money* 30, no. 6 (June 2001).

ILLUSION OF TIMING THE MARKET

The third way overconfidence impacts you is that you get a feeling that you can time your entry and exit from the market to reap extraordinary profits. And when you gain such overconfidence, you are constantly looking for *tops* and *bottoms* in the stock price movement; you study various charts, observe the volume of transactions taking place and then act. You basically try to enter the market when you feel that it has come to its bottom and from here it will rise and rise. Similarly, you try to exit the market when you feel that it has topped and from here it will only fall and fall.

Now let me tell you something. Nobody and with 'nobody' I really mean nobody can predict the tops and bottoms of the market precisely and nobody can execute this entry/exit thing to reap any material benefit which would exceed the simple 'buy-and-hold' strategy. Not yet convinced. Well, let me show you some maths.

Imagine you had invested ₹100 on 1 April 1979 (the day when the Sensex Index was started with the base value of 100) in Sensex. This means you had invested ₹100 to purchase shares of top 30 companies in the Indian stock market. Further, imagine that you didn't do anything with your money thereafter. You never added a single rupee and neither had you withdrawn a single paisa. Moreover, you never followed any business news channel and, hence, never had any urge to trade or enter/exit the market. You just stay put in the market all along and at the end of 31 December 2017 you find that your ₹100 has grown up to ₹34,506, thereby delivering you a handsome return of 15 per cent per annum.

Now I did some analysis on the earlier Sensex data and the results of this analysis is something you should always remember. In this period of 38 years, there were 8,892 trading days. And out of these 8,892 trading days, only 30 days had the daily return which exceeded 6 per cent. So if you are one of those investors who are always on the lookout for *timing the market* and if you happened to miss those 30 days then your money wouldn't have reached to the level of ₹34,506. Rather, it would have been just ₹3,124. Think for it sometime and let it seep into your subconsciousness.

Laszlo Birinyi, who is a noted investor, in his book *Master Trader*, studied a longer period and calculated that a buy-and-hold investor would have seen one dollar invested in the Dow Jones Industrial Average[11] in 1900 grow to $290 by the start of 2013. Had that investor missed the best five days each year, however, that dollar investment would have been worth less than a penny in 2013.

So what do we conclude from the earlier two studies? It's simple and the conclusion is that market timers risk missing the infrequent large sprints that are the big contributors to the performance of overall market. So the next time you think that you can enter or exit the market at just the right time, think again. The probability of you missing those brilliant 30 days in those 9,000 days is very high and chances of your wealth shrinking from ₹34,506 to ₹3,124 are very bright.

Remember, decisions that are driven by greed or fear are usually wrong, usually late and very unlikely to be reversed correctly. And when it comes to real money, my only suggestion to you would be to don't even consider trying to outguess the market or outmanoeuvre the professionals to 'sell high' and 'buy low'. You'll fail, perhaps disastrously and spectacularly.

CAUSES OF OVERCONFIDENCE

Now let us turn our steering wheel to see what the possible causes of *overconfidence* are and how we can learn to be more realistic about our investment results and protect our wealth from ourselves.

---

[11] Dow Jones Industrial Average is to the USA what Sensex is to India, that is, both of these indices comprise of top 30 stocks of their respective market.

SELF-ATTRIBUTION BIAS

One of the reasons of this overconfidence is what the psychologist call is *self-attribution bias*. What essentially this means is that we link our successes—our good outcomes—to our own skills and abilities, and we tend to rationalize bad outcomes as resulting from unusual external events which were beyond our control.[12]

In the world of investments, when an individual starts investing, he/she is usually oblivious of his/her abilities. He/she infers his/her ability from his/her successes and failures. The only problem is that in assessing his/her ability, he/she takes too much credit for his/her success while blaming failures to external factors such as market conditions or probably some bad decisions taken by the RBI or the government.

Similarly, in a bullish market when most of the stocks tend to do well, people who select stocks on their own think that because they chose those stocks on their analysis, it is doing well, while, in reality, almost every other stock would be doing well. Don't confuse between bulls and brains. *When there is a bull run, every brain seems to be working correctly and when the bear roars; the brain goes for a hibernation.*

CONFIRMATION BIAS

The second reason for this overconfidence stems from *confirmation bias*. Usually when we believe something to be true, then we look for reasons why it is true and ignore evidences which show that your belief isn't true. Say one of your friends has invested in a stock XYZ and it has done fairly well in the past. Over your coffee break, you hear him/her say about his/her investment in XYZ and how he/she picked this stock. So you go back to your screen and start looking for this stock and since this particular stock has done fairly

---

[12] B. Fischhoff, P. Slovic, and S. Lichtenstein, 'Knowing with Uncertainty: The Appropriateness of Extreme Confidence', *Journal of Experimental Psychology: Human Perception and Performance* 3 (1977).

well, there will be numerous articles on media (media worships past heroes) praising this stock. You were already biased that this stock is good from your friend and on your personal research you find enough reasons why you should invest in this stock and immediately put some money in this stock. However, there must also have been reports why this company may not be a good stock at this point of time because its price has increased too much. But you would have silently ignored those reports and evidences. Paul Simon has rightly said that 'A man hear what he wants to hear and disregards the rest'.

SELECTIVE MEMORY

The third reason for our overconfidence is our tendency of compartmentalizing our successes and failures. We tend to remember those activities, or areas of our portfolios, in which we succeeded and forget those areas where we made losses as remembering those losses gives us pain and we tend to avoid such pains. Erik Davidson, who is the chief investment officer, at Wells Fargo says, 'Much like our human predisposition toward nostalgia about the past, where we only remember the good times and gloss over the bad, investors likewise tend to take a nostalgic view of their past winners but forget about their past losing investments'.

Understand that we have a selective memory of success. We remember our successful investments and often boast about it and tell stories how we made the killing. Rarely, I have come across where someone would admit how he/she had been wrong in some of his/her investments. And since we remember our heroics and fail to remember where we came out as loser, we tend to be overconfident of our abilities.

This tendency of ours to compartmentalize success and failures is particularly dangerous because it distracts us from what should be our main focus: the whole portfolio. Remember, in our portfolio, there would always be some winning stocks and some stocks which have seen a decline in recent times. But performance of individual stocks rarely matters to our overall wealth. What really matters is how our overall portfolio is doing and that is what our focus should be. Rejoicing our successes and burying our failures not only builds up unnecessary confidence, it forces us to ignore the overall failure of our asset allocation and overall portfolio strategy. As a result, we earn below par long-term returns for the simple reason that we choose to overlook our overall portfolio.

OVERCONFIDENCE IN INVESTMENT INDUSTRY

Now you must be thinking that normal investors tend to be over-confident and this impacts their investment decisions. But what about professionals? Do they also tend to be overconfident in their abilities? And whether our money that we hand over to them to take better care suffers losses because of this overconfidence? The answer is a big YES!

It has been found in numerous studies that experts are generally more overconfident in their abilities than the amateurs. James Montier who is a renowned investor, professor and author of mul-tiple books on finance, once asked a sample of more than 600 pro-fessional fund managers about how many of them were above average on their jobs and an impressive 74 per cent responded in affirmation.[13]

Further, in one of the studies[14] on stock market professionals (portfolio managers, stock analysts, stockbrokers) and common people (undergrad students from the psychology department of a university) on their respective confidence and performance in the stock market, it was found that students were around 59 per cent confident in their stock picking abilities; however, the

---

[13] James Montier, *The Little Book of Behavioural Investing* (Hoboken, NJ: Wiley, 2017).

[14] Gustaf Torngren, and Henry Montgomery, 'Worse Than Chance? Performance and Confidence among Professionals and Laypeople in the Stock Market', *Journal of Behavioural Finance* (2004).

professionals averaged 65 per cent confident. Then both the groups were asked to select one stock from a pair as being likely to outperform the other every month based on every public information that one can get on any stock.

And when their stock picking abilities were analysed, it was found that the students picked the right stock 49 per cent of the time, while the professionals picked the right stock less than 40 per cent of the time. That is to say, you should have been able to beat both groups just by tossing a coin!

From this study, two things can be concluded very easily. First, an average person (either professional or amateur) is overconfident of his/her ability. Second, even if the professionals might know more than the amateurs in their chosen field, they tend to underperform.

IS BEING OVERCONFIDENT REALLY BAD?

Let us be very clear here. Our overconfidence and unrealistic optimism are not at all bad for ourselves. Overconfidence in ourselves makes us feel good about ourselves by creating a positive outlook with which to get through life's experiences. Further, it has been found out that the proportion of overconfidence among the entrepreneurs and self-employed is higher than the proportion among employees. Also, the unrealistic optimists, whether self-employed or employees, have a more positive attitude towards work than the realists: they work for longer hours, anticipate longer careers and are more likely to think that they would never retire.[15] Meir Statman in his book *What Investors Really Want* says:

> *Optimism, even if unrealistic, is mostly a blessing. Optimists are happier than realists; they recover faster from surgery and adjust more smoothly to major life transitions, such as leaving home for college, looking for a job or healing after a divorce. Optimists*

---

[15] Manju Puri, and David Robinson, 'Optimism and Economic Choice', *Journal of Financial Economics* 86 (2007).

respond to negative feedback with a positive sense that they are good, skilful, and effective, whereas realists perceive the same negative feedback accurately and integrate it into their sense of themselves. Optimism bolsters self-control necessary to over-come temptation on our way to our goals.

But there is a flip side to this overconfidence and false optimism, and this reversal becomes more visible when it comes to investing where an overconfident investor trades more and loses more. Remember, optimism may be a good life strategy, but it definitely is not a good investment strategy.

LESSONS FOR THE INVESTORS

- People are usually overconfident of their abilities and it becomes more prominent in their investment decisions.

- Overconfident investors tend to think that they can pick winning stocks and/or mutual funds on a regular basis through their research, while it has been proven time and again that they can't.

- Overconfident investors trade and speculate more and, as a result, lose a lot of their money by paying huge fees and commissions to their brokers and other financial intermediaries.

- Professional investors on an average are more overconfident of their skills and tend to underperform.

Quiz Answers: 64; 1312; 3783; 1929; 12742; 1779574; 155015; 104; 1853; 261

Loss and Gain: Not the Same
We Hate Loss Much More Than We Love Gain

One of the best gifts from Daniel Kahneman and Amos Tversky to the field of decision-making is the idea of *prospect theory* which not only challenged the 250-year-old *utility theory* but also ushered in a new era of looking at how we make our decision when we are buying and/or selling our stocks and how our irrational decisions impact our wealth.

So, before we proceed, let us first revisit the *utility theory* proposed by Daniel Bernoulli in 1738 which almost remained unchallenged till Kahneman and Tversky published their seminal paper in 1979[1] to fully appreciate how prospect theory affects our decision in buying and selling of stocks.

Bernoulli had suggested that we human beings assign utilities (also called values) to different things, and money is one such thing. However, he said that not every equal increment in your wealth increases your happiness by the same amount. For example, he argued that a gift of 10 ducats (currency used in Europe till the 20th century) has the same utility to someone who already has 100 ducats as a gift of 20 ducats to someone whose current wealth is 200 ducats.

Bernoulli was right at this perspective. The following chart shows a version of utility function that Bernoulli calculated.

---

[1] Daniel Kahneman, and Amos Tversky, 'Prospect Theory: An Analysis of Decision under Risk', *Econometrica* 47, no. 2 (1979).

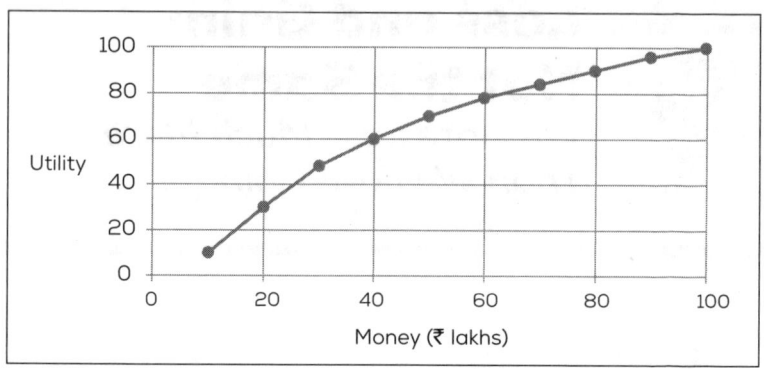

You can see that adding a sum of ₹10 lakh to your initial wealth of ₹10 lakh increases the utility level from 10 points to 30 points. However, the same addition of ₹10 lakh doesn't increase the utility points that much when your wealth is ₹90 lakh. This is the essence of Bernoulli's utility theory which states that *happiness and joy of a person depend on his final state of wealth at that time and any further increment in the wealth decreases in value as the person becomes richer and richer*. Gifting a beggar ₹1,000 will give him much more happiness than gifting the same ₹1,000 to someone who had just come out of a 5-star hotel after having a sumptuous dinner.

Another implication of this utility function is that people are risk-averse as they tend to assign lower values for the same amount of money as their wealth increases. For instance, if your wealth is ₹20 lakh and I offer you the following two choices:

- An addition ₹1 lakh for sure
- A 50 per cent chance to win ₹2 lakh

And if you are like most of the people, you would opt for the first option (the sure thing) because you value the second as you would win in the gamble less than the first, so you are not willing to risk losing that first ₹1 lakh in an attempt to get ₹2 lakh.

While Bernoulli's utility theory was right in some parts, it had one serious flaw which Kahneman and Tversky explained in their paper—the reference point from which we look at our final state of wealth. For example, take the following scenarios:

Ram and Shyam each have ₹50 lakh today. However, yesterday, Ram had ₹20 lakh and Shyam had ₹80 lakh. Are they equally happy (do they have same utility) today?

Bernoulli's theory assumes that the utility of a person's wealth is what makes him/her happy (or sad). So Ram and Shyam each having ₹50 lakh today should be equally happy, but you do not need a psychology degree to know who is happier and who is sad. And it was this gap—the reference point—which was filled by Kahneman and Tversky in their *prospect theory*.

Kahneman and Tversky said that people's choices are motivated not by their final state of wealth but by the values they assign to gains and losses (the changes in their wealth). Further, losses are considered far more undesirable than equivalent gains are desirable. They called this behaviour *loss aversion*. So how much people hate loss more than they love gain. To know this, let's play a game.

I will toss a fair coin. If it comes head, I will pay you ₹600 and if it comes tail, you pay me ₹500. What are the chances that you would play the game?

If you are like most of the people, then you wouldn't play the game even though it's a positive pay-off[2] game for you. Why is it so? It is because you are probably risk-averse meaning you hate loss more than you love the corresponding gain.

Now assume I change the rules as follows. Head: I will pay you ₹1,000; tail: you pay me ₹500. Would you play the game now?

Chances are that you would play now because your gain from this game is twice as big as the loss you would incur. Kahneman and Tversky conducted this study over a large sample of people

---

[2] Since the coin is fair, the probability of coin showing *head* or *tail* is equal. So the expected pay-off to you is ₹50 (0.5 × 600 – 0.5 × 500). Hence, if you are risk-neutral, you will play this game.

and concluded that losses were nearly 1.5 to 2.5 times as undesirable as equivalent gains were desirable.[3] The following chart shows the typical emotion (joy or pain) people have when they witness a gain or loss in their portfolio. As can be seen, a gain of ₹50,000 will give you 2 units of joy. However, a loss of the same ₹50,000 will give you 5 units of pain.

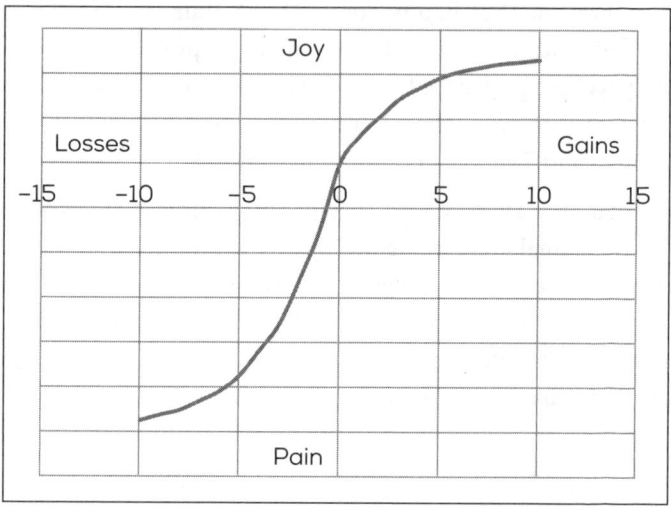

It is a fact that loss gives you pain, and most people tend to avoid this pain at any cost. Frank Armstrong, who is a financial advisor, writer and ex-military pilot, observes: 'I have known men who have routinely faced death in the sky with equanimity but became physically ill when their portfolios declined 5 percent'.

You will notice from the earlier chart that the utility doesn't depend on the level of wealth as in Bernoulli's utility theory but in changes in wealth from the current level. And it is this point—the frame of reference—from which we make our decisions which made the prospect theory so popular and appealing.

---

[3] Daniel Kahneman, *Thinking Fast and Slow.*

THE DISPOSITION EFFECT

Now before we proceed, let us again answer one simple question which most of us face when we have invested our money in the equity market.

Suppose you bought two stocks X and Y last month at the same price of ₹500 per share. Since last month, the price of X has gone up to ₹600 and the price of Y has dropped to ₹400. You need money for some urgent need, and you need to sell one of the two stocks. Which one would you sell?

(a) Definitely X (b) Definitely Y (c) Probably X (d) Probably Y

Now if you are like most of the people, your answer would be either (a) or (c), that is, you are most likely to sell stock X which has gone up in value and hold on to Y. Why do people do so? It is because we are humans and we tend to avoid losses (prospect theory). Second, we also have our sense of pride and we like to maintain it even if it would cost us some money.

As we discussed earlier, we take decisions based on a reference point. So the moment we purchase a stock, our reference point becomes the price of the stock at which we purchased it and our future decision whether to hold that stock or sell it is greatly influenced by whether the stock has moved up or below that reference point. And many a times, we become fixated on this reference point so much that we exclude any other information regarding that stock. Our entire decision then becomes based on one single criteria: has the stock gone up or below the reference point? And since we tend to avoid losses, we hold on to stocks that have gone down in value and sell those on which we have realized some profit.

Second, when we invest money in the stock market, we not only put our money but also our pride and intelligence go along with the money. And if the money is not very large, then we can withstand the loss of the money but it's very hard for us to see our pride and intelligence being melted away in the market. And that is why we find it very difficult to admit, even to ourselves, that we have made a bad stock market decision. On the other hand, we are usually quite proud to tell the world about our successful investments that produced large gains. So whenever we face such a situation, we sell winning stocks and hold on to losers. Selling a stock that has risen enables us to realize profits and build our self-esteem and provide us an opportunity to boast of our investment successes to our friends and colleagues. And if we sold our losing stocks, we would realize the painful effect of regret and loss. Also, we feel that if we hold on to a losing position, it will eventually recover, and feelings of regret will be avoided. These emotions of boosting our self-esteem and regret avoidance is one of the reasons behind the tendency of investors to hold on to their losing positions and to sell their winners. And this tendency of investors to hold on to losing stocks and sell the winning stocks is called *disposition effect*.[4] Holding onto a stock that has done poorly keeps alive the possibility that we will not have to confront the finality of our failure.

Now the question comes why it is a bad decision to sell winners and hold losers.

Well, logically it seems foolish to sell winning stocks and holding on to losing stocks. Why? It is because when we purchase stock, we look at its future prospect and evaluate how the stock will do in future. But at the time of selling, we don't look prospectively. Rather, we look retrospectively and see if the stock has risen above or fallen below its reference point (the purchase price of the stock). A bad way to approach your investment decisions.

The correct approach should be to see which stock has better prospect in the future and then sell the one with a not-so-promising future. Remember, decisions on your investments must be made on a forward-looking basis. What has happened in the past cannot

---

[4] H. M. Shefrin, and M. S. Statman, 'The Disposition to Sell Winners Too Early and Ride Losers Too Long: Theory and Evidence', *Journal of Finance* (1985).

be changed. It is a 'sunk cost'. When prospects don't look good, sell the stock whether or not you have a loss. And similarly, if the prospects look good, hold on to it irrespective of its past movement.

Second, if you see from a tax perspective then this disposition effect again makes no sense. Ideally, investors should sell stocks which have fallen in value because the losses realized from selling the losers would help in reducing the tax. Further, holding on to the winners would help by postponing taxable gains and in case investors hold the stock for a longer period then the tax rate on the capital gain also comes down.

But you would say 'what if the stocks which have fallen in price recover'. It was the same feeling which our professor Terrance Odean from Chapter 8 had, and he decided to investigate whether investors were correctly betting on recovery of the losers. Sadly, he found that winners that were sold outperformed the losers that continued to be held by an average of 3.41 per cent over the next one year and by 3.58 per cent over the next two years.[5] Yes, winners continued to do better, and losers continued their downfall. And in case you still trust on your instincts that your fallen prince would recover and become a king one day, it would still make sense to sell that loser and take tax benefit. And once you sell the losing stock, purchase a stock with similar characteristic (probably from the same industry and similar risk profile) so that your portfolio's overall risk exposure doesn't change.

Now you may be wondering: 'Okay, agreed. We individuals are prone to such biases and take irrational decisions which impact our wealth. What about the professionals? Do they also exhibit similar trait, and does it impact their performance?'

Yes, our professional investors are also humans and they also suffer from the same set of biases. In one such study,[6] it was found out

---

[5] Terrance Odean, 'Are Investors Reluctant to Realize Their Losses', *Journal of Finance* 53, no. 5 (1998).
[6] Andrea Frazzini, 'The Disposition Effect and Under-Reaction to News', *Journal of Finance* 61 (2006).

that across all mutual funds, 17.6 per cent of gains were realized, but only 14.5 per cent of losses were realized. Further, it was found out that the best performing funds were those with the highest percentage of losses realized. Thus, the fund manager who was the least loss-averse did better than others. So this problem of disposition effect is not only present in individuals but in professional fund managers as well.

YOUR PORTFOLIO IS NOT YOUR CRUSH

I remember the days of my undergrad when I used to have frequent crushes. It was also the time when online messengers and social media were the means through which you talked to everyone probably except with your parents. So whenever I used to come back from my class, I used to see whether my present crush is online. If yes, ping her. If no, just see the 'last seen at' timestamp and wait for her to come online. And now with the advent of smartphone, teenagers keep looking at the 'last seen at' timestamp of their crushes in mobile and hit them up the moment they see the green button.

Now this constantly monitoring the online presence of crushes is not only restricted to teenagers, it has increased its span and its tentacles have reached adults in their 30s and 40s who keep checking their smartphone frequently. The only thing is that it's not their crush who they stalk, it's their portfolio which they keep monitoring day and night.

Now the obvious question comes: 'How this constantly monitoring of portfolio affects my wealth?'

The answer lies in acknowledging the fact that you are most likely a risk-averse person who doesn't like to see, witness and realize a loss. However, the more you check your portfolio, the more likely you are to encounter a loss simply because of the volatile nature of stock prices. The thing is that if you buy stocks, it is very much likely that its value will drop below the price you paid, if but for a short time, soon after your purchase. And we have already seen how our nature of loss aversion makes this decline very disturbing to us. However, since the long-term trend in stocks is upwards, if you wait for some period of time before checking your portfolio, the probability that you will see a loss decreases. In fact, researchers have found that people are willing to invest more when they see the performance of their holdings infrequently.[7]

To see how this 'monitoring frequency' impacts the investor's wealth, two economists conducted a 'learning experiment' in which they allowed individuals to see the returns on two unidentified asset classes.[8] One group was shown the yearly returns on stocks and bonds, and the other group was shown the same returns, but instead of annually, the returns were aggregated over period of 5, 10 and 20 years. The group were then asked to pick an allocation between stocks and bonds.

The group that saw yearly returns invested a much smaller fraction in stocks than the group that saw returns aggregated into longer intervals. Why did they do so? It was because in the short term, stocks are highly volatile (meaning they fluctuate a lot and, hence, appear risky) and it was this short-term volatility of stocks which dissuaded people from choosing that asset class, even though over longer periods, was clearly a better choice.

This tendency to base decisions on the short-term fluctuations in the market is known as *myopic loss aversion*. And since over longer periods (5, 10 and 20 years), the probability of stocks showing a loss becomes smaller and smaller, our loss-averse investors are more likely to hold stocks if they monitored their performance less frequently.

---

[7] M. S. Haigh, and J. A. List, 'Do Professional Traders Exhibit Myopic Loss Aversion? An Experimental Analysis', *Journal of Finance* 60 (2005).

[8] Shlomo Bernartzi, and Richard Thaler, 'Myopic Loss Aversion and the Equity Premium Puzzle', *Quarterly Journal of Economics* (1995).

Researchers have found that in the long run, stocks are less risky than other asset classes. Further, over a period of 20 years and above, stocks have far exceeded in delivering better returns than any other asset class. So the question that comes to mind is: 'Why doesn't everybody buy stocks?'

It is because most of the investors are short-sighted. In one of his studies, Richard Thaler estimated the risk horizon of the average investor to be about one year. And since for an investment horizon of one year the stocks are risky, people tend to avoid holding stocks.

One of the reasons why investing in real estate is more popular among Indian investors than investing in stock[9] is because people can't monitor the present value of the land/home/office they purchased in the real time. They simply buy that piece of real estate and sit over it. Had there been a system where people could constantly monitor the performance of their real estate investment, then real asset wouldn't be as popular an investment vehicle as it is now among the investors. Behavioural finance experts have found both in their research lab and in the real world that investors who never look at their portfolios expose themselves to higher risk and earn higher returns than those who examine their holdings frequently. Think about your house or the one which you would have rented out. It's a good thing that you can't check its value every day, or even every month or every year. You happily hold onto it, oblivious to the fact that its actual market value may have temporarily declined 20 per cent on occasion.

Remember, the constant monitoring of your portfolio is not only injurious to your health as it increases your anxiety and blood pressure, it is also detrimental to your wealth. It never ceases to amaze me that some fund managers actually have access to their portfolio's performance in real time; they can see exactly how

---

[9] It should not be inferred as if real estate is a better asset class than stocks and equities. It's not only the nature of the asset class which delivers the result to investors, it's also how investors behave with those asset classes.

much they are winning or losing second by second. Many fund managers and stock analysts have this habit of looking at their portfolio the moment they get up from their bed. I can't imagine a more destructive process than this. If I've done my homework and selected stocks that I think represent good value over the long term, why on earth would I want to sit and watch their perform-ance day by day, let alone second by second. I rarely examine the performance of my personal portfolio at such frequency and neither should you.

LESSONS FOR THE INVESTORS

- We investors are normal people and we hate losses much more than we love gains.

- The idea of selling winning stocks and holding on to losing stocks is not a good idea. What has happened in the past is a past and all investment decisions should be taken based on the future prospect.

- Constant monitoring of your portfolio is not good for your health and wealth.

10 Trampled by the Herd
All of Us Are Part of the Crowd

When I was a kid, my father used to tell me a story about sheep where a herd of sheep is following one of them. As the events turn in the story, the one who was leading suddenly fell into a well. Seeing this, other members of the herd joined that fellow and jumped into the well. Why would they do that? I used to ask. And my father's reply was that everyone was just following the crowd.

I thought for some time on this and said to myself, 'maybe they are animals and that's why they did that'. But what if they were humans? Would they also do the same?

Robert Shiller in his book *Irrational Exuberance* says, 'a fundamental observation about human society is that people who communicate regularly with one another think similarly'. It is a fact that we human beings are supremely social animal. We enjoy talking to people, associating with friends and colleagues, and particularly love sharing our ideas and interests with the like-minded people. And it is this association with people and society at large which influences how we think and take decisions. For example, Marwaris and Gujratis going for CA or starting their own business, Biharis going for UPSC, Bengalis going for Art & Literature and Punjabis going to Canada is nothing but the influence of others' thinking on our own thinking.

Most importantly, the way we think is also influenced by the trending fashion prevalent in our culture during a particular time period. How else can we explain why men wore bell-bottom trousers during the 1970s and early 1980s? Why bobby print was a craze at one point of time and then suddenly lost its sheen and gave way to new and contemporary design?

All these phenomena in the behaviour of crowd is often called 'group thinking'. And when we are stuck to choose between two often close but confusing alternatives, we go with what the crowd suggests, even though it may be an incorrect choice. Why it is so? It is because group of individuals often reinforce one another into believing an incorrect point of view into something true.

In 1950, the social psychologist Solomon Asch conducted a famous experiment where people were presented with four lines and asked to pick the two that were of the same length. The right answer was obvious, and anyone could have answered it correctly if they were asked independently. But when associates of Dr Asch gave wrong answers, the subjects often succumbed to the group's view and gave the incorrect answers.[1]

Why did people give wrong answers when it was very clear what the right answer was? Was it because people wanted to be the part of group and giving the right answer (which was different from the group's consensus) would make them look different? Was it that people just wanted to conform to the group? Well, initially it was thought so as Asch conjectured that social pressure caused participants to pick the wrong line even when they knew that their answer was correct.

However, a follow-up experiment three years later which was a slight variation of Asch's experiment confirmed that it was not social pressure that led the subjects to act against their own best judgement but their disbelief that a large group of people could be wrong.[2]

---

[1] Solomon Asch, *Social Psychology* (Englewood Cliffs, NJ: Prentice Hall, 1952).
[2] Morton Deutsch, and Harold Gerard, 'A Study of Normative and Informational Social Influences upon Individual Judgement', *Journal of Abnormal and Social Psychology* 51 (1955).

We are often made to believe that at times an individual can be wrong, but a group of people cannot be wrong. And that is the reason why people gave wrong answers (even when the correct answer was obvious) because they thought a group of 6–7 people cannot be wrong with the same choice. This wisdom of crowd is perhaps best illustrated from a real-life example—showcasing the famous *information cascade*[3] behaviour—which most of us would have encountered sometime.

Assume you visit a new city and your smartphone Internet is not working. You are hungry and reach to a place where you found yourself choosing between two restaurants. The two restaurants are pretty close by; however, one restaurant is slightly crowded and the other relatively empty. Now, one perfectly rational way of deciding at which restaurant you should eat is to see which restaurant is busier since there's a good chance that at least some of the customers would have tried both restaurants and have now chosen to eat at the better one. But when you chose to eat at the busier restaurant, you are increasing the chance that the next diner, using the same rational reasoning, will also eat there and so on. Eventually, everybody will be eating at that one restaurant even though the other could have been much better.[4]

Now you would be thinking that we humans tend to exhibit herd behaviour in other areas of life. But what about our investments? Do we exhibit herd behaviour in our investment decisions also?

In various studies across different economies, it has been found that investors everywhere run in herds, large or small, bullish or bearish. For instance, Chinese investors herd as they speak to one another about their investments and infect one another with their bullishness or bearishness. Further, this investment infection

---

[3] D. S. Bikhchandani, David Hirshleifer, and Ivo Welch, 'A Theory of Fashion, Social Custom and Cultural Change', *Journal of Political Economy* 81 (1992); and Abhijit Banerjee, 'A Simple Model of Herd Behaviour', *Quarterly Journal of Economics* 107, no. 3 (1992).
[4] I had the good opportunity to listen to this example directly from Professor Ivo Welch (one of the economists who analysed this effect) during my Master of Financial Engineering course at UCLA Anderson School of Management.

in China spreads most easily among neighbours who share broker-age branches.[5] Similarly, Americans draw one another into the stock market, and drawing power is especially strong in sociable communities.[6] And this herding of American investors extends beyond stocks to industries. Investors who are bullish on a stock of a company tend to be bullish on stocks of other companies in its industry.[7]

And the most interesting of herd mentality was found among the investors of Finland. In one of the studies,[8] it was found that Finnish investors join the herd of stock market investors when their neighbours have gained in the stock market. Yet neighbour's stock market losses don't discourage stock market investing among other investors, probably because neighbours tell neighbours about gains but keep quiet about losses (a perfect example of pride and regret from Chapter 9).

THE COST OF CONFORMING

Imagine you entered your office and the first thing that you noticed on the newspaper lying on the front desk was about the sudden increase in the valuation of an XYZ company. You reach to your desk and your colleague tells you about that XYZ company and how he/she had invested his/her money in that stock six months back which has increased more than four times now. He/she further tells you that he/she will buy some more stocks of this company as various research reports are showing it to grow even further. You start working on your regular schedule and then there's a message on your phone from one of your old friends who sleeps/eats/lives the stock market suggesting you buy stocks of

[5] Lilian Ng, and Fei Wu, 'Peer Effects in the Trading Decisions of Individual Investors', *Financial Management* 39 (2010).

[6] Jeffery Brown, Zoran Ivkovic, Paul Smith, and Scott Weisbenner, 'Neighbours Matter: Causal Community Effects and Stock Market Participation', *Journal of Finance* 63 (2007).

[7] Russell Jame, and Qing Tong, 'Retail Investor Industry Herding' (working paper, Emory University, Atlanta, GA, 2009).

[8] Markku Kaustia, and Samuli Knupfer, 'Learning from the Outcomes of Others: Evidence from the Stock Market' (working paper, Helsinki School of Economics, Helsinki, 2009).

that XYZ company. Now you think you cannot miss to invest in this stock. All your friends are getting rich and you definitely don't want to be left behind. So what do you do? You search for that company on the Internet reading the expert's opinion and a green bar showing a 'must buy' recommendation and after you convince yourself with the good financial performance of the company in past few months you place a buy order for XYZ stock. As Charles Kindleberger who is a noted economic historian has stated, 'There is nothing so disturbing to one's wellbeing and judgement as to see a friend get rich'.

Remember, when everyone is excited about the market, you should be extremely cautious. Stock prices are not based just on economic values but on psychological factors that influence the market. Yale economist Robert Shiller, one of the leaders of the behavioural finance movement, has emphasized that fads and social dynamics play a large role in the determination of asset prices.[9]

While the conventional wisdom may work in your social and corporate life but when it comes to investment, the conventional investment wisdom may not be always right. *If everyone believes that a particular stock or a fund is the best thing available in the market, then what it tells you is that everybody already owns them.* This, in turn, means two things. First, because everyone has bought them, prices are high and future returns are low. And second, and more important, that there is no one else left to buy these stocks. And since there are no more investors left to buy, sooner or later somebody will give up and the price will fall just like a stack of cards. The investors who had participated in the dot-com bubble thinking that just because their friends made money by investing in Internet companies had learnt this lesson the hard way.

[9] Robert Shiller, 'Stock Prices and Social Dynamics' (Brookings Papers on Economic Activity, Brooking Institutions, Washington, DC, 1984).

Robert Shiller, in his book *Irrational Exuberance,* has noted that the process feeds on itself in a *positive feedback loop.* The initial price rise encourages more people to buy, which, in turn, produces greater profits and induces a larger and larger group of participants. Eventually, one runs out of greater fool.

Remember, money is not made when everyone knows that a particular stock or fund is good. If everyone agrees with you that Bajaj Finance is a good stock, then the price will reflect that today and you won't be able to profit by investing in that company. If, however, you have some informational advantage or understand sentiment better than others, then only you can make some profit out of it.

LESSONS FOR THE INVESTORS

- We tend to exhibit herd mentality in almost all areas of life including our investment decisions.

- While conforming to the social pressure may be one of the reasons, the primary reason for herd mentality is the notion that wisdom of the crowd is better than that of an individual.

- When we participate in the herd, we inflate the bubble and deflate the burst and our timing of entry into and exit from the market often causes serious losses to our portfolio.

The Folly of Forecasting
Money Lies in Predicting; Not in Following the Prediction

Human life consists of events which can be broadly classified as deterministic or probabilistic. Deterministic events are those whose outcomes are known with almost surety. For example, you know for sure that if you drop an egg from 10 feet, it will break. Probabilistic events, on the other hand, are those, whose outcomes are not known for sure and we try to make the best guess on the basis of our experience, knowledge, intuition and heuristics, that is, we forecast the possible outcomes of the event and try to guess which outcome is most likely to happen. For instance, if you jump from a height of 10 feet, you don't know for sure whether you will break your leg or not. Chances are that you will be as fine as earlier, and chances are that you might end up with a plaster around your leg.

As you would appreciate on the basis of your experience that our life presents us with a host of occasions to forecast. Every entrepreneur forecasts how his/her business will do in 2–3 years down the line and whether it is worth taking the risk. Book publishers forecast the sales of a book and predict who all can be the target audience. Contractors forecast the time required to complete the project. Politicians forecast how a particular measure or decision is going to impact their vote base. Military veterans forecast the casualties. Engineers estimate the amount of bricks and concrete required to make a building. And economists forecast what would be inflation, growth rate and unemployment one year down the line.

But what about us—the investors? Do we forecast?

I guess, I don't need to tell you the answer. Since investments in an equity market is a probabilistic endeavour,[1] we investors love to forecast and if we feel that we lack the skills to do it on our own then we take the help of the so-called market experts who make their living by forecasting. Yes, just like astrologers make their living predicting the future course of someone's life, we have financial astrologers who make their living predicting the future course of stock market. And while the traditional astrologers portray to lead a simple and minimalistic life so that people believe that they are not after the money; the financial astrologers portray to lead a high-flying life giving an impression that because of their market knowledge they have made money and with their knowledge you too can make money. And while the traditional astrologers charge you their fees upfront, the financial astrologers are the worse of the lot. Usually, they will give you free advice and you become happy saying they are so kind-hearted. But, in reality, what happens is that once you believe in their advice, you buy their product and services, and pay much more fees and commission to them, either directly or indirectly.

Why do we love to forecast our investment outcomes and why do we love to listen to the self-proclaimed market gurus?

ILLUSION OF KNOWLEDGE

When it comes to investing, we seem to be addicted to inform-ation as if more information will give us better insight and help us become a better investor. Unfortunately, in the world of capital market, where the end investors are right at the bottom of the information chain, where they receive information after all its juice has been extracted out by the corporate executives, policymakers,

---

[1] Many investors are not aware of this fact that investments in capital market is a probabilistic event and one needs to have a good understanding of probability and statistics to appreciate how the capital market behaves.

fund managers and stockbrokers that any information that the common investors receive is nothing but the residual which should ideally be thrown out and dumped rather than be consumed.

The illusion of knowledge is the tendency for the investors to believe that the accuracy of their forecasts increases with more information. So dangerous is this misconception that Daniel Boorstin once said, 'The greatest obstacle to discovery is not ignorance—it is the illusion of knowledge'.

There are certainly some pieces of information and data that have some predictive element of the future economic activity. But the problem is that the information is not privy to you. The reality is that everyone knows, watches and analyses the information that you have with you. And the result is that any material value that can be derived from such information has already been factored into the stock prices. For instance, you watch your TV news channel and came to know that the RBI will be easing interest rates, and this will be good for the stocks. And then you have a host of panel discussions on how this RBI decision is going to be beneficial for the market and investors. So what do you do? Do you place bet on the upward swing of the market and place more buy orders? If you do so, then you are doing a grave mistake. When you get to know about the RBI's decision, the rest of the world knows it too, and stocks have already risen because of it. So your buying decision based on this information is not going to help you in any way. Bernard Baruch once observed that 'Something that everyone knows isn't worth knowing'.

DESIRE TO GAIN CONTROL OVER FUTURE

While we fret over our past, we live in fear about our future. We don't know what lies ahead for us and we sometime become a cripple in fear of such uncertainty. So we seek out to know what's there in the box so that we can live peacefully in present knowing that we are going to get our goodies. And in case we get to know that there are no goodies in the box, we try to take corrective measures so that our box gets filled with the goodies which we would relish in the future. The astrologers—both financial and otherwise—exploit this human weakness to their advantage by claiming that they have an expertise to predict the future. So we flock to them to get an access to their third eye which would enable us to see if there are any goodies for us and if not then what we should do to get them.

DENYING RANDOMNESS

If there is one skill that makes us superior to both the animals and our computers is our ability to recognize highly abstract pattern and to make some sense of the randomness surrounding us. We all rely on pattern recognition in our everyday lives, from complex professional jobs to mundane things such as taking the route to our work. Nassim Nicholas Taleb discusses this pattern seeking behaviour of humans in his book *The Black Swan,* where he introduced the concept of narrative fallacy to describe how flawed stories of the past shape our views of the world and our expectations for the future. He says that narrative fallacies arise inevitably from our continuous attempt to make sense of the world. He further suggests that we humans constantly fool ourselves by constructing flimsy account of the past and believing they are true.

Remember, humans can't accept randomness; otherwise, for every decision, they would need to bring their System 2 into action which is time-consuming and painful. So we try to seek pattern in everything and try to adjust so that our System 1 takes most of the decisions for us. But in investing, this talent is rather counterproductive. The simple reason is, for the most part, the stock prices follow a nearly random path in the short term; that is to say there are almost no patterns. In such a chaotic world where randomness rules over everything in the short term, the search for patterns is not only futile, it is downright injurious.

Another interesting human bias is that once we are told that something is a random event, we expect the outcome to be totally random, while, in fact, in the short term the outcomes may not be as random as we would like them to be. For instance, Kahneman and Tversky conducted experiments on tossing of coin (a complete random events) and the participants of the experiment routinely judged the sequence of coin flips H-T-H-T-T-H to be more likely than H-H-H-T-T-T, which does not appear random.[2] However, simple statistics tell us that each of these sequences is equally likely because of the independence of multiple random events. Remember, being random doesn't mean that its outcome has to look random. What it essentially means is that looking at the past outcomes, we can't predict the future outcomes. And the same applies to our stock prices. But most of the investors when they see a pattern similar to H-H-H-T-T-T in the stock prices think that they have found the logic and can forecast its future movement. Alas! The real world is not as predictable as some people believe it to be.

REPRESENTATIVE ERRORS

There is one simple law of statistics which I think every investor should know and understand if they want to fully appreciate the nuances of investments in the equity market. This law is rather simple and highly intuitive and is known as the law of large numbers.

This 'law of large numbers' is an important law and it teaches us, for instance, that the percentage of heads in a sequence of coin tosses is likely to be closer to 50 per cent when we toss a coin a large number of times, say 800, than when we toss it a small number of times, say 8.

---

[2] Daniel Kahneman, and Amos Tversky, 'Subjective Probability: A Judgement of Representativeness', *Cognitive Psychology* (1972).

Rational investors or investors who have undertaken university-level statistics course know this law of large number. But what about the common investors? They believe in law of small numbers (there is no such law per se; it's just a false belief of common investors). They believe that a random sequence, such as a coin toss, will generate close to 50 per cent heads not only when we toss the coin a large number of times but also when we toss it a small number of times. Unfortunately, it doesn't work that way in the real world. You may toss a coin 3 times and chances of getting all 3 heads or all 3 tails is quite high.

Now, one manifestation of this belief in the law of small numbers is that four good years of return out of five is considered as a representation of the skill of a mutual fund manager rather than as a representation of a chance. So what do we do? We put our money in the hands of the fund manager who have delivered better than market results, never questioning how many such funds in the market are and what is the probability of a fund manager to get four heads in five tosses. This approach of ours often leads to serious investment mistakes because more often than not we substitute chance with skill thinking we will get the same superior return going forward also.

But once we note that this fund manager is one among thousands of fund managers, we can appreciate the fact that it is highly likely that there would be lucky coin tossers who would get four heads in a row and lucky fund managers who beat the benchmark four times in a row. Nassim Taleb in his book *Fooled by Randomness* says:

> *If one puts an infinite number of monkeys in front of (strongly built) typewriters, and lets them clap away, there is a certainty that one of them would come out with an exact version of the Iliad. Upon examination, this may be less interesting a concept than it appears first: such probability is very low. But let us carry*

> *the reasoning one step beyond. Now that we have found that hero among monkeys, would any reader invest his life's savings on a bet that the monkey would write the Odyssey next?*[3]

RECENCY BIAS

Another reason why we investors tend to forecast and why often our forecasts go wrong is because we give too much weight to the recent past and suffer from recency bias. We believe that immediate past is predictive of the long-term future. For instance, if the market has lately been doing well, investors think that it will continue to do well and extrapolate the most recent past creating rosy pictures and imagining all the possible wealth they could make. During such bull runs in the market, investors forget about the bear markets that might have occurred in some distant past and keep buying stocks feeling good about their prospects. Investors, thus, increase their exposure to the risk and may forget about the diversification or portfolio management prudence. Then a bear market hits, and rather than being prepared for it with shock absorbers (read asset allocation) in their portfolios, investors instead suffer a massive drop in the value of their portfolio and may sell out stocks when the market is low.

Why do investors exit when the market starts to decline? It is because here again they extrapolate the recent fall in the market and think that market is likely to fall going forward also. And when the market is down, investors become convinced that it will never go back up; they reduce risk at exactly the wrong time and stick their heads in the ground. But because of the mean reversion, stocks do go up and by the time investors plan to get back into action, the market is already back to its usual.

This behaviour of individual investors is what the institutional investors like and it is them who reap benefits from such biases of

---

[3] Nassim Taleb, *Fooled by Randomness* (New York, NY: Random House, 2005).

individual investors because it is mostly them on the other side of trade when the investors buy during market peak and sell during the bottoms.

THE FINANCIAL SOOTHSAYERS

Lao Tzu, the 6th-century BC poet and philosopher, once observed: 'Those who have knowledge don't predict. Those who predict don't have knowledge'. Yet most of the financial industry seems to be obsessed with predicting the future. You open any business magazines or any business channel on your TV and you will find all the executives from top brokerage houses, donning the cloak of Oracle, predict where the market is headed and how some key financial decisions taken by the government are going to impact the market. Further, this business of prophecy telling gains momentum when the market becomes volatile and everyone seems curious to know what will happen to their portfolio. William Bernstein in his book *The Four Pillars of Investing* has put it down very aptly. He says:

> It is said that there are only two kinds of investors: those who don't know where the market is going and those who don't know that they don't know—the overconfident fellas. But there is a rather pathetic third kind—the market strategist. These highly visible brokerage house executives are articulate, highly paid, usually attractive, and invariably well-tailored. Their job is to convince the investing public that their firm can divine the market's moves through a careful analysis of economic, political and investment data. But at the end of the day, they know only two things: First, like everybody else, they don't know where the market is headed tomorrow. And second, that their livelihood depends upon appearing to know.[4]

---

[4] William Bernstein, *The Four Pillars of Investing*.

Once such an expert was asked why they forecast even though it is such a futile attempt, his answer was crisp and clear: 'We forecast because the clients want them'.

Now, one may ask if there is any validity in such predictions and whether they add any value to the viewers and readers investing so much time watching them speak.

Well, the answer was provided by psychologist Philip Tetlock at the University of Pennsylvania who explored these so-called expert predictions in a landmark 20-year study, which he published in his 2005 book *Expert Political Judgement: How Good Is It?*

So Tetlock interviewed 284 people whose profession was to comment or offer advice on political and economic trends, and he gathered more than 80,000 predictions both in the areas in which they specialized and in fields whether they had little knowledge. Later, these predictions were compared with the actual outcomes and the result was something which none of the so-called experts would like to face or admit. The experts performed worse than what a kid would have done by simply guessing the outcome. In other words, people who spend their time, and earn their living, studying a particular topic produce poorer predictions that the ones that would be produced by a Grade 5 student.

Why did experts perform so badly? It is because as the person acquires more knowledge, he/she develops an enhanced illusion of his/her skill and becomes unrealistically overconfident. And since they can't simply guess as it would cast shadow on their knowledge, they try to use their knowledge thinking that they are skilled and, as the results show, they are wrong more often than they are right.

So much for the art of forecasting or rather the folly of forecasting. It's time to wrap up some of the important lessons from this chapter before we plunge into the real world of investment business. Yes, we are now progressing from the classroom to the street where you will meet the security analysts, the fund managers, the stockbrokers and the financial journalists and how they go on to do their respective jobs and what all important lessons you can learn from them.

LESSONS FOR THE INVESTORS

- Predicting the future, though may seem to be enticing, is a futile attempt to earn superior returns.

- Knowing and understanding the past in no way helps in predicting the future.

- When someone claims to predict the future, don't listen to them. Either turn off the TV, close the magazine or if the person is standing in front of you ask him/her to go and grab some Snickers and in case that doesn't work then run away from him/her.

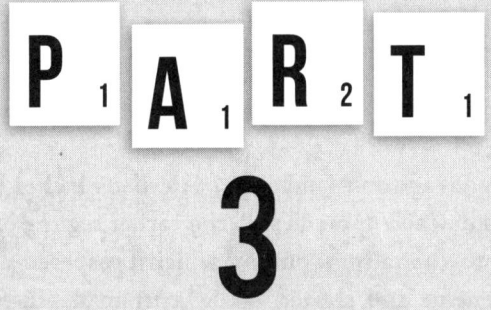

PART

3

THE BUSINESS OF INVESTING

12

Welcome to the Jungle
The Real World of Investment Business

A few decades ago, in a land called *Growthatica* when the industrial revolution dawned upon its soil, the earlier regime of the socialist gave way to capitalist economy which prospered as the people saw its benefits and started taking part in it. The corporations which were born out of this new economy soon started issuing stocks and bonds to the common people so that they can also become part owner (shareholder) and lender (bondholder) to these corporations and reap fruits from their growth.

Almost immediately, a group of elephants came forth to assist these investors. These elephants were old and wise, lived a quiet and peaceful life for themselves and had no greed for fees and commissions. They had earlier assisted the investors in the neighbouring country in owning stocks and bonds of their respective economy. Seeing that owning the shares of the entire stock market was in the best interest of the investors, they invited people to give them money, with which they would buy a cross-section of all the newly issued securities. Investors too considered this a reasonable idea and since everyone wanted to grow together, they handed their money to the elephants and soon everyone held a piece of *Corporate Growthatica* on the basis of their invested capital.

Elephants, upon completing their initial task, did rebalancing of individuals portfolio when a new company issued its initial public offering (IPO) or some company delisted from the exchange or whenever there was a merger/demerger of the companies.

However, such events were not frequent. Further, since everyone held the same portfolio (as the portfolio of every investors had the same stocks, though the quantity of the shares differed based on the money invested by the investor), the elephants didn't have to spend much time and effort in such rebalancing. Accordingly, the elephants took very minimal fees from the investors and were content with their simple life. And the people too enjoyed the set-up and focused their energy to pursue other interesting things in life. Now, this set-up meant two things:

- All the investors earned the same return as delivered by all the corporations of Growthatica Inc. put together, that is, all investors earned the total stock market return. So there was no winner and no looser. All grew together at the same rate.

- The net return earned by the investors decreased marginally from the total return of Growthatica Inc. as the elephants charged fees for their service, though it was very minimal.

But very soon, there came a bunch of chimpanzees who claimed to have advanced degrees in finance. Some even showed their MBA degrees and financial certifications to the investors of *Growthatica* to impress them and asked them to hand over their money as they had learned all the financial skills which would enable them to earn returns higher than their neighbours. Initially, some of the investors fell for the greed and soon everyone followed the suit. The elephants having witnessed such situations in their earlier job knew what was going to happen and silently left for the woods, though few stayed teaching people about the wisdom of their earlier method of investing.

Now all these chimpanzees were extremely happy as they had all the money of *Growthatica* at their disposal. However, all the chimps had three peculiar characteristics. First, they were extremely jealous of each other and wanted to beat others in any way possible. Second, they loved throwing darts. Third, they wanted to eat bananas—a lot of bananas—and loved driving the latest high-end luxurious cars. So what did these chimpanzees do? Well, they did two things. First, they started picking stocks based on where the dart projectile fell on the stock page wishing that with some divine intervention their dart does a better job than the dart of the other chimps. Second, they started charging a much higher fees from the investors on the pretext of their MBA degrees and by giving an illusion to the investors that they would deliver a better return than what their neighbours would get. This new set-up now meant four things for the investors of Growthatica:

- Over any given period of time, some of the chimpanzees will be lucky and obtain a higher return than others.

- The past performance of a chimp at selecting stocks has no bearing on his/her future performance. Last year's winner was the last year's winner. The next year's winner is completely unknown as even the chimps don't know where the dart will fall the next year and how the stock selected by the dart would perform.

- The average performance of all the chimps will be same as the entire market. Since only chimps are managing the total investment pool of Growthatica, the stock market return is the average return earned by all the chimpanzees.

- The net return earned by the investors as a group will be the market return minus the fees and commissions charged by chimpanzees for their bananas and cars. And since the chimpanzees are charging a much higher fees than the elephants, the net return earned by the investors decreases considerably.

Now with the aforementioned set-up, each chimpanzee has a 50 per cent chance of beating the market (remember, market is nothing, but all the chimpanzees put together) because the chimp will either be above average or below average. But since these chimps are charging 2 per cent fees, instead of 50 per cent beating the market, only 40 per cent of them do so. Further, the 40 per cent of the chimps who beat the market has no guarantee that it will be them who would again beat the market next year because the darts have their own mind. So with the passage of time, the law of averages catches up with all but the luckiest chimps. And after 20 years, only 1 in 10 beats the market by more than 2 per cent annual fees and expenses. So the odds of your picking that winning chimpanzee are 1 in 10.

Now, my dear readers and investors, I have some bad news for you. For the past several decades, economists and researchers have been studying the performance of all these chimpanzees and their message is very clear. The elephants are more peaceful, trustworthy and supportive to the well-being of humans than the chimpanzees.

And yes, I now extend my hand inviting you to the real world of investments. 'Welcome to the Jungle'.

INDEXES: PROXIES FOR THE MARKET

Now comes the question. What is this stock market return? How do we compute it? And what it means to 'beat the market'? So before we answer this, let us first understand what we mean when we say stock market or, simply, market. The stock market is nothing, but all the 5,500 stocks listed on either of the two most popular exchanges in India, that is, BSE and NSE. It is like the portfolio consisting of all the 5,500 listed stocks.

Now all the companies generate return for their investors. In a given time period, some may generate good return, some would deliver an average return and some would bring losses to its investors. And when we combine the returns of all these 5,500 listed companies, we get the *stock market return*.

But calculating the returns of all these 5,500 companies is tedious, cumbersome and time-consuming. Also, the bottom 5,000 companies are very small and their impact on the overall market is rather very small. So, for most of our practical purposes, we would consider the top 500[1] companies by their market size to be the stock market. And the return generated by these 500 companies would be called the stock market return.

Now there is something called stock indexes. These indexes are like the basket of stocks based on some similarities which are combined together to calculate a single value for all its constituents. For example, BSE Sensex is an index consisting of top 30 stocks (by market size) listed on BSE. Similarly, Nifty is an index consisting of top 50 stocks (by market size) listed on NSE. So whenever the newspaper report that Sensex increased 80 bps yesterday, it basically meant that combined value of top 30 companies increased by 80 bps (you may consider it to be a portfolio of top 30 companies and with Sensex increasing by 80 bps, your total portfolio value also increased by 80 bps). Further, these two popular indices serve as a proxy of our stock market (consisting of top 500 companies) in the sense that when Nifty increases by 1 percentage point, it can be easily inferred as that the entire stock market consisting of top 500 companies increased in value by approximately 1 percentage point.

In addition to Sensex and Nifty which are restricted to large-cap stocks, there are other popular indices in the Indian stock market which include mid-cap and small-cap stocks as well. For example, there are BSE 100 (consisting of top 100 companies by market size), BSE 200 and BSE 500. Similarly, there are Nifty 100, Nifty 200 and Nifty 500.

Now there are mutual funds (index fund to be precise) which invest in different indices without doing any analysis (the analysis has already been done by the market as it sorts those stocks in top 100 or top 500). These mutual funds just see which are the top

---

[1] Value of Top 500 stocks is almost equal to 95 per cent of total stock market value.

100 or top 500 companies in a particular index and invest money in them and sleep over it. They don't engage in looking for under-valued stocks and simply accept whatever the market presents them on its plate. Further, they don't churn their portfolio and hold it till eternity. So when you invest in an index fund of BSE 200, it essentially means that you have invested in top 200 companies (by market size) belonging to various sectors. And since the indices are composed of the companies, weighted by the value of their market capitalization, the portfolio based on such indices never needs to be rebalanced by buying and selling shares due to changing stock prices. And this saves a lot of brokerage costs as virtually there is no trading involved. Further, the fees of index fund are very small (0.2–0.5%). So net return earned by the investor of index fund is the stock market return less its fees (0.35%).

And if you have invested in a typical mutual fund (active mutual fund) which hand-picks stocks from these 200 stocks, then the return generated by this mutual fund would be either higher than the return generated by BSE 200 index or it will be lower. Further, this mutual fund will entail cost as you would need to pay stock analysts and fund managers for their expertise and labour in picking stocks. Additionally, these funds keep looking for undervalued stocks and accordingly churn a lot (meaning they buy and sell stocks very regularly in an attempt to deliver superior return). Usually, the fees for the analysts/managers and brokerage costs in addition to other costs is around 2.5 per cent.[2] So the net return received by the investor is the return generated by that particular mutual fund less 2.5 per cent.

Now whenever a mutual fund generates net return to its investors, which is more than the stock market return,[3] it is said to have *beaten the market*. And whenever such events occur (as you will see later,

---

[2] We will learn the various costs incurred by mutual funds in detail in Chapter 15: Death by a Thousand Cuts.
[3] Remember, you don't need to apply any skill in earning the stock market returns. Simply invest in top 200 or top 500 companies via an index fund and the returns that you would earn will be the stock market returns.

these are not so regular events), the stock analysts and fund managers of those mutual funds are awarded with huge bonuses and exotic vacations. And who pays them such bonuses and their foreign trips? It is the new investors who upon seeing the good performance pour in their money into the fund thinking that it will again deliver the market beating return. Alas! Not every story has a happy ending.

Now almost the entire mutual fund industry runs with this single agenda—*the agenda of beating the stock market*. If there was no such agenda of beating the stock market, then there wouldn't be any active mutual funds. Further, there wouldn't be any job of stock analysts and fund managers as earning the stock market returns don't need any such skills. All you would need to do is invest in an index fund, switch off your TV and go to sleep.

The problem with the Indian investors is that many of them are not aware of this agenda (of beating the market) at the first place. They even don't know that why they are paying so huge fees and commissions to the mutual fund managers when there is a low-cost alternative to diversify their portfolio and take part in the equity market. Worse, many investors are not aware that they are paying high fees to their mutual fund managers. And these are the investors who earn a suboptimal return and blame the market.

Coming back to our earlier discussion, you have now two options to invest in a mutual fund. Either invest in an index such as BSE 200[4] or invest in a (active) mutual fund which would pick some 50–60 stocks from this pool of 200 stocks in an attempt to beat the return generated by these 200 stocks. The first approach of investing is often called the passive approach and the second is called the active approach.

And if we refer to the earlier example of our fictitious country of *Growthatica*, the elephants had taken the passive approach as they

---

[4] You may choose to invest in other indices such as Sensex, Nifty, BSE 100, Nifty 500 and so on.

considered the stock market to be more intelligent than themselves and they knew it would be impossible to beat the market continuously. The chimpanzees, on the other hand, were following the active approach as they considered themselves to be smarter than the other chimpanzees (the other chimps too considered themselves to be smarter than the rest of the chimps) and thought they can beat the market continuously. While in the former approach, there are no winners and no losers as everyone earns the same return generated by the total stock market, in the latter case, it is the investors as a group who are the ultimate losers and it is the chimps who are the real winners and who go away with lots of bananas and many new SUVs.

A LOSERS' GAME PLAYED BY PROFESSIONALS

Now before we proceed, let us see how the landscape of equity market has changed over the past few decades and why it has become so difficult for anyone to beat the market consistently.

Earlier, the market was dominated by individual investors where an individual used to buy/sell stocks on his/her own (through his/her stockbroker) directly. However, that has gone a drastic change over the past few decades. Now, the institutions, such as I-Banks, mutual funds, brokerage firms, pension funds, insurance companies and foreign institutional players, have taken up the place of individual investors. Most of the individuals[5] now take part through these institutes (like mutual funds and insurance companies). So all these big boys together now constitute the entire market. And this change in the market participants have made all the difference. No longer is the active investment manager competing with the amateurs (individual investors) who are

---

[5] There are some bold (or most probably ignorant) investors who invest in stock market directly, but their combined amount of money invested/traded in the entire stock market is less as compared to the total stock market size and we can safely ignore them when we talk of the overall stock market.

mostly out of touch with the market, he/she is competing with others who are equally intelligent, well informed and as networked as him/her. Accordingly, in this new game, you don't win by playing some super shots, but you win when you exploit the mistakes made by the other players.

Confused? Let us see how.

In today's world, the stock market has been swarmed up with too many professional investment managers who are competing with each other fiercely with all their teeth and nails. A lot of new mutual funds with new fund managers and stock analysts are entering the market every year. And all these fund managers are bright and brilliant people. They are among the best in their business schools and possess top finance certifications such as CA, CFA and so on. In short, they are the 'best and the brightest'— disciplined, intelligent and mostly rational. Further, they are supported by hundreds of stock analysts who are equally highly qualified, motivated, hard-working and very competitive. Thus, all these professional investment managers are so good in their job, they make it nearly impossible for any single professional to outperform the rest of them.

Remember, for any fund manager to outperform the other professionals (and thereby the market), he/she doesn't rely on his/her skill as much as he/she relies on the mistakes made by other professionals. If a fund manager thinks that stock XYZ is undervalued and he/she should have it in his/her portfolio then he/she can't go and ask the company to issue more shares to him/her directly. He/she needs to buy it from the secondary market and, hence, relies on the stupidity of other professional who would think that the same XYZ stock is overvalued and is ready to sell. And since every fund manager is looking for mistakes made by other professionals, the probability of any fund manager to consistently beat others is as low as finding a live seal in a tank full of sharks. Hence, in this intense competitive market, where every player is as smart as the other, the secret to winning has now become lose less than the others lose. And that is why the present-day investment business has become a loser's game. Charles Ellis in his book *Winning the Loser's Game* shares an important insight about the business of active investing. He says:

> *The business of active investing has one fundamental characteristic in common: They depend on errors of others. Whether by omission or commission, the only way in which a profit opportunity can be available to an active investor—in an individual stock or group of stocks—is that the consensus of other professional investors is wrong.*[6]

The reality is that with so many equally smart and intelligent stocks analysts and fund managers seeking superior insights to find the undervalue stocks and with so much information being passed instantaneously among the investing community, the chances of discovering the undervalued stocks and (most importantly) exploiting those opportunities to reap real benefits are certainly not richly promising.

Remember, the basic assumption and the underlying principle of all the active mutual fund managers is that they can beat the market. It is this assumption on which the entire mutual fund industry is running. Unfortunately, the basic assumption that most mutual fund managers can outperform the market is false. The institutions—the mutual funds, I-Banks, pension funds—are the market. They cannot, as a group, outperform themselves.

THE REAL SPEED BREAKER

While the environment under which our typical active mutual fund manager works, where his/her opponent is as smart as him/her and that there is not one opponent but hundreds of them, is

---

[6] Charles D. Ellis, *Winning the Loser's Game.*

one of the big hindrances for him/her to succeed, the other major obstacle for him/her to win the race is the cost associated with active investing.

As we discussed earlier, there is a cost that has to be incurred when you invest in the capital market. This cost, as we will see in Chapter 15: Death by a Thousand Cuts, is in the range of 2.5 per cent for most of the active mutual funds. Now observe carefully what happens in the real market.

Assume the stock market, as a whole, provides a gross return of 15 per cent in a year. So all those people who would had invested in an index fund replicating the stock market would have earned a net return of 14.50 per cent (cost of investing in index fund is in the range of 0.2–0.5%). Now, all the active mutual funds would try to beat this stock market return of 15 per cent. So there would be some mutual fund who would do better and there would be some who would do worse. Why? It is because the stock market return is the average return of all the big boys. Hence, there would be someone above average and someone below average. The rule of mathematics tell that everybody cannot be above average.

Now if we aggregate the returns of all investors who did better, their returns must be offset by the aggregate returns earned by all of those who did worse, and by precisely the same amount. That is to say, if someone earned a gross return of 17 per cent (an extra return of 2% over the market return), then someone else has to earn a gross return of 13 per cent (a return lesser by 2%).

And since all these active mutual funds entail cost, the net return earned by the investors would be net off this cost. Hence, the investors of the winning mutual fund would earn a net return of 14.5 per cent and the investors of the losing mutual fund would earn a net return of 10.5 per cent. The following table summarizes the result.

	Total Stock Market Return: 15%		
	Index Fund	Active Mutual Fund	
	All of Them (%)	Winner (%)	Loser (%)
Gross return	15.00	17.00	13.00
Cost	0.50	2.50	2.50
Net return	14.50	14.50	10.50

The fact that our winners net return after expenses merely match the net stock market return and our losers lose by 4 percentage points suggests why garnering even the stock market return is so difficult for the active mutual funds. Some of the active fund may be lucky to earn more than stock market return, but their cost pulls them down heavily and, in the end, it is the retail investors (who have invested with them) suffer. Fund managers and the stock analysts are happy with their bonuses as they had beaten the market. But have the end investors really done better? Well, the mutual fund companies don't answer such questions. As Warren Buffett has said, 'When trillions of dollars are managed by Wall Street managers charging high fees, it will usually be the managers who reap outsize profits, not the clients'.

Now the immediate question that would come to your mind is what if I select that active mutual fund which beats the stock market consistently. Well, as we will see in Chapter 16: The Mirage in the Desert (on consistency of mutual fund performance), it is not an easy task and that is why on an average the people who have invested in the active mutual fund earn less than the people who have invested in the passive index fund. John Bogle in his book, *The Little Book of Common-Sense Investing*, says:

> In the casino, the house always wins. In horse race, the track always wins. In the Powerball lottery, the state always wins. Investing is no different. In the game of (active) investing, the

> *financial croupiers always win, and investors as a group lose... Owning the stock market over the long-term is a winner's game but attempting to beat the stock market is a loser's game.*[7]

Remember, this mathematics of *gross return – cost = net return* is so simple that most of the people turn a blind eye to it. The most thoughtful and intelligent investors of our present times and the past including Peter Bernstein, Benjamin Graham, James Vertin, John Bogle, Burton Malkiel and Charles Ellis have said it time and again, and their message to the common investors is very clear.

Because the gross returns of all the active investors (as a group) and passive investors (holding the portfolio of stock market) are same and because of the cost of active investors are substantially high, the net return earned by the active investors has to fall below the return earned by passive investors.

Remember, it is not that an active mutual fund can't earn above stock market return. The question is whether they can beat it to that extent to cover their cost, so that the net returns earned by the real investors increase. As it turns out, it is an extremely difficult task and most of the active mutual funds fail to cover their cost.

NOTHING SPEAKS LIKE THE NUMBERS

Now you would be thinking: 'Okay. Enough of the talk between active versus passive, and enough of the theory that active mutual fund can't beat the market consistently'. But do we have any numbers to support this claim? Well, it looks like that we do have some numbers which speak of itself.

S&P Indices versus Active (SPIVA) has been comparing the performance of active mutual funds and passive mutual funds (index fund) across all major economies of the world and they come out with half-yearly report with their findings. The following

---

[7] John Bogle, *The Little Book of Common-Sense Investing* (Hoboken, NJ: Wiley, 2007).

figure shows the performance of active mutual funds (for both large cap and mid cap) versus the relevant market index for the Indian stock market. And from the figure, it is very much obvious that around 60–70 per cent of active mutual funds are being outperformed by the index, that is, the index fund is winning handsomely with a win ratio of nearly 60–70 per cent.[8]

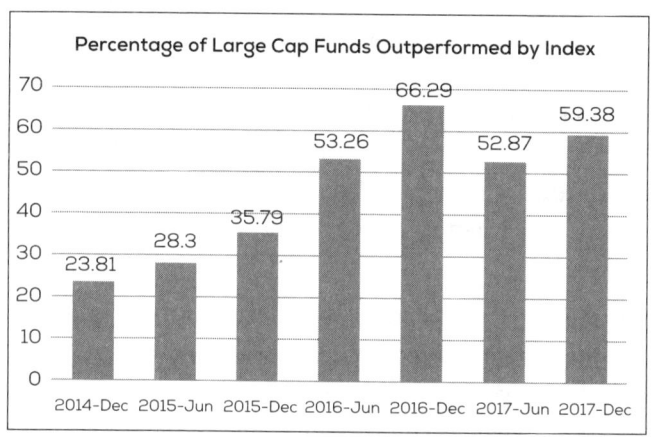

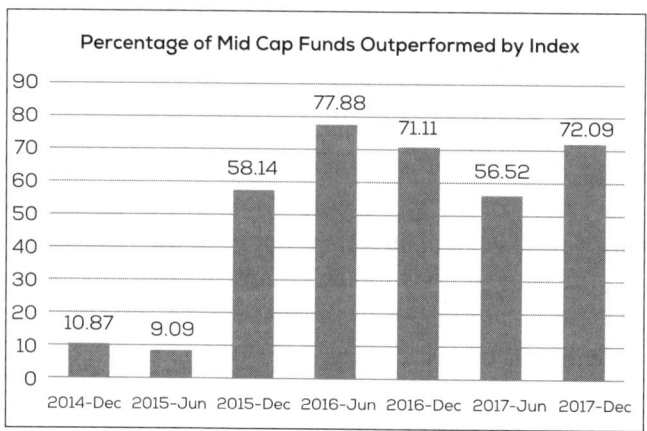

Source: SPIVA.

---

[8] In the US stock market, which is considered to be a highly competitive and efficient, the index fund wins by nearly 90 per cent. As Indian stock market develops with increasing number of players taking part in the market, the win ratio of the index fund in Indian stock market is too likely to move towards that level of 90 per cent.

As you would notice from the earlier figure that in the earlier period, active managed funds performed better than the index fund in India. So is it that they were doing a better job at that time and have lost their sheen now? No. They are doing the same job as they were doing earlier and their performance as a group is more or less the same. The reason why index funds might have underperformed earlier in India is that in early days of their inception they were not so properly defined and robust (many of the indices started as late as in 2004–2010). So it was slightly difficult to calculate the return generated by the index fund. However, now that there is a proper and scientific approach to define the index, the returns are easier to calculate, and the results show why being passive is a much better strategy than to be active and trying to beat the market.

Second, Indian capital market is still at a nascent stage as compared to the developed economies of the USA, UK and Japan. So, in India, the percentage of money invested/traded by individual investors is still high as compared to those in the developed economies. And since the number of individual investors is high, they provide a good opportunity to the institutional investors to reap benefit from them (yes, individual investors who invest/trade on their own are the biggest loser in this game). And that is one of the reasons why active funds did better 10 years ago. However, as people are getting more educated and are routing their investment via mutual funds and as more and more of the fund houses are entering the market, the winning ratio of active funds has started to come down. Further, as and when more fund houses would keep on entering, they will increase the competition among themselves which will ultimately make their performance worse. For instance, in the USA, the percentage of active mutual funds getting beaten by passive funds for a 20-year period is as high as 94 per cent. Yes, only 6 per cent of active mutual funds beat the index fund in a developed economy such as the USA. And as Indian economy progresses and as Indian capital market becomes more intense and more competitive, the win ratio of index fund in India is also going to increase.

It is important at this point to understand that this concept of index fund is not something new. As we will see in the subsequent chapters, this concept has been into practice since the 1960s in the USA. The first index fund made available to the common investors like you and me was issued by Vanguard in as early as 1976 in the USA. However, since the common investors are ignorant of this concept and since popularizing this fund would stop the fees and commissions earned by all the stockbrokers, mutual fund managers and other intermediaries, none of them took initiative to spread the awareness among the investors. Worse, they started writing articles on why active mutual fund is better than passive investing in India and dissuaded people to invest in index funds. They had their own agenda and they have been pretty successful in their agenda till now.

Now it is up to you to decide what is your agenda, and then work towards it. Your job should be to make yourselves rich and not to make your stockbrokers and mutual fund managers drive the fancy SUVs bought from your money. However, if you would like to indulge in philanthropy activities then there are more deserving and needy people out there and you would do a better job of donating your money to them then to simply pass your hard-earned money to the millionaire fund managers and greedy stockbrokers.

LESSONS FOR THE INVESTORS

- The entire business of investment management which is based on single basic belief that 'professional investment managers can beat the market consistently' appears to be false.

- The exciting truth is that while most investors are doomed to lose if they play the loser's game of trying to beat the market, every investor can be a winner. All we need to do to be long-term winners is to reorient ourselves and concentrate on realistic long-term goal setting, sound policies to achieve our goals and bring in the requisite self-discipline, patience and fortitude required for persistent implementation.

- The index fund does all this at a very minimal cost.

13

The Parrot's Prophecy
Flaws of the Fundamental Analysis

It's 8 a.m. in the morning and you are getting ready for your office. While you are having your breakfast, you switch on the TV and there comes a neatly dressed man talking about the stock market, the bull run the market is witnessing and his recommendations about which stocks you should buy or hold, or sometimes sell. He tells you that his recommendations are based on some analysis. And since he has been in the market for so long, he can analyse the stock price movement very well and help people reap benefits from his expertise. And what analysis usually he does? Well, I don't know what analysis they really do but they claim to follow one of the two analyses—the fundamental analysis and the technical analysis. Now, let us see what these two analyses are and whether they serve any purpose for you as an investor or it is just a tool to make you feel that only the professionals who can do such analysis are privileged to handle your money.

FUNDAMENTAL OR TECHNICAL

Technical analysis is all about studying the past prices of stocks, finding pattern in the movement of the prices and trying to jump the gun so that they can reap profit. The technical analysts also called chartists (as they are busy in reading and studying price charts) don't care whether they are studying Infosys or Reliance, neither do they care about the fundamentals of the companies such as earnings, profit margin and so on nor about the business that particular stock is involved in. For them, a particular stock is just an animal who loves galloping—definitely not so randomly—and you can shoot them and take home for your dinner if you are able to predict where it will land before it takes yet another jump.

Definitely, these analysts don't believe in EMH and the intrinsic value of a company as for them EMH is rather an absurd concept and has almost no validity in the real world. Further, they think that past prices of stocks have all the predictive power and can help them in determining the future path the stock price would take. Needless to say, technical analysis is not carried out for the purpose of long-term investments but to find the right time to buy and sell; hence, it is used by traders for speculative purposes only. Hence, in the world of investments, it is looked not so favourably and with respect in the public, though it has its own following and cult. And where do these chartists work? They mostly work for a trading or a brokerage firm.

Fundamental analysis, on the other hand, is all about trying to find out the intrinsic value of the company and then seeing if it is undervalued or overvalued by comparing the computed intrinsic value with the present price. Hence, if it is undervalued then buy that stock and if overvalued, sell it as sooner or later the stock price will converge to its intrinsic value. The practitioners using this analysis are called security analysts and they love playing with the numbers (they find inferences crunching numbers rather than deciphering the stock price charts). They also study stock on Infosys and Reliance differently as they belong to different industry and have different business model. Needless to say, this analysis is claimed to be used for investment purpose and all the security analysts take pride in that.

And where do these security analysts work? They usually work in the typical mutual fund companies and I-Banks. So whenever you invest in a mutual fund, understand that the stocks selected in that fund are based on the analysis and recommendation of a security analyst using the technique of fundamental analysis.

THE QUEST TO FIND THE HOLY GRAIL

Assume there is a company called Abhishek Inc. specializing in printing and publishing educational material on personal finance and investments, and which is listed on BSE. The company in its last annual report has declared that it would give out a dividend of ₹15 per share the next year. The security analyst has the numerator of the Gordon growth equation readily available. In the quest to find the intrinsic value of the company, his/her most important job is to find the growth rate of this dividend and the interest rate by which these dividends must be discounted.

To find the growth rate of the company, the analyst has to estimate the future earnings growth of the company. The first thing the analyst does is that he/she would study the past record of Abhishek Inc., review its past financial statements, balance sheets, etc. Then he/she would have a first-hand visit to and appraisal of the company's management team to gauge their view on company's future performance and outlook. And since the general prospects of a company are strongly influenced by the economic position of its industry, the analyst would study the printing and publishing industry in detail. Based on all this information, the analysts then estimate the future earnings of Abhishek Inc. The analyst hopes that a thorough study of industry conditions, company's history and the future prospect as suggested by the company's management will help them to project the company's earnings precisely. So the analyst comes out with his/her *growth rate* for Abhishek Inc.

Now the analyst has to determine the appropriate discount rate. The discount rate is the interest rate the investor demands from holding this stock and as we saw in Chapter 3, the greater the risk in holding the stock the higher the return our investors demand. So, in essence, the analyst has to analyse the riskiness of this stock. Usually, the more respectable a stock is, the less risk it has. Stocks of the so-called blue-chip companies, for example, are said to deserve a quality (or stability) premium. And since most investors prefer less risky stocks, these stocks (of blue-chip companies) therefore can afford to provide a lower return to its investors. Risky stocks, on the other hand, has to offer a higher return in order to induce the investors to bring in their money. So after analysing all this information and taking everything into consideration, the analyst comes up with an appropriate discount rate commensurate with the company's risk.

And with the expected dividend pay-out, the growth rate of Abhishek Inc.'s earnings and the appropriate discount rate, our security analyst finds the intrinsic value of Abhishek Inc. And if it is below the present market price, sell the stock and if it is high buy the stock. Looks easy! But let me tell you that it's a daunting task to arrive at such precise figures of growth rate and discount rate and it's almost impossible to find the true intrinsic value of a company. Let us now see what makes the work of security analyst so challenging and why you should not always rely on the face value of their recommendations.

PRECISE FORECASTING IS NOT DIFFICULT: IT'S IMPOSSIBLE

As we have already seen, in an attempt to predict the growth rate and discount rate, the analyst looks at multiple factors such as growth of the economy, the industry trend, the company's present business and its future plans of growth and expansion, taxes, foreign exchange, government policies, investors sentiments and so on and so forth. And when something is dependent on so many factors, it stands to reason that you can't obtain precise figures by using these many indefinite factors.

Let's say you invest according to the following process: forecast the overall economy, forecast the interest rate, forecast the sectors which will do well within that environment and finally forecast which stocks will do well within that sector.

Now suppose you are very good at forecasting which means that you are right on each forecast 60 per cent of the time (anything above 50% accuracy is considered good). If you require all four forecasts to be correct, then you have just 13 per cent chance of actually getting your pick right.[1] Now think about the number of forecasts an average analyst's model contains—sales, costs, margins, taxes, interest rates and so on. No wonder these guys are never right.

There have been numerous studies on the validity of security analysts forecasting abilities. In one such study, it was found that the careful estimates of security analysts did little better than those that would be obtained by simple extrapolation of past trends and that Wall Street top analysts failed to predict earnings accurately in every single industry both in one-year period and five-year periods.[2]

Another reason why forecasting company's earnings is so difficult is that there are random events which influence the company's business and its earnings. And what are these random events? Well, random events are those events whose occurrence cannot be predicted. It is said that most of the important changes that affect the basic prospects for corporate earnings are essentially random. For example, the Indian IT companies which derive much of its revenue in USD as they export their services to US clients is presently booming with the rupee depreciation. But what if because of some unforeseen reasons the rupee appreciates against the USD. The revenue of all these companies will get impacted and estimates of the security analyst will go for a toss.

Now some of you may be thinking what if the analyst had taken the case of rupee appreciation in his/her estimates. Well, chances are that he/she would have taken that into consideration, but he/she wouldn't be able to say when and to what level the rupee would appreciate because movement of currency depends again on a lot of factors such as government policies, FDI investment, imports,

---

[1] This assumes that all the four forecasts are independent events.
[2] J. C. Cragg, and Burton Malkiel, 'The Consensus and Accuracy of Some Predictions of the Growth of Corporate Earnings', *The Journal of Finance* 23, no. 1 (1968).

exports, geopolitical events and so on. And predicting the precise level of all these factors is very difficult to make.

Remember, the policies of the Indian government and decisions taken by regulatory bodies such as the RBI, SEBI can have enormous implications for the fortunes of individual companies. So can the removal of key members of company's management, the discovery of a major new product or some fault in existing line of product, the entry of new competitors and price wars between them, a labour strike, a trade war between the countries, terrorist attacks, election results and natural disasters such as flood, earthquake, fire and so on. And if you would notice, all these are random events. You can't predict them and every one of them can have a material impact on the companies' earnings.

Let me share you something about the work that I did as a credit analyst for over six years. The job of a credit analyst working in a bank or some other lending institute is no different from that of a security analyst.[3] While I never worked as a security analyst, I did almost the same kind of job and carried the same analysis. So as part of debt financing for the companies by way of extending loans, we used to analyse the industry in which the company operated, the impact of any government policies and regulations on that particular industry, the company's business model and how it stands in comparison to its peers, its management, operation and financials. We also used to have first-hand information by interacting with the company's management and often used to go to the company's manufacturing unit to see the company's operation at the ground level and often interacted with the staff working there. And with all this information at our hand, we used to estimate the company's earnings and its bottom line for the next few years. Say it is 2019. So in our analysis, we used to estimate

---

[3] A company is financed partly by equity and partly by debt. Security analyst analyses the company from the equity perspective and credit analyst do it from the debt perspective. Apart from this, there is no major difference in the duty and role of the two.

the company's earnings for 2020, 2021 and 2022 (depending on the tenure of the loan being extended). And once we made the estimates, the report was submitted to our management committee.

Now our job was not just to appraise the company only once at the time of extending loans but also to review them at some regular interval. So after one year when the company's actual results were out, we used to compare the real results of 2020 with the estimates that we had projected in 2019 for 2020. And guess what, those figures never matched. Why? It is because no matter how much objective we tried to be in our approach, a large part of our predictions was based on our subjective interpretations of multiple factors. And since no one can be always right in his/her subjective interpretations, the estimates never—I repeat never—matched with the real figures. And what do we used to do in 2020? Well, we used to write a report why our estimates didn't match with the company's results. And it was much easier to do because it's always easy to justify things in retrospect. But predicting future, I can very easily tell is almost impossible. And in case your prediction happens to be true, then it's not that you are intelligent, or you have some divine power, it's just that it was a mere coincidence and you were lucky. That's all. As Samuel Goldwyn used to say, 'Forecasts are difficult to make—particularly those about the future'.

TRYING TO FIT IN: REVERSE ENGINEERING

Assume you are a security analyst trying to find the intrinsic value of Abhishek Inc. The company has declared a dividend of ₹15 for the next year. And after a careful analysis of the economy, the industry, the company and its peers, you arrive at a discount rate of 10 per cent and growth rate of 5 per cent. So you input these numbers in the Gordon growth equation and you get the stock price of ₹300. The current stock price of Abhishek Inc. is though ₹320. However, based on your subjective judgement and what you know about this company through your informal network, you believe that the stock price of Abhishek Inc. is presently undervalued, and you should buy it even though the intrinsic value which you just calculated is lower than the present market price. Also, your peer and competitor analyst working in a different mutual fund company has included it in his/her pool of stocks and you wonder probably your calculation is just isn't right. So what do you do? You increase the growth rate from 5 per cent to 5.5 per cent, feed in the numbers in your calculator and bingo. You get the stock price of ₹333—an increase of ₹33 from your last calculated value with just a mere increase of 0.5 per cent in the growth rate. You run to your fund manager and show him/her your analysis and calculation, and tell him/her that the stock of Abhishek Inc. is undervalued, and they should definitely invest in it. You also explain how the competitor mutual fund house has included this stock in their portfolio. The fund manager buys in your idea and ultimately buys the stock of Abhishek Inc. So much for the analysis.

The problem with fundamental analysis is not that it's wrong in its approach. The problem is that the *calculation of stock price is highly sensitive to the values of discount rate and growth rate.* A mere increase of 1 per cent in the discount rate can decrease the stock price by ₹50 and a mere increase of 1 per cent in the growth rate can increase the stock price by ₹75. The following table illustrates the point.

Dividend	Discount Rate (%)	Growth Rate (%)	Stock Price
15	10	5	₹300
15	11	5	₹250
Change	+1	–	–₹50

Effect of change in stock price by 1 per cent change in discount rate

Dividend	Discount Rate (%)	Growth Rate (%)	Stock Price
15	10	5	₹300
15	10	6	₹375
Change	–	+1	+₹75

Effect of change in stock price by 1 per cent change in growth rate

And this explains why the target price of the stock as set by the security analysts and as reported by the brokerage firms in their neatly crafted 'investors insights' is at the whims and wishes of the analysts or fund manager. In most of the cases, the target price of the stock is set beforehand, and analysts play with the inputs to get the result (a perfect example of reverse engineering). Just increase or decrease the discount rate or growth rate by 0.5 per cent and you get your desired value. Remember, there is always some combination of growth rate and discount rate that will produce any specific price you want. In this sense, it is almost impossible to calculate the intrinsic value of a company's stock price. And yes, nobody will question the security analyst why they chose growth rate of 5.5 per cent and not 5 per cent. After all, they put all their assumptions somewhere at the end of report with the smallest fonts permissible.

THE CREATIVE ACCOUNTING

Burton Malkiel in his book *A Random Walk Down the Wall Street* says that 'a firm's income statement may be likened to a bikini—what it reveals is interesting but what it conceals is vital'. Now having worked as a credit analyst for 6 years and perusing annual reports and financial statements of over hundred companies, I can easily vouch for it.

As per the regulatory requirement, the firms and corporations in India have to follow the Indian Accounting Standard (Ind-AS)

when they report their earnings and other details in their financial statement which is then made public to the security analysts and other investors. And these financial statements reveal what is happening in the company; how the company is using its capital (the money that you invest in a particular stock goes to the company as part of its equity capital) and how much they are earning so that the profits could be shared with its shareholders (investors). But more often than not, the financial statements of many companies (especially the mid-cap and small-cap ones) doesn't truly reveal what is cooking inside, and this creates a different view of the company in the eyes of analysts and investors alike.

In an attempt to create a better impression in the market, the companies use multiple tricks to pump its earnings and to fool investors and security analysts alike. Most of the senior accountants working in these companies are experts of all the accounting rules and they try to find some loophole in the accounting standards and then take advantage of that. Additionally, there are many legal ways in which a company can boost its sales without selling a single product. While the regulations require that the company's financial statements be audited by a statutory auditor, there have been multiple instances where even the best of the auditors have failed to check the fraud the company was doing—either by overlook or when they agreed to work in connivance with the company itself.

Take the classic case of Satyam Computer Services itself. Many investors lost their money just because the company was simply boosting its sales and profit, and the auditors didn't do their job properly. And many security analysts' recommendation went haywire not because their analysis was wrong but because they were simply acting on wrong and misleading information. And yes, this is not one of the cases. The misrepresentation of financial numbers is much more rampant that what you thought, though it may not be up to the level and scale of Satyam Computers.

Even we credit analysts were told by our seniors not to believe everything that is reported in the company's financial statements and we were given specific instructions to read all the footnotes and star-marks printed in smaller fonts because it is where the company used to put their disclaimers and assumptions. Remember whenever there are assumptions, chances of getting and being creative increases and as per Ind-AS there are many accounting parameters which are based on company's assumptions.[4] So the next time you read any of the company's financial statement, don't forget to read their assumptions.

Another major problem that the security analyst has in interpreting current and projecting future earnings is the tendency of companies to report the so-called pro forma earnings as opposed to actual earnings computed in accordance with Ind-AS. In pro forma earnings which the companies submit to the security analysts, they very wisely decide to ignore certain costs that are considered unusual—meaning these costs are not incurred by the company in their normal operation. But it is not unusual to see one or the other unusual cost appearing in the actual financial statement as submitted by the company to regulatory authorities every year. Pro forma earnings are often called 'earnings before all the bad things that could happen to the company' and give firms license to exclude any expenses they consider to be 'extraordinary' or 'non-recurring'. And this usually overstates the company's earnings. In short, they present their best edited profile picture for their matrimonial purpose. No wonder our security analysts have extraordinary difficulty estimating the future earnings of the company.

CONFLICT OF INTEREST

Even if we assume that the stock analysts, despite their so many difficulties and challenges, are able to determine the intrinsic value of a company and put their recommendations in their 'investors insights' report or ask their fund manager to invest in their selected

---

[4] It is perfectly legal to state these financial parameters based on the company's assumptions as long as the company discloses those assumptions in their report.

stocks, chances are that you as an investor won't get a fair and unbiased recommendation from them. Why? It is because there is an inherent conflict of interest between the analyst and the companies they cover.

While to the world the job of the security analyst would appear to be to come up with the intrinsic value of a company and provide recommendations whether the retail/institutional investors should buy/sell/hold those stocks, it is often claimed that the real value these analysts provide is granting access to some of the big investors an access to the high-level executives working for the companies they cover. The big investors (either HNI retail investor or institutional investors) want to talk to the company's executives to get the first-hand information directly from the horse mouth and don't rely much on the analysts' recommendations. So what do they do? They pay equity research firms and security analysts for getting access to the insiders of the company they want to invest it. In an article published in U.S. News, it was said that equity research firms were paid roughly $2 billion by clients in 2016 for access to meetings with company executives and insiders.[5]

Now, these companies are under no obligation to grant this type of special access. But since the research analysts develop a rapport with the executives of these companies over a period of time, they grant them such favour. And since such favours can't be one-way always and have to be returned in cash or kind, the analysts covering these companies return their favour by assigning 'buy' recommendations to them.[6] Remember it is $2 billion at stake for the research firms and our analysts don't want to lose that amount by assigning a 'sell' rating to these companies and pissing

[5] Available at https://money.usnews.com/investing/investing-101/articles/2017–08-10/stock-analysts-are-more-biased-than-you-think (accessed on 9 January 2020).
[6] Ratings assigned by the research firms have an effect on the stock prices of those companies. Usually, a strong 'buy' rating pushes the stock price up and a 'sell' rating brings down the stock price. Naturally, all companies want to get a 'buy' ratings from the equity analysts.

off their executives. And that is why no security analyst advises a 'sell' rating to a particular stock so easily. And if you do get to see a 'sell' rating from a research/brokerage firm, then understand that this brokerage firm no longer expects to get any benefit from the company which they just recommended to be 'sell'.

This *you-hit-me-I'll-hit-you* unwritten rule between research firms and companies has major implications on the approach analysts take to their work. In December 2016, *the Economist* conducted a study of all the equity analyst ratings for the 500 stocks in the S&P 500 index. The study found that 49 per cent of the total ratings on those stocks were 'buy' ratings, 45 per cent were 'hold' ratings and only 6 per cent of total ratings were 'sell' ratings.[7] So much for the analysis, and fair and unbiased report.

Another conflict of interest comes between the sell-side division of the I-Bank (research division) and the capital raising arm of the bank, popularly called investment banking department (IBD). Security analyst working in the research division do their job of analysing companies and writing reports and recommendations. And the IBD helps the companies raise money from the capital market. And from where do the I-Bank makes most of its money? It is from its IBD where underwriting of new issues such as IPO can fetch the bank hundreds of crores of rupees. So if an I-Bank wants a business from a company seeking to raise money from the capital market, it should come as a no surprise that its research team would hardly come up with a negative report on it.

While this conflict of interest between the research team and the IBD was pointed out to the regulatory authorities and there have been regulations placed since then to check such conflict of interest, stock analysts are still influenced by the fear that negative comments about a company could result in a loss of underwriting business in the future. And since they can't afford to lose hundreds

---

[7] Available at https://www.economist.com/finance-and-economics/2016/12/01/sell-side-share-analysis-is-wrong (accessed on 9 January 2020).

of crores of rupees, their report on the companies are obviously not completely true. In the investment and academic community, such analysts are called *affiliated analysts* (meaning they are affiliated to the IBD wing which is carrying out underwriting of stocks and bonds of such companies). And in one of the researches, it was found out that stocks that affiliated analysts recommend as 'buy' perform more poorly than 'buy' recommendations by unaffiliated analysts prior to, at the time of, and subsequent to the recommendation date.[8] Further, a study from investors.com found that investors lost over 50 per cent when they followed the advice of an analyst employed by a Wall Street firm that managed or co-managed the IPO of the recommended stock.[9] Needless to say, affiliated analysts are highly biased in their recommendations.

To be sure, when an analyst says 'buy' he/she actually means 'hold', and when he/she says 'hold' he/she probably means to 'sell' those stocks as soon as possible. This, however, doesn't mean that you should never buy stocks. What it means is that you cannot rely on the recommendations made by the stock analysts on their face value. Further, whenever any expert doles out his/her recommendations on future movement of any specific stock, it would be better if you take their advice with a pinch of salt.

JUDGING THE MARKET'S VIEW ON VALUATION

Now all the challenges that the security analysts face in their job which we discussed so far are like trivial when we compare them to the real villain which is nothing but finding the future P/E ratio of the company. This task of predicting the correct P/E ratio gives the security analysts a real nightmare and they sometimes feel

---

[8] Roni Michaely, and L. Kent Womack, 'Conflict of Interest and Credibility of Underwriter Analyst Recommendations', *The Review of Financial Studies* 12, no. 4 (1999).
[9] Burton Malkiel, *A Random Walk Down Wall Street.*

helpless in their job of finding the undervalued stocks. And the reason they dread so much of this is because this is not part of the fundamental return but of speculative return which, in turn, depends not on any maths and formulas but on psychology—the investor's sentiments. And if you don't know what your spouse mood will be tomorrow, how can you determine what would be the mood of millions of investors 30 days down the line.

The investor's sentiment on valuation of a stock is usually determined by the stock's P/E ratio. This ratio, in addition to other factors, also depends on the growth rate of the company. Usually if a company has a higher growth rate, the market values it higher by assigning a higher P/E ratio. For example, two companies being identical in almost every respect except for their growth rates would have different prices. Why? It is because investors like growth and are ready to pay a higher price to have that differential growth. Academicians have conducted numerous researches on the relationship between P/E ratio and growth rate and their conclusion is very similar to the following chart.[10]

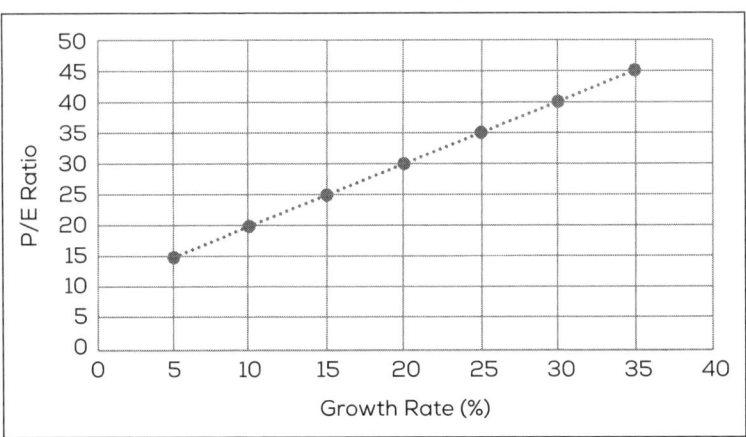

---

[10] It's a representative chart to show the typical relationship between P/E ratio and growth rate. Readers should not draw absolute numerical inference from this chart.

From the earlier chart, we see that market values different growth rates at different P/E multiple. For example, for a growth rate of 5 per cent, the market assigns a P/E multiple of 15 and for a growth rate of 25 per cent, the market assigns a P/E multiple of 35.

So if you were a security analyst and you arrived at a growth rate for a particular stock at 15 per cent, then from the earlier chart you knew that this particular stock should have a P/E multiple of around 25. And if the stock's P/E was less than 25, then that stock is a bargain and should be purchased. And if its P/E was, say something like 30, then you knew that it is overvalued, and you would reject the idea of buying it.

While it may appear a relatively easier task, the catch is that the market doesn't value the growth rates of the companies at the same level always. When the market is having its one of those bull runs, it will increase the P/E multiple of all the companies for all the levels of growth rate. And if there is a bearish trend, then it will bring down the P/E ratio level for all the range of growth rates. Most importantly, even during the normal times the market may value the growth rates differently. For example, if the growth rate of 5 per cent is presently having a P/E multiple of 15 then tomorrow the market may assign the same growth rate of 5 per cent to have a P/E multiple of either 18 or 8. The thing is that you don't know and you can never know for sure what would be the P/E multiple for a particular growth rate tomorrow.

And that is why all the security analysts dread doing this part of their job. Even if they are able to come up with a precise growth rate (which we already know that it's not easy to get) they can never be sure to ascertain what P/E multiple the market will assign to this growth rate tomorrow or day after tomorrow.

Also, the entire idea of finding the undervalued stock is that market will realize its mistake sooner or later, and it will rectify its mistake by increasing the price of undervalued stock to its fair intrinsic value. For instance, upon your analysis you found the growth rate of Tata Steel to be 5 per cent. As per the industry norm, the company in this group with 5 per cent growth rate has a P/E multiple of 15. But Tata Steel has a P/E multiple of 11. So you buy it, thinking that the market will increase its valuation and bring its P/E multiple to 15, in line with the industry norm.

But suppose, a few weeks later, stocks with 5 per cent growth are now selling at a P/E multiple of 10. So even if the analyst was correct in its growth estimate, his/her investors won't benefit from his/her skill because now the Tata Steel is not under-valued but overvalued. Yes, the market may correct its mistake by revaluing all stocks downward, rather than raising the price of Tata Steel.

TAKE ADVICE BUT DON'T BE BLIND

The job of fundamental analysis or security analysis whether done with all the honesty, integrity and with full conviction of benefiting the end investors like you and me doesn't appear to be as useful as claimed by its practitioners. It has been found that the stocks which fund managers sell after doing their fundamental research and the stocks they don't buy typically do as well as the stocks they do buy. Why? It is because most of the time all these fund managers are buying and selling from each other and as the time progresses and as the law of averages spread its wings, the stocks sold do almost as good as the stocks bought which brings us to think if such analysis are fundamentally right or practically useless.

The problem is not that these professionals are not intelligent or doesn't have any good intention to help the investors. The problem is that all of them are handicapped in one way or the other and their recommendations and/or selections of stocks for their respective mutual funds should never be trusted on their face value.

LESSONS FOR THE INVESTORS

- Fundamental analysis, though may appear as a scientific approach of calculating the intrinsic value of a company, is not a full proof method as it relies on the quality of inputs.

- Forecasting the company's earnings and growth rate is very difficult and even the best of the brains fails to accomplish this task.

- Analysts are usually biased in their report as there are multiple conflicts of interest in their job.

- Market valuation is highly whimsical, and it makes the job of security analysts all the more difficult.

14 The Curious Case of Chimpanzees
Fund Managers Fail to Find the Alpha

I have few of my friends who are working as security analysts and portfolio managers in some of the major mutual fund companies in India. And I usually pull their legs by calling them chimpanzees and their method of picking stocks to be nothing better than throwing darts. While they understand that I don't exactly mean that, they are very much aware of the limitations and constraints under which they work which makes it extremely difficult for them to provide any superior return to the investors what a normal buy-and-hold an index fund strategy would deliver.

Now, while in Chapter 13 we saw the challenges of the security analysts, it is now time to see how our fund managers perform and why the (active) funds they oversee can't do any better than the normal buy-and-hold index fund would do.

NOTHING FAILS LIKE A SUCCESS

In a short span of past two decades, the Indian mutual fund industry has grown from a kind of cottage industry to almost like a financial behemoth. The great Indian mutual fund industry boom has multiplied equity fund assets like never before. In the past decade, the average asset under management of the Indian mutual fund industry has increased from ₹5.41 lakh crore (2008) to ₹23.96 lakh crore (2018).[1] That is more than four and half times increase in

---

[1] *Source*: Association of Mutual Funds in India

size is just 10 years. Well, it's a good sign for the growth of the economy and the corporates who are benefitting from the increased participation of the retail investors, the same can't be said about the investors themselves.

Have you ever wondered what happens when a fund earns high returns? The fund advertises it, media propagates it and the investors notice it. And since most of the mutual fund investors are not so financially literate in understanding and appreciating certain financial laws such as 'reversion to mean' (RTM) they pour in their money in hundreds of crores in a matter of week. Consequently, the fund size balloons and so does the bank balance of its fund manager.[2] And what happens when the asset under management (AUM) of the fund increases? Usually, its performance decreases. In one of the studies on size and performance of the mutual fund, it was found that fund returns both before and after fees decline with the fund size.[3]

So now comes the obvious question why does the performance of mutual fund decline with the increase in the fund size? Well, there are not one or two, but three reasons why it happens. Let us see them one by one.

SHRINKING UNIVERSE

When the fund is small and growing, it has ample scope to find good investing opportunities. So it pools in all the good stocks it deems fit in its portfolio. And if the luck works in their favour, their performance is better than the average. So our performance chasing investors keep on pooling money into such funds and its fund manager keeps on buying 'good' stocks until it runs out of 'good' stocks. Yes, you can't have an infinite number of under-valued stocks to invest it.

---

[2] Salary and bonus of mutual fund manager are directly linked to the fund size—its AUM and not on the performance of the mutual fund.
[3] Joseph Chen, Harrison Hong, Ming Huang, and Jeffery D. Kubik, 'Does Fund Size Erode Mutual Fund Performance? The Role of Liquidity and Organization', *American Economic Review* 94, no. 5 (2004).

Now when the fund size swells, its manager gets loaded with lots of money and he/she is left with very few choices—all of them bad. So he/she has three options. Either he/she can keep that money safe for a rainy day, but then the low returns on cash will crimp the fund's results if stocks keep going up. The second option is that he/she can put the new money into the stocks he/she already owns—which have probably gone up since he/she first bought them and will become dangerously overvalued if he/she pumps in more money. Third, he can buy new stocks he didn't like earlier as they were already overvalued. All these factors make the job of fund manager extremely difficult and that is why the fund performance decreases when its asset size increases.

This phenomenon of 'shrinking universe' of 'good' stocks is one of the reasons why some of the reputed mutual funds often shut their door to new investors because they know they can't repeat the performance which they had with an AUM of ₹5,000 crore when their AUM increases to ₹20,000 crore. But yes, such cases are rare in Indian mutual fund industry as of now and most of the fund managers still prefer to keep on increasing the fund size (and their own bank balance) even if it comes at the cost of end investors wealth.

The reality is that good investments are scarce and with the increase in the size of the mutual funds, such opportunities to find good investments become scarcer. It may sound a little counter-intuitive, but it is much easy to deploy ₹1 lakh in a good stock than to invest ₹1,000 crore in the same good stock. Why? It is because the total value of that free float stock was only ₹100 crore. Further, this is especially true of funds that focus on small companies, given that there are strict rules about how much of a single company a fund may own. If a mutual fund has ₹5,000 crore to invest and is only able to invest an average of ₹50 crore in a single small-cap stock, then it needs to find at least 100 such companies to invest in. As a result, the fund might be forced to lower its standards when selecting companies to invest in, which subsequently lowers the return earned by the investors.

PROCESS WINS OVER JUDGEMENT

If any one of you have worked in a growing organization, you would appreciate that after some time the process and bureaucracy impede your work, as much of your time goes in doing the paperwork and following the process. The same is true of the mutual fund industry as well. John Bogle in his book *Common Sense of Mutual Funds* says:

> As an organization expands, the impact of an individual portfolio manager wanes and the impact of an institutional investment process waxes. No longer are there a few portfolio managers with messy desks, bright ideas, and decisive minds, supported by a handful of analysts and traders, and modest administrative building. Now there are horde of funds (as many as 100 or more), plus an organization chart, an investment process, committees to approve transactions and then to appraise them, meetings, exhaustive legal and regulatory filings, red tape, and a focus on process. The manager who used to invest heavily in his best ideas can no longer afford to do so.[4]

Given the earlier handicaps, it comes as a no surprise that why an active mutual fund delivers below par performance when its asset size increases beyond a certain level.

Now the obvious question comes: why do funds allow size to get out of hand? Why do they keep on accepting money from new investors when they know they can't deliver the past superior return (if any) when they already are sitting at such a big pile of asset?

---

[4] John C. Bogle, *Common Sense on Mutual Funds: New Imperatives for the Intelligent Investor* (Hoboken, NJ: Wiley, 2010).

It is because, for advisors and fund managers, 'nothing succeeds like success'. Most of the fund companies know that an average investor in addition to looking at the past performance (a bad benchmark) also look at the AUM of the fund and usually they go for the larger AUM as it appears to be a sign of investors' confidence. Second, and most important, the mutual fund companies love large size because the amount of fees it earns rises linearly with the fund assets. The larger the asset, the larger the fees. And as the fund size increases, the mutual fund company's profit grow; even if the returns of the end investors decrease. But again, they are there to make themselves rich and they have been doing impressively well as far as their own wallet size is concerned. And what about the wallet size of the end investors? Well, if in a group of three (mutual fund company, fund managers and investors); two of them (fund company and the fund manager) are making money; then it's a good deal. Isn't it?

Remember, a fund's large size tells only one thing with certainty, that is, in the past it has done a good job. However, it indicates one more thing. And what is that? Well, it gives enough hint that the fund's performance is very much likely to come down in future. Warren Buffett put it succinctly when he said, 'A fat wallet is the enemy of superior returns'.

BAA BAA BLACK SHEEP

Once a fund becomes successful, that is, it is able to attract more and more investors, its fund managers become timid and imitative. As we already saw, with the growth in the fund size, its fees become lucrative, making its fund managers reluctant to change his/her portfolio. Now that they have won the crown of best fund manager in the town, they don't want to look stupid.[5] So what do they do? They play a much safer game shunning away all the undervalued

---

[5] You can afford to look stupid when no one knows you. But you cannot afford to look stupid when everyone knows you.

stocks because they appear to look risky on the face. Hence, the very risk that the managers took to generate the initial high returns for the fund may now appear too risky and could jeopardize their reputation in case their bet doesn't pay off. Accordingly, the fund managers play a safer game as their motive is no more to deliver a high return to the investors but to maintain their superstar status and the fat fee income they are generating for the mutual fund.

Imagine there are two stocks, HDFC Bank and Bandhan Bank. One is definitely the investors' favourite and the other is not that favourite. However, to a fund manager, the Bandhan Bank appears to be a good buy based upon his/her analysis and research. Now, he/she has two choices. Either buy HDFC or Bandhan. Guess how many would buy Bandhan. Not many. Why? It is because if he/she buys HDFC and it goes bad then no one will question his/her stock picking ability but will say, 'What's wrong with HDFC lately?'. But if he/she happens to buy Bandhan and it goes bad then everyone will ask him/her, 'What's wrong with you? Why you bought Bandhan?'. John Keynes said it aptly when he wrote, 'Worldly wisdom teaches that it is better for reputation to fail conventionally than to succeed unconventionally'.

As you would have guessed it by now, most of the mutual funds have filled their portfolios with the popular stocks (one having a very high P/E ratio) because everyone is talking about them and missing such stocks would appear to be foolish on fund manager's part. And when you have your portfolios consisting of HDFC, ITC, Infosys and the likes, you know what to expect from such a fund. A below par result!

Remember, a fund manager is not as much concerned about delivering superior net return to his/her investors as he/she is concerned with earning fees and keeping his/her job intact. And that is why most of the fund managers are reluctant to buy stocks which may appear to be against the conventional wisdom. Remember you can't lose a job losing your clients money in HDFC, but you will definitely be questioned, grilled and, in worst case, fired if you happen to lose a lot of your client's money in Bandhan. Jason Zweig who is a senior writer at *Money* magazine says:

> *The biggest funds resemble a herd of identical and overfed sheep, all moving in sluggish lockstep, all saying 'baaaa' at the same time. Nearly every growth fund owns Cisco and GE and Microsoft and in almost identical proportions. This behaviour is so prevalent that it is nothing less than the herding. By protecting their own fee income, fund managers compromise their ability to produce superior returns for their outside investors.[6]*

Another reason why fund managers exhibit the herd mentality is their obsessiveness to the index they are tracking. Remember, fund managers get bonuses only when they beat the market—the index that they have set as their benchmark. So instead of finding the undervalued stocks from their raw research, they mostly keep a track on the stocks that are being added/removed from the index. And if a company gets added to an index, hundreds of mutual funds compulsively buy it—all saying 'baaa' together. If they don't buy that stock and it then does well, the managers will look foolish; on the other hand, if they buy it and it does poorly, no one will blame them. Why? It is because every other fund has that stock and when you conform to the group you appear as someone rational and intelligent. Jeremy Grantham, who is a noted British investor, says:

> *A fund manager's biggest risk is career risk, the risk that he substantially underperforms compared to the fund's benchmarks or to other funds that are classified as peers and loses his job as a result. If the fund loses a lot of money when all of its peers also lose a lot of money, that is less likely to result in a change*

---

[6] Commentary by Jason Zweig in the book *The Intelligent Investor* authored by Benjamin Graham.

of fund manager, than if a fund manager takes a conservative stance and misses out on a big market rally. This situation leads to herding among fund managers. There is less career risk for fund managers to make decisions similar to one another.[7]

So why this herding behaviour of fund manager is injurious to your wealth? It is because you are paying your fund manager to be different and deliver a superior result. If all he/she does is what his/her peers are doing, then his/her result will be what his/her peers would have. And if that is the case, then there is no point in paying excess fees to your mutual fund manager. You could very easily get the same or perhaps better result from the index fund and that too at a very cheap cost.

THE CURSE OF GROUPING

Now that you are reading this book, you know that it pays to be a long-term investor, and short-sightedness will often bring you considerable losses. Unfortunately, not all investors know this fact and it is this short-sightedness of other investors which impact your own return. Now you might be wondering how on earth other investor's mistake can impact your own investment result. Well, the fact that the mutual fund that you have invested with not only manages your money but of thousands and lakhs of other investors; it is the collective action and reaction of all the investors which ultimately has a final say on the fund's performance.

In the mutual fund industry, there is something called *standard client patience time*. This is the amount of time that a client (the investor) is likely to stay with a fund manager if the fund's performance does not meet the client's expectations. A fund manager who makes investment decisions that are substantially different

---

[7] Available at https://blog.folioinvesting.com/2012/04/27/why-mutual-fund-managers-may-not-act-in-your-best-interest (accessed on 11 January 2020).

from his/her peers or who takes some risks which he/she thinks would pay off in the long term has a difficult time implementing this strategy. Why? It is because in his/her long term when his/her strategy is likely to pay off, there would be times when his/her portfolio performance would deliver a below par result. And when that happens, then the investor—who may not be as long-term player as you or your fund manager is—is likely to pack their bags, dump this fund and switch to another fund which has shown a momentarily better performance.

And since a fund manager loves a bigger asset size more than anything else, he/she constantly focuses on strategies which he/she thinks would be best in the short term. But since there are no such short-term strategies which would give superior result consistently, his/her best alternative is to match his/her result to his/her peers so that he/she doesn't lose his/her existing clients. And since every other fund manager also suffers from the same set of problems, they also think alike. Result, everyone suffers. It's like everyone agreeing to let their investors get drown in the turbulent water of volatility while they themselves float on their fat fees.

It is not that fund managers are not intelligent or don't want to work in the best interest of investors. It is because of the relatively short patience time of the investors that the fund managers feel handicapped to execute the best investment strategies that would be really helpful for the investors. Further, evidence suggests that you have more to lose (AUM, fees or at the extreme, your job) by following your belief if it goes against the crowd than you have to gain if it turns out to be correct.

Remember, a fund's income depends on the total amount of money being managed and not directly on the performance of the fund. If investors dump their shares, AUM drops and consequently the fund's income drops. So the fund manager rarely thinks of the long-term result. What he/she mostly thinks of is how to achieve the result in the short term so that the investors don't run away.

The reality is that most of the retail investors are looking for easy money in the short term and it is this short-sightedness of other investors which, through the action of your fund manager, impacts your results.

Now if you would have invested in an index fund, you know for sure that the other investors who also have invested in that index fund is a long-term investor (the very basic premise of index fund is buy-and-hold strategy and, hence, the investors it attracts are mostly the like-minded people looking for an investment horizon of 10–15 years or probably more). So you don't have to worry about their behaviour and that is yet another reason why index fund delivers better results than most of the (active) mutual fund.

Another reason why action of other investors impacts your wealth is that when the performance of the fund starts falling (though it may be just a temporary decline), short-term investors start pulling their money back. Now, the fund manager needs to pay them and if he/she doesn't have sufficient cash surplus to return them, he/she would be forced to sell some stocks from his/her portfolio which he/she would have otherwise kept. This forced selling of stocks impacts your wealth in two ways. First, it incurs transaction cost which would have otherwise been avoided. Second, it pushes the price of the mutual fund further down and there would be a corresponding decline in your wealth.

THE INCUBATED FUNDS

This is one part of the mutual fund industry which is mostly unknown to many of the investors. There is something called the *incubated funds*. So what happens here is something that you would have seen in a laboratory in a sci-fi movie where they grow something out of an experiment. If it fails, dump it and if it succeeds then sell it ferociously.

The similar strategy is used by some of the mutual fund companies which specialize in 'incubating' their funds—test driving them privately before selling them publicly. Usually, in such cases, they start with some 15–20 funds deploying different investment strategies. Typically, in such cases, the only investors in such funds are employees and affiliates of the fund company itself. Further, they keep the size of these funds pretty small (remember big funds often deliver poor results) and by keeping them tiny, the sponsor uses these incubated funds as guinea pigs for risky strategies that work best with small sums of money.

Now if the strategy fails, they kill these funds and remove their entries from their track record as if it wasn't tested at all. And in case its strategy succeeds, the fund company starts advertising it all over the place luring investors to bring their money to them. Also, in such instances, the fund manager waives management fees during the trial period, which further boosts the net return. But when it is able to attract plenty of investors, it slaps their regular fees on them. Accordingly, the returns of these incubated and fee-waived funds often come down heavily once the outside investors have poured lakhs and crores of rupees into them. In one of his studies on returns from investing in equity mutual funds, Professor Malkiel says:

> A number of mutual-fund management complexes employ the practice of starting 'incubator' funds. A complex may start ten small new equity funds with different in-house managers and wait to see which ones are successful. Suppose after a few years only three funds produce total returns better than the broad-market averages. The complex begins to market those successful funds aggressively, dropping the other seven and burying their records.[8]

Now you would say that it's such a misleading practice and how can something be allowed per se. While it may appear to be

---

[8] Burton Malkiel, 'Returns from Investing in Equity Mutual Funds 1971 to 1991', *The Journal of Finance* 50, no. 2 (1995).

misleading, the mutual fund companies disclose in their documents and prospectus that these returns are hypothetical returns obtained in an incubation trial. But did you read those fine lines when you invested in your mutual fund? And even if you read, did you fully understand what those hypothetical returns mean?

THE LEAPING FROGS

While most of the mutual fund success, if any, can be easily attributed to mere luck, few fund managers seem to have some kind of Midas touch. And since such skills are very rare, all fund companies would want to have them on their board. Further, many of the star fund managers often leave the mutual fund company they work for and start their own fund. Now the mutual fund which you would have invested with and was doing a pretty good job would become a kind of orphan without its star manager. Needless to say, the performance of the fund is very much likely to come down when its fund manager leaves it.

It is important to note that instances of such fund managers having the Midas touch is rare. However, even if we assume some fund managers have such skills and they are able to systematically outperform the market, then it is very much likely that these fund managers would charge appropriately high fees to capture all the advantages they provide to investors. After all, it is the fund manager who would have the rare skill of picking the right stocks and not the typical investor. Usually when a fund manager skill gets known to the public, the investors compete among themselves to place money with such superstar fund manager. And when you have a long queue of investors standing outside your window waiting to deposit their money with you, then what do you do? You increase your fees, though some of the incremental fees may not be so obvious to the investors. In the end, it would be highly unlikely that uninformed investors could earn excess returns by investing in some manager's actively trading fund.

In one such study on assessing the skill of the fund manager and its benefits being passed on to the end investors, it was found out that the average fund manager is skilled (a big sigh of relief for all the fund managers out there) but all the benefits of such skills go to the fund managers in the form of high fees and commission. The researchers observed that because investors compete in capital markets, the excess return[9] over the index to end investors is zero, that is, fund managers capture all the economic benefits themselves. Further, they found that an investor cannot generate positive excess return by investing with the best funds.[10]

Now the question comes, does it really matter whether the fund manager picks stocks by using his/her skills or by simply throwing darts on the stock board? As long as you are not getting any benefit from their stock picking ability, it doesn't make sense (at least to me) to go with such (active) mutual funds. The index fund serves the purpose of delivering the stock market return and that too without any of the earlier handicaps and constraints the typical fund manager faces. Moreover, it comes at a very low cost.

MUTUAL FUNDS CANNOT SHORT

The entire premise of fundamental analysis lies on the idea of finding the intrinsic value of a company. And if the present price is below this intrinsic value, then buy this stock and if it is higher then sell it. Suppose, in one such analysis, you found that TCS is overvalued and you should sell it as its price is going to fall to its intrinsic value. So if you have TCS in your portfolio, you sell it. But what if the TCS was not there in your portfolio to begin with? Can you still sell it to reap profit? The answer is no.

Usually when you don't own a stock and still want to sell it because you think that its overvalued, you can do so by 'shorting' the stock.

---

[9] Excess return is the return that you get over and above the return generated by index. So if the excess return of any fund is zero, it simply means that the fund is generating the same return which its benchmark index fund is generating.
[10] Jonathan B. Berk, and Jules H. van Binsbergen, 'Measuring Skill in the Mutual Fund Industry', *Journal of Financial Economics* (2015).

Unfortunately, mutual funds are not permitted to 'short' stocks because the regulatory bodies considering 'shorting' to be too risky. So even if your fund manager knows that TCS is likely to fall in its price going further, he/she cannot profit from such knowledge and pass on the resultant gains to you.

THE SPECIALITY RISK

These days, the job of fund managers is so competitive that to remain in the race they are often expected to specialize. Just as in medicine the general practitioner has given way to the specialists such as neurologist, paediatric, gastroenterology, cardiologist and the likes, the fund managers have also become specialists of 'small growth' stocks, or 'mid-sized value' stocks or 'large blend' stocks. And their portfolio consists of stocks belonging to only that category. They are usually not permitted to include stocks which fall outside their category definition.

So what happens in the real world is that if a stock which a fund manager specializing in 'small growth' category had thought to be undervalued and included in his/her portfolio turns profitable (in line with the fund manager prediction) and it breaks the 'small' threshold and enters into 'mid-size' category, then that fund manager would be forced to sell that stock even if he/she would have loved to have that stock in his/her portfolio.

No wonder why fund manager can't help you earn superior return.

LESSONS FOR THE INVESTORS

- Fund managers are among the smartest of the professionals you are likely to meet. But since every other fund manager are equally smart, their skill of stock picking turns out to be worthless for the investors.

- They care more for their own reputation and fat fees and less for the net return that their investors earn.

- The risk of losing job makes them pick stocks which may not be optimally suitable for their investors.

- Since fund managers manage money for both the long-term and short-term investors, the action of short-term investors impacts the return earned by the long-term investors.

- The past record of the fund may be very much of a trial run and it is the duty of the end investors to read the fine lines of the fund prospectus to see if it was a real return or a dummy one.

- It is the fund manager which reaps benefits of their skills (if any) and investors don't earn any superior return.

15

Death by a Thousand Cuts
All About Fees and Commissions

In ancient China, there was a practice called *Lingchi*[1] which was known to the outside world as *death by a thousand cuts*. It was one of the cruellest forms of torture and capital punishment where a knife was used to methodically remove portions of the body over an extended period of time, eventually resulting into death. The practice was banned in 1905.

If you would observe closely to what is happening to your wealth in the today's modern world, you would realise that the victim is the average Indian investor, and the proverbial knife is the excessive fees that slowly but surely bleeds the investor dry. The problem is that the victim is being punished for no fault of his/her own.

But you would say, 'Hey, I know I am paying a 1 per cent fees to my mutual fund manager. The expense ratio in the mutual fund prospectus showed it was close to 1 per cent. So how this little fee of 1 per cent is bleeding my savings and investments away?'

First of all, the total fees that you are paying to your (active) mutual fund is much more than 1 per cent. *It's in the range of 2.5–3 per cent of your total invested amount.* Second, this apparently looking small fees is taking away more than 50 per cent of your entire savings that you would otherwise have. Not yet convinced. Let us see how.

---

[1] Timothy Brook, Jerome Bourgon, and Gregory Blue, *Death by a Thousand Cuts* (Brighton, MA: Harvard University Press, 2008).

ENTER SHERLOCK HOLMES

Just after the financial crisis of 2008, there was a guy called Robert Hiltonsmith who graduated with a PhD in economics and decided to take a job with policy think tank Demos. While he learnt almost everything about his subject in his college, it didn't prepare him for how to create a successful investment strategy—mind you, he had a PhD in economics.

Being a responsible guy who cared about his future, he started making dutiful contribution to his retirement fund. However, he noticed one peculiar thing. He observed that even though the market was rising, his retirement account would rarely rise with it. He knew something was wrong, so he decided to take this assignment as a research project for his work. As he progressed in his research, he found an entire catalogue of almost 17 different fees that were being charged to him. There were also additional costs that weren't direct fees per se but were passed onto and paid for by the investors, nonetheless.

After a month or so of research, Hiltonsmith concluded that there wasn't a chance that his retirement account would flourish with these excessive and hidden fees acting as a big hole in his boat. In his report titled 'The Retirement Savings Drain',[2] he calculated that an average worker with an annual income of $30,000 per year and saving 5 per cent of his/her income each year will lose nearly $155,000 to mutual fund fees over his/her lifetime.[3] In other words, people would lose nearly five times of their annual income just to pay fees to their mutual fund manager.

Now as Hiltonsmith was carrying out his research, there was another guy called Ty A. Bernicke who is the president of Bernicke Wealth Management. He wrote an article on *Forbes* magazine titled 'The Real Cost of Owning a Mutual Fund' where he peeled back the

---

[2] Robert Hiltonsmith, 'The Retirement Savings Drain: The Hidden & Excessive Costs of 401(K)s' (New York, NY: Demos, 2012).
[3] Robert Hiltonsmith and his research were featured on a Frontline documentary called 'The Retirement Gamble', which first aired on PBS on 23 April 2013.

layers of different mutual fund fees—both obvious and hidden—dissecting the actual cost and arrived at a heart-stopping total: *the average cost of owning a mutual fund is 3.17 per cent per year.*[4] It is not 1 per cent of 2 per cent as your stockbroker or fund manager says; it is 3.17 per cent and to me that is a huge fee anyone could afford to pay.

LET'S PEEL OUT THE FEES

Now let us spend some time to see what these fees are and how they impact your final wealth. I have tried to make the main findings of Hiltonsmith and Bernicke as simple as possible so that you can understand them easily. Remember, it is important to understand what you are paying to your fund manager and stockbroker because if you don't know what you are paying for; it is very much likely that you will get what you had never desired for. The following chart summarizes the different fees a typical (active) mutual fund charges to its investors.

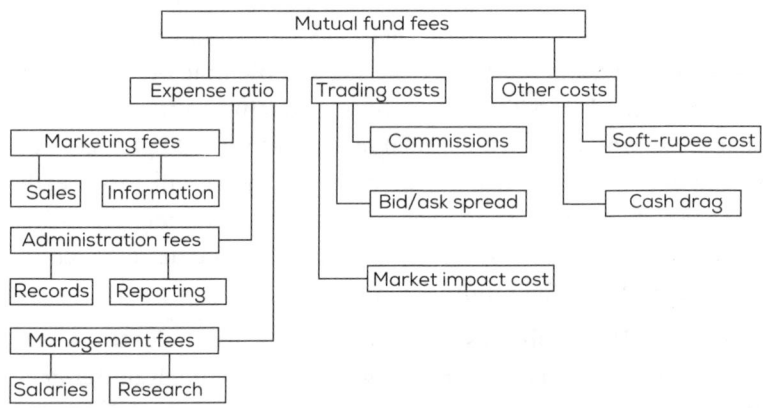

Note: Adapted from Richard W. Kopcke, Francis Vitagliano, and Dan Muldoon, 'The Structure of 401(k) Fees' (Issue in Brief 9–3, Center for Retirement Research at Boston College, Chestnut Hill, MA, 2009) and updated to include the findings of Ty A. Bernicke.

---

[4] Available at https://www.forbes.com/2011/04/04/real-cost-mutual-fund-taxes-fees-retirement-bernicke.html (accessed on 11 January 2020).

EXPENSE RATIO

This is the main 'price tag' the mutual fund companies want us to focus on and they have been pretty successful in their agenda so far. Most investors think that the fund's expense ratio listed in the prospectus and annual reports is the true cost of investing in the mutual fund. But the reality can be very different than what you are made to believe. As you would have already observed in the earlier figure that the expense ratio is not the only cost and an investor pays much more than that.

Now, the question comes what exactly this expense ratio is and how much it costs an investor. Well, this expense ratio comprises of administrative fees (for keeping records, providing statements, processing transactions, ensuring the fund complies with applicable regulations, customer service, etc.), marketing fees (for informing savers and potential savers about the mutual fund and its 'exemplary' track record including advertisements, brochures and other information materials) and management fees (for salaries and bonuses to stock analysts and fund managers). While there have been many studies with the findings on the expense ratio, many of the large mutual funds have realized that 1 per cent ballpark expense ratio is something which they can easily sell to their prospective customer.

TRADING COST

This is the cost incurred by the mutual fund when buying and selling securities. Now you would be thinking why the mutual funds are trading when I have given my money to them to invest. Well, the fact that you have given your money to an *active* mutual fund who by their very nature (and definition) are constantly looking to buy undervalued stocks and sell overvalued stocks, they trade a lot, which essentially means that they churn their portfolio making the portfolio composition dynamic. And, as a result, they incur a hefty trading cost.

Another reason why mutual funds trade is because each time an investor buys shares of the mutual fund, it must then purchase additional assets, incurring a trading cost. And each time an investor sells shares, the fund must pay the investor either out of its cash reserves or by selling some of its assets, also incurring trading costs. So while you thought that you are being a prudent investor by following the buy-and-hold strategy and won't incur much trading cost, the reality is not what you believed. Why? Because there are too many stupid investors who also have also invested in that mutual fund and are always buying and selling shares of the fund.

Thus, trading costs increases the more active the mutual fund's investment strategy is, and the more investors trade the shares of the mutual funds itself. Now let us see what the key components of this trading cost are.

Commission

Now each time a mutual fund buys or sells a share of a company, it can't do this on its own. Buying and selling of shares can be done only by a stockbroker. So to carry out any single activity of a trade, the mutual fund companies pay stockbrokers their commission. Now, the regulations require that the mutual fund company reports these costs to the investors. And our mutual fund companies do report such commissions, but they are presented in such an obscure manner in such a place that it requires the effort of Sherlock Holmes (Hiltonsmith and Bernicke) to find out where it is.

Bid/Ask Spread

The bid/ask spread is the fees that is paid to the 'market maker'. A stock is always bought at a slightly higher price than its selling price to provide the market maker with a profit (most financial markets require a market maker—someone who brings together buyers and sellers, and who maintains a supply of securities for immediate buy/sell to ensure smooth functioning of the market).

Market Impact Cost

The third component of the trading cost is very peculiar and is very costly for a mutual fund. Nobody talks about it and no one reports it in their brochure because it is very difficult to quantify and come to a specific number. To understand it, let's consider two cases.

Let's say that you think that the stock of XYZ company is a good buy. You call your broker and without too much fuss, you purchase ₹50,000 worth of that share. It is unlikely that anyone has noticed your order—hundreds of crores of rupees worth of company stocks are traded every day, and your purchase would not produce even a ripple in the stock's activity.

But suppose you are a fund manager and you have ₹500 crore to invest in the stock. Now you have a big problem. You will not be able to complete your purchase without dramatically inflating the stock price. Another way of saying this is that at today's price, there is not nearly enough stock available for sale to meet your needs—and in order to bring sufficient shares out of the woodwork, the price must be raised. The amount you pay for your shares will be considerably higher than if you had only a small order, and your overall return will be commensurately smaller. The opposite will happen if you decide to sell a large block of stock: you will seriously depress the price, again lowering your return.

This decrease in return experienced by large traders is called 'impact cost', and it goes straight to the bottom line of a fund's return. Unfortunately, it is almost impossible to measure and more unfortunately it is borne by the end investors themselves.

Now as you would have noticed that the combined effect of all these trading costs is not so easy to calculate. But there have been brave hearts and there will always be. Three economists, in one of their studies, found that the average trading costs for a typical mutual fund is 1.44 per cent per year.[5] This means that these trading costs are perhaps the most expensive component of investing in a mutual fund, but the industry has deemed it too tough to quantify, and, thus, it goes unreported in the brochures.

OTHER COSTS

While there are multiple other costs, the following two are the major ones and need to be explained. So here we go.

Cash Drag

It is the cost of having cash in your portfolio. Cash is frequently held by mutual fund managers to maintain liquidity for potential transactions and potential redemptions by mutual fund owners. This usually brings down the return of the investor as cash held earns 4 per cent but stocks on an average earn in the range of 10–15 per cent. According to a study, the average cost from cash drag on large-cap stock mutual funds over a 10-year time horizon was 0.83 per cent per year.[6]

Soft-Rupee Cost

One of the most difficult mutual fund expenses to estimate is called soft-rupee cost. This cost comes into play when mutual fund managers are buying and selling stocks within the mutual fund's brokerage account(s). Frequently, mutual fund managers may direct the money being managed to brokerage companies providing them with research and/or other services, even if the brokerage companies are not providing the most cost-efficient brokerage commissions involved with buying and selling stocks. Essentially, this is a quid pro quo arrangement.

---

[5] Roger Edelen, Richard Evans, and Gregory Kadlec, 'Shedding Light on "Invisible" Costs: Trading Costs and Mutual Fund Performance', *Financial Analyst Journal* 69, no. 1 (2013).
[6] William O' Reilly, *Dealing with the Active* (2000). Available at https://www.etf.com/publications/journalofindexes/joi-articles/1159.html (accessed on 11 January 2020).

The mutual fund manager gets special services and/or research, and the brokerage company gets the brokerage business at a premium rate. This effectively keeps this cost out of the public's eye, giving a fund the artificial appearance of lower than actual expenses. A research study by Stephen M. Horan suggested that US soft-dollar brokerage commissions may total $1 billion annually, or up to 40 per cent of all equity trading costs.

Now all these are a whole lot of fees that you are paying to your mutual fund company.[7] And when we combine all of them together, it comes a whopping amount of 3.17 per cent per year.

A PERCENTAGE OF WHAT?

Now you would say, 'Okay, I agree. The cost of investing in a mutual fund is 3 per cent. But what this 3 per cent is going to do to my wealth?.

Before I answer your query, let me ask you a question. What is this 3 per cent of? Is this a per cent of your total invested amount or your total income? The answer is this 3 per cent is of the total invested amount. For every ₹100 that you invest in a mutual fund, you pay ₹3 to your mutual fund company and brokerage houses. But is it your true fee—the true cost that you are incurring? The answer is no. You are incurring a bigger cost than what you have been taught by your fund manager and stockbroker. Let us see the following example.

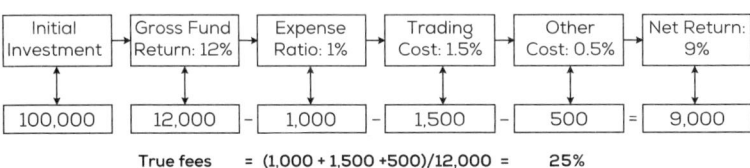

Initial Investment	Gross Fund Return: 12%	Expense Ratio: 1%	Trading Cost: 1.5%	Other Cost: 0.5%	Net Return: 9%
100,000	12,000	− 1,000	− 1,500	− 500	= 9,000

True fees = (1,000 + 1,500 + 500)/12,000 = 25%

Note: Adapted from Demos Analysis and updated to include the findings of Ty A. Bernicke.

---

[7] Thanks to Hiltonsmith and Bernicke for bringing out these fees so that the common investors can understand what they are paying to their fund managers and stockbrokers.

I hope I don't need to explain any further. The amount of ₹1 lakh that you invested is your own money (which you most probably earned and saved from your salary or business income). It was there with you before you invested and is rightfully yours. And as the terminology goes, this ₹1 lakh is not your investment income but the principal. The income that you earned from your investment is ₹12,000 (not ₹1 lakh) and it is from this ₹12,000 that you are paying the total fees of ₹3,000. So total fees that you are paying to your mutual fund company is 25 per cent of your income.

As I have told you earlier also, the entire business of investment has been made so obscure and so misleading that the common investors get confused and often intimidated by the whole process. And to bring these innocent investors, the fund managers and stockbrokers express their fees as something as just 1 per cent or 2 per cent and from the figure itself it appears as if they are charging so less fees. Imagine, mutual fund companies selling their fund saying, 'We charge 25 per cent of your income as our fees. Invest with us'. What are the chances that anyone will ever go to that fund? Nil. But when they say, 'We charge 2 per cent as our fees', everyone rushes to them. Yes, it's all about framing and making a fool of the common investors.

Now, one of the justifications which the fund managers cite for quoting fees as a percentage of AUM and not as a percentage of investment income is that since the investment income varies every year, it is difficult to estimate the fees as a percentage of income and, hence, they quote it as a percentage of AUM. In fact, upon hearing their justification, I thought shouldn't they charge investors only when they help investors make some money and, hence, express their fees as a percentage of income. But then I thought, maybe I am thinking too good about them.

The reality is that fund managers and stockbrokers are charging nearly 25 per cent of your investment income and if you still feel that it is very less and cheap then my best wishes are with you.

I would just pray that somehow you don't fall prey like Robert Hiltonsmith who once quoted in an interview, 'I save in it. It hasn't seemed to go up. It's awful. I kept checking the statement. I'd be like, "Why does this thing never go up? This is weird"'.

Now let me tell you one thing. If the maths is working against you, then even the sincerest of the prayer may not work for you.

THE IMPACT OF COSTS

Now, the question comes: what is the impact of these fees that you pay to your fund managers and stockbrokers and whether it's really worth paying that much of money?

Many people with whom I have interacted on this topic say that fund managers and stockbrokers are doing their job and, hence, they should be compensated. True, they should be compensated for the hard work they do but when it comes to your money which is going to be used to pay their salaries and bonuses, you should ask yourself a question whether you really need their service and whether they really do something which justifies the high fees and commissions they ask for. We all have been taught since our childhood that if we want to get something good, we need to pay a higher price for it. Unfortunately, in investment, that maxim doesn't work because every rupee that is paid in fees and commission is a rupee less that we receive on our investments.

As we have already seen that given the circumstances under which our analysts operate, their job of analysing securities and picking stocks is as good as throwing darts on the stock page. Second, we also saw that more than 60 per cent of active mutual funds don't even match to the performance of index fund. So what is happening is that you are paying all these fees and commissions to your fund manager for underperforming the stock market and giving you a suboptimal return. Well, it's so bad a choice that even a grade 6 kid would say you are killing yourself one cut at a time. David Swensen, the chief investment officer of Yale University's endowment fund which he has grown from $1 billion to nearly $24 billion and often called as Warren Buffet of institutional investing says, 'Overwhelmingly, mutual funds extract enormous sums from investors in exchange for providing a shocking disservice'. In the article, 'The Blame Game', *the Economist* of London puts it straight and to the point:

> *The truth is that, for the most part, fund managers have offered extremely poor value for money. Their records of outperformance are almost always followed by stretches of underperformance. Over long periods of time, hardly any fund managers have beaten the market averages.... And all the while they charge their clients big fees for the privilege of losing their money.... It is better to invest in an indexed fund that promises a market return but with significantly lower fees.[8]*

Now let us see the impact these fees have on your final wealth. Imagine you invest ₹10,000 in a mutual fund at the age of 25 and leave it to grow with time. Now, assuming this particular fund has been able to deliver an average annual return of 15 per cent per year, your investment would grow to ₹26.78 lakh. But wait, you won't get all of that. Assuming you pay a very modest fess of 2 per cent (of your AUM) per annum what you would get at the end is ₹13.27 lakh (less than 50% of the total money). And if we consider the fees to be 3 per cent (much more realistic), you will end up with ₹9.30 lakh. So what is happening is that you put your money, take all the risk and end up with just ₹9.30 lakh and your fund manager and stockbroker run away with ₹17.48 lakh. No wonder the average investors are so pissed off with their return from the stock market that they think it is the market, which is the villain, but the reality is something else.

---

[8] *The Economist*, 'The Blame Game' (3 July 2003).

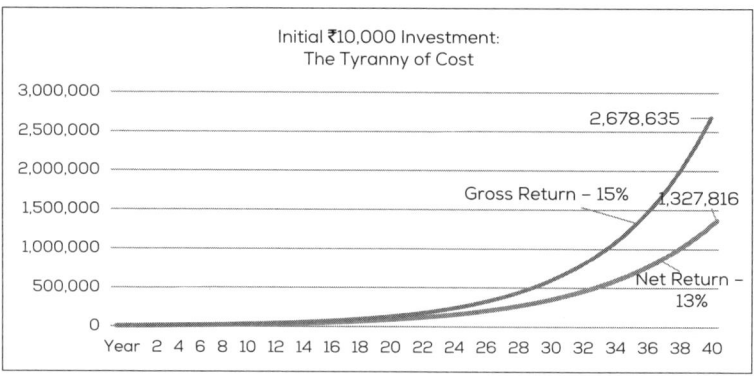

The harsh reality is that our fund manager and stockbrokers, sitting at the top of the investment food chain, eat an excessive share of the returns delivered by our financial market and that too without investing a single paise of their own. The real investors like you and me, who are inevitably at the bottom of the food chain, are left with a shockingly small share. Well, you don't need to incur that much of loss if you chose to invest in a low-cost index fund that tracks the broad stock market.

Remember, investment is a probabilistic event—you don't know what you will get. But your cost is a deterministic event—you need to pay 3 per cent of your AUM; no matter what. And it doesn't take much of a genius to realize that the only way to increase your net return is to bring down the quantum of this deterministic event (cost) as much as possible because anyway we don't have much control on the gross return since it is probabilistic.

The Financial Research Corporation, which provides research and strategic consulting services for investment products once conducted a study to determine which of the 11 common predictors of future mutual fund performance worked. The predictors studied were morningstar ratings, past performances, expenses, turnover, manager tenure, net sales, asset size, alpha, beta, standard deviation and the Sharpe ratio. And their study's conclusion was that *the expense ratio is the only reliable predictor of future mutual fund performance.*[9]

HOW INDEX FUND WINS?

One of the reasons why index fund delivers a better return on an average to its investors is that with index fund you save a lot on various fees and when you save that money, it comes back to your own pocket. Further, when these are compounded over time, the result is something you should never miss. Remember, with an index fund you *don't* need to pay:

- Marketing fees: Index fund doesn't spend money in marketing and advertising.

- High management fees: Since index fund is not trying to beat the market but simply mimic it, its fund managers are not paid any huge bonuses. Further, the salaries paid are much less as they don't hire any 'expert' stock analyst as their job is just to invest in stocks which are present in the index. No brain applied here as the job has already done by the market.

- Trading cost: Index fund doesn't trade and, thus, you are able to save all those commissions to stockbrokers, bid/ask spreads and market impact cost.

- Other cost: Since investors in an index fund hold their investment for a longer period, the index fund doesn't hold much cash, and this increase the return of an index fund.

However, for active mutual fund when we subtract these costs, the returns of investors as a group fall short of the market return by an amount precisely equal to the aggregate amount of those costs. This is the simple, undeniably reality of investing and you can't

---

[9] Mel Lindauer, Taylor Larimore, and Michael LeBoeuf, *The Bogleheads' Guide to Investing* (Hoboken, NJ: Wiley, 2014).

escape this fact. In the words of John Bogle, 'we investors as a group get precisely what we don't pay for. If we pay nothing, we get everything'. Definitely, we can't have a situation where we don't pay anything, but the index fund comes pretty close to that.

LESSONS FOR THE INVESTORS

- Cost is an integral part of the investment just as return is.

- Increasing your cost doesn't guarantee a higher gross return. What it guarantees is a lower net return.

- Viewing mutual fund fees and commissions as 3 per cent of AUM is a wrong idea. The correct approach is to consider the fees as 25 per cent of your investment income.

- Over your investment life of nearly 35 years, you would pay more than 50 per cent of your gross return to your fund manager and stockbroker if you chose to invest in the typical active mutual fund.

16 The Mirage in the Desert
Chasing Past Performance Is Injurious to Wealth

Imagine that you are sitting in your home browsing on the Internet. You search 'best mutual funds to invest' or 'top performing mutual funds' and there you have a list of all the mutual funds which are topping the chart. You check their past performance, their AUM, the stars provided by different rating agencies and read different reports written by the 'experts'. Once you get yourself convinced that this particular fund is a good fund, you invest your hard-earned and even harder saved money into the fund thinking that it will repeat its past performance and you would be able to multiply your wealth just like those 'experts' are predicting. But one year down the line when you check your account balance, you don't see the appreciation (which you had expected) in your invested money and just like our Robert Hiltonsmith you think where all the fund's superior performance went. Welcome to the mirage of the financial market!

Most of the individual investors when they decide to invest in an (active) mutual fund the three things that they usually look before investing are the past performance of the fund, its AUM and the star rating as assigned by the different rating agencies. Of these, the past performance (particularly the most recent ones) is the most watched criteria by the investors. There have been multiple studies on mutual funds flow and it has been found across the studies that flow of new money to mutual funds were driven primarily by the past year's fund performance, that is, the best performing funds attracted most of the money confirming that new money indeed chased the best performers.[1] A similar study by three economists also confirmed that investors buy funds with strong past performance. In the study, it was found out that over half of all the fund purchases are of funds ranked in the top 25 per cent of funds based on their last year performance.[2]

Also, some of the investors also look at the fund manager, their educational qualifications and their track record. Now of all these parameters, we have already seen how a bigger AUM plays a destructive role in bringing down the fund performance and how the skills of the fund manager (if any) do no good to end investors as all the benefits of such skills are eaten away by fund manager himself. Now we will see why chasing the past performance is a futile effort and a bad benchmark to decide which fund to invest with. And yes, those stars that rating agencies assign to the fund are as misleading an indicator as the claims purported by the fairness cream in their advertisements.

REVERSION TO MEAN

One of the primary reasons why chasing performance is a futile effort is because stock returns tend to mean revert. We have already encountered this phenomenon in Chapter 3 where we discussed how a period of good returns is followed by a period of low returns and vice versa. This RTM is so pervasive that no stock or fund can escape from this. John Bogle, the founder of Vanguard, calls this phenomenon Newton's law of gravity in the financial market. Further, this force of gravity becomes more powerful the farther someone is away from their mean, forcing them to revert to their mean sooner rather than later. The only thing is that no one knows for sure when such a phenomenon would occur, that is, when a

---

[1] Zoran Ivkovic, and Scott Weisbenner, 'Individual Investor Mutual Fund Flows', *Journal of Financial Economics* (2009); Erik Sirri, and Peter Tufano, 'Costly Search and Mutual Fund Flows', *The Journal of Finance* (1998).
[2] Brad Barber, Terrance Odean, and Lu Zheng, 'The Behaviour of Mutual Fund Investors' (working paper, University of California, Davis, 2000).

stock or fund going up will start to decline and similarly when a stock falling freely will suddenly change its course and start its bull run.

Now before we proceed further, it is important to understand one important aspect about this mean reversion process which many people find confusing and misleading. Most people confuse RTM as something which hovers around the value of zero. So going by this hypothesis, people think that if a stock has delivered a return of 10 per cent in one year then it is likely to deliver a return of negative 10 per cent the next year. This is a wrong way of looking at the mean reversion process.

What mean reversion essentially means is that the stock return tends to move to its *mean return* over a period of time, that is, the *stock return will converge to its long-term norm over time*. Hence, period of exceptional returns is very much likely to be followed by periods of below average performance and vice versa. So if a stock has a mean return of 12 per cent, that is, its fundamental return (comprising of dividend yield and earnings growth) has been around 12 per cent and if this stock delivered a return of 15 per cent last year then it has a good chance of delivering a return which would be below 15 per cent the next year; so that the average return of the two years regress towards the historical average return of 12 per cent.[3]

Daniel Kahneman shares an interesting story on RTM in his book *Thinking Fast and Slow* when he was teaching flight instructors in the Israeli Air Force about the psychology of effective training. When Kahneman told the instructors that 'rewards for improved performance work better than punishment for mistakes', one of the instructors said:

---

[3] This is just an example to demonstrate the mean reversion process. Further, it is not necessary that RTM works every year. There have been instances when a stock witnesses a bull run for 7–8 years continuously and then reverts to its mean return thereafter. Similarly, a stock may continue to decline for 4–5 years before the hammer of RTM pulls it up.

> *On many occasions I have praised flight cadets for clean execution of some aerobatic manoeuvre. The next time they try the same manoeuvre they usually do worse. On the other hand, I have often screamed into a cadet's earphone for bad execution, and in general he does better on his next try. So please don't tell us that reward works, and punishment doesn't, because the opposite is the case.*

Kahneman then goes on to say that the observation of the instructor is correct: occasions on which he praised a performance were likely to be followed by a disappointing performance, and punishments were typically followed by an improvement in the performance. But the inference he had drawn was completely wrong. Naturally, the instructor praised a cadet only when he delivered a performance which was far better than the average. But the cadet was probably just lucky on that particular attempt and, therefore, likely to deteriorate regardless of whether or not he was praised. Similarly, the instructor shouted into the cadet's earphones only when the cadet's performance was unusually bad and, therefore, likely to improve regardless of what the instructor did.

A similar experience I had encountered while working as a corporate banker. One particular year, our department had bagged certain good deals and the fees that the bank earned was huge. In fact, the fee income was so high that almost all the top management started praising our department and the people who had worked on those deals. As everyone started to send congratulatory mails, they ended their message with, 'Keep up the good work. Let's work together to achieve higher and earn better income next year'.

When I was reading those mails, I thought to myself, 'Are they in some kind of illusion or simply motivating their lower cadre to keep working hard?' I was not sure what was their intention but one thing I was very sure that this performance is not likely to be repeated the next year. And guess what, our department performance the next year was much lower than the last year. And many of the people were rounded up for not keeping up and matching to their performance.

The aforementioned two stories again reveal the principles of the RTM in action. Until and unless we are working as a pre-programmed robot, our performance in any activity is likely to be affected by random fluctuations. And any superior performance on a particular day or in a particular attempt is likely to be followed by a not-so-superior performance the next day. Similarly, any below par performance is likely to be followed by a much better performance. Fortunately, or unfortunately, the stock return is also impacted by the same RTM. Benjamin Graham in his book *Security Analysis* says:

> *Abnormally good or abnormally bad conditions do not last forever. This is true not only of general business but of particular industries as well. Corrective forces are often set in motion which tend to restore profits where they have disappeared, or to reduce them where they are excessive in relation to capital.*[4]

Remember, rarely do companies have an impenetrable competitive advantage which can protect it from all its competitors always. We all have witnessed how some great companies flounder and are pushed back into darkness and how bad companies rise from their ashes to become every investor's heart-throb. And that is why it is said that time doesn't remain the same for everyone. With time, great companies become less great. Bad companies become less bad. And good companies become average. And the stocks prices reflect all these realities sooner or later.

Now the question comes: why does stock return exhibit such mean reversion phenomenon? Well, one reason as stated earlier is that

---

[4] Benjamin Graham, and David Dodd, *Security Analysis*.

the fundamentals of the company change over time and, hence, there is a mean reversion phenomenon. This particular explanation has more to do with the seasonality and business cycle of the company and the industry overall. However, another reason theorized by the Nobel Prize winning economist Richard Thaler is that it is the investor's overreaction to the meaningless stock price movements that creates the conditions for mean reversion. Thaler along with his student De Bondt, who later became his colleague and is now an eminent professor, speculated that investors overreact to short-term, random fluctuations in stock prices, and this overreaction causes the stock prices to temporarily depart from their intrinsic value.[5] And as the investors come to the reality, the stock price moves back to the level where it should be.

In their study, Thaler and De Bondt made two portfolios at regular intervals: the *Winner* portfolio consisting of best performing stocks in the preceding period and the *Loser* portfolio consisting of worst performing stocks and observed their return over the next period. And what they found out was something which many of the investors who pick funds based on their past performance wouldn't like much. *They found that portfolios of prior 'losers' outperformed the prior 'winners'.* And nearly 36 months after the portfolio formation, the stocks which were labelled as 'losers' earned about 25 per cent more than the 'winners' stocks.

RTM works as flawlessly in the stock market as the law of gravity works in our physical world. Just as the apple cannot fly to the sky, so are the stocks. Yesterday's winner will most likely be tomorrow's loser and vice versa. The mutual fund industry is well aware of this phenomenon and know that nearly all top performers eventually lose their edge. Then the question arises why do all the mutual fund companies indulge in expensive and misleading advertising and promotion of their most successful past performers. It is

---

[5] Werner F. M. DeBondt, and Richard H. Thaler, 'Does the Stock Market Overreact?' *The Journal of Finance*, Vol 40, No. 3, 1985.

because promotion of funds with high past returns brings in lots of new money from the gullible investors to the fund houses and with this also come the fat fees to the advisors and bonuses for the fund managers. Yes, the fund managers are highly rewarded for their transitory past success which they are very much unlikely to repeat. John Bogle explained this (mal)practice of the mutual fund industry when he said:

> *Despite compelling evidence of that outcome, fund advertisers consistently hawk top performers. Fund organizations know full well that today's idols have feet of clay. But as long as there are believers in witchcraft, the purveyors of witches' brew will create and peddle elixirs and panaceas, engendering costly and counterproductive investment choices that inevitably come to grips with yesterday's realities, not tomorrows.[6]*

Another question that you should ask is if you have ever seen the promotion of a fund that has had either a low absolute return or a subpar relative return? Chances are that you wouldn't have seen. Why fund houses would advertise them when they have a hero in a group of nine other zeros? They will showcase that hero in every media outlet and lure investors to bring in their money. Remember, promotion of funds based on past performance lead you in the wrong direction. Ignore them. Chances are that it won't make a cut the next year.

DEAD MEN TELL NO TALES

The second reason why looking at the past performance to gauge the future performance is a very bad metric is because the past data that we see are not what the reality is. It is not that the past data have been fudged. The reality is that the past data of the mutual fund

---

[6] John C. Bogle, *Common Sense on Mutual Funds.*

performance that we investors get to see are not complete. Why? It is because the past data don't include the performance of the mutual funds which have been killed, removed or merged with some other fund.

Yes, just like the mutual funds are born, they also die. To put it using a more appropriate word, the mutual funds are *killed* by the mutual fund companies. Naturally the funds which are killed are not the top performers but the ones lying in the bottom. So to improve their report card, the fund houses simply remove their laggards from the card itself. Just like the racing horse who stops performing are sent to the slaughterhouse, so are the mutual funds which have stopped delivering superior results. While killing the racing horses is illegal and unethical in many countries, killing of mutual funds is perfectly legal. And whether it is ethical? That I would leave up to you to decide. John Bogle said the same thing in his usually unforgiving tone:

> *The reality is that the mutual funds that we hear the most about are those that have lit up the skies with their glow of past success. We don't hear much about those that did well for a while— even for a long while—and then faltered. And when they falter, they often go out of business—liquidated or merged into other funds. Either way, they vanish, consigned to the dustbin of mutual fund industry.[7]*

Remember, when you look at the past fund performance in your daily newspaper, or even a sophisticated mutual fund database, you are not looking at the complete sample of funds. What you look at are those funds which have done good in the past and survived. The losers are not present there because they didn't survive. The mutual fund company killed them and removed their

---

[7] John Bogle, *The Little Book of Common-Sense Investing.*

record so that their average performance looks better than what it really is. This phenomenon is called *survivorship bias* in the mutual fund industry. The funds that were recently put out of their misery because of poor performance do not make it into record unless you don the hat of Sherlock Homes and go out of your way to find them. It's estimated that including these defunct funds would decrease the performance of (active) mutual fund performance by about 1.5 per cent every year.[8] Yes, actively managed funds are even worse than they appear to look.

Vanguard, which is the world's second largest mutual fund company, conducted a study on the long-term returns of mutual funds from 1970 to 2005 on 355 equity mutual funds that existed in the US market in 1970. Of the total 355 mutual funds that were live and breathing during 1970, 223 of the funds went out of business by 2005.[9] In other words, two-thirds of the funds couldn't live for more than 35 years. Now if your fund cannot last that long and if you are prudent enough to be a long-term investor, then can you really afford to invest with such funds?

But you would say that these data are of the US market. What about India? Well, for Indian market we don't have data for as long as 35 years, but we do have data for the past 10 years. And as per the SPIVA report for the year ending 2017, the survivorship rate for the equity mutual fund in India was around 70 per cent[10]—meaning that of the 100 funds that was present in 2007 only 70 of them survived in 2017 and the remaining 30 were removed and put out of sight of the common investors in a span of 10 years.

Killing of the bad performing funds and the phenomenon of survivorship bias is not only a thing of the West. It is the inherent nature of the mutual fund industry across all economies. The fact

---

[8] William Bernstein, *The Four Pillars of Investing.*
[9] John Bogle, *The Little Book of Common-Sense Investing.*
[10] S&P BSE Indices, 'SPIVA India Scorecard', Year-ending 2017 (New York, NY: S&P Dow Jones Indices).

that they are so bad that mutual fund companies have to kill them is nothing but a slap on the face of investors who had entrusted the savings of their lifetime into the hands of those fund companies. The sad part is that most of the investors even don't know that they are getting slapped.

PERSISTENTLY UNPERSISTENT

When we look at the historical performance, it is very easy to identify the winners. However, there is little evidence that such performance persists in the future. You look at the newspaper, magazines or Internet portal and say, 'Hey that fund has done pretty well. I think I should invest in that fund'. Now before you go ahead with your investment, you could do yourself a favour by asking one simple question. Does this fund have the persistence to be among the best going forward? If yes, then it makes sense to invest in them and if no, chances are that you are betting your money on the horse which is going to finish in the bottom half in the next race.

So before we make any judgement on the persistence of the mutual funds' performance, it's time we first have a look at some empirical data. SPIVA which monitors the performance of active mutual fund versus the passive (index) fund prepares a research report every year on the persistence of the past performances of the active mutual funds. So for the period ending 2017–2018, it was found that of the total of 571 equity funds that were in the top 25 per cent (based on their past performance) in the US stock market in 2013, only 1 of the funds remained in the top quarter in 2017 and the balance 570 funds had fallen below that top performance category. So just in a period of 4 years, the top performing funds have gone out of the limelight and their place has been taken over by other funds (who were mostly in the bottom quarter in 2013). A clear example of yesterday's winner becoming tomorrow's loser.

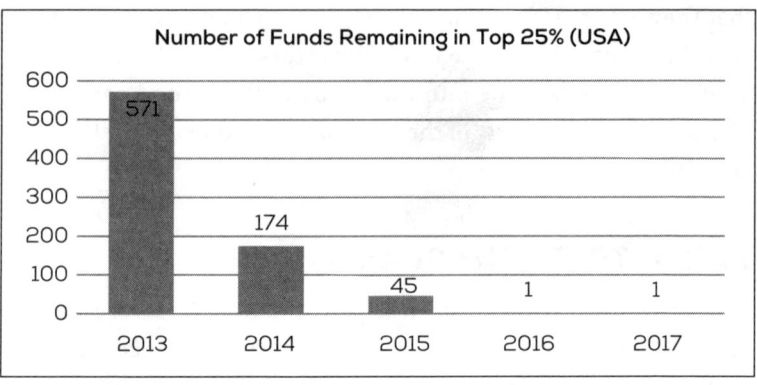

Source: SPIVA: The Persistence Scorecard (USA), July 2018.

But you would say, these data are of the US market and doesn't tell much about the Indian stock market as both the US and Indian market are not the same. Unfortunately, SPIVA hasn't done such research on the Indian stock market but has done for other emerging markets such as Brazil and Chile. Now we can safely assume that the Brazil economy is very much similar to Indian economy and that is our best case to analyse what would be the persistence of mutual funds' performance when such study was done for Indian market.

So looking at the persistence scorecard for the Brazil, we see that of the total 101 equity mutual funds in the top 25 per cent in 2013, none could maintain their record 4 years down the line. The yesterday's winner has given way to someone else and no fund—no matter who the fund manager is—can maintain its top position even for as little as 3 or 4 years.

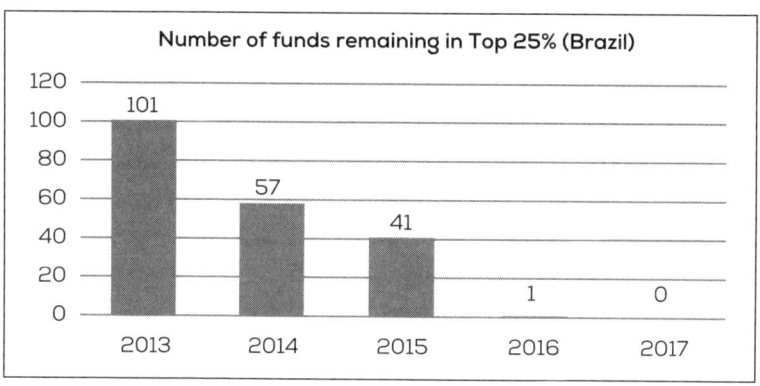

Source: SPIVA, Persistence Scorecard: Latin America, May 2018.

The following table shows the persistence performance of equity mutual funds for four economies and the result is clear and unambiguous. No fund can claim to be good enough to maintain the top position beyond 3–4 years.

Economy	Fund Count in Top 25% at the End of 2013	Percentage Remaining in Top 25%			
		2014	2015	2016	2017
USA	571	30.47	7.88	0.18	0.18
Australia	75	33.30	17.30	0.00	0.00
Brazil	101	56.44	40.59	0.99	0.00
Chile	11	9.09	9.09	0.00	0.00

Source: SPIVA.

But you would say that there are few funds which have shown consistency for 1 or 2 years. So why can't we invest in those funds and reap the benefit before it lapses. The answer is you don't know for sure which mutual fund will break the heart of its investors in year 1 and which will do so in year 2 and so on. Even the fund manager of mutual funds can't say where they will stand the next year, but yes, they will always say, 'We have been doing pretty good till now and we *expect* to do so in near future as well'. Notice the presence of 'expect' and absence of 'will'. And this replacement of one word makes all the difference. Alas! The investors are too busy looking at the past performance that they miss this little crucial point.

Now the question comes: why the mutual funds and their fund managers can't maintain their top status and almost everyone— more than 99.82 per cent of them—falls to the bottom quarters after 4 years. Well, there are multiple reasons why the superior performance of mutual funds doesn't persist. And one such reasons is the chimpanzee's random stock picking methodology of throwing the darts. Nassim Nicholas Taleb shares an interesting insight in his book *Fooled by Randomness*. He says:

> Assume there are 10,000 investment managers. Toss a coin; heads and the manager will make $10,000 over the year; tails and he will lose $10,000. We run (the contest) for the first year. At the end of the year, we expect 5,000 managers to be up $10,000 each and 5,000 managers to be down $10,000. Now we run the game (with 5000 winning managers) a second year. Again, we can expect 2,500 managers to be up two times in a row; another year 1,250; a fourth one, 625; a fifth, 313. We have now, simply a fair game, 313 managers who made money for five years in a row. Out of pure luck... a population entirely composed of bad managers will produce a small amount of great track records.[11]

Given the competitiveness of the present-day stock market, the skills of fund managers have become nothing but a hygiene factor which allows them to remain in the job but don't give them an edge to outsmart the other fund managers. On seeing such

---

[11] Nassim Taleb, *Fooled by Randomness.*

cut-throat competition and the impact of randomness in the market, Taleb adds to his coin toss analogy and says, 'the number of managers with great track records in a given market depends far more on the number of people who started in the investment business, rather than on their ability to produce great profits'.

John Bogle shares the same insight, though in a rather amusing way. He says:

> [I]f you pack 1,024 gorillas into a gymnasium, and teach them each to flip a coin, one of them will flip heads ten times in a row. Most would call that luck, but when that happens in the fund business we call him a genius!

And, what are the odds it's the same gorilla after the next 10 flips?

The thing is that though we can't call everything happening in the stock market to be entirely random but random events do have a say in what a fund manager or an average investor can get from the market. Further, this 'say' of the random events is even more powerful when we look at short intervals such as one to five years.

There is a well-known example in the sports world called 'Sports Illustrated Jinx'[12] where it is claimed that an athlete whose picture appears on the cover of the magazine is doomed to perform poorly the following season. Now, one of the reasons why it happens is that an athlete who gets to be on the cover of *Sports Illustrated* must have performed exceptionally well in the last season, probably with the assistance of a nudge from luck—and the luck is fickle.

Now the same analogy holds true of the mutual fund and the fund manager. The fund that you hear the most, the one who appears on the top of all the magazines, newspaper and the business channels have delivered a superior result in the past, probably with the

---

[12] Daniel Kahneman, *Thinking Fast and Slow.*

assistance of a nudge from luck. And since the luck is fickle, the past performance of the fund is unlikely to be repeated. And this explains why we can't find much persistence in the mutual funds' performance. In fact, Mark Carhart who is a noted investor and a professor of finance conducted a study and subsequently published a research paper which has now become the most authoritative study on the subject of mutual fund performance persistence. He concluded:

> *Individual funds do not earn higher returns from following the momentum (persistence) strategy in stocks.... Funds that earn higher one-year returns do so not because fund managers successfully follow momentum strategies, but because some mutual funds just happen by chance to hold relatively larger positions in last year's winning stocks.... Further, the results do not support the existence of skilled or informed mutual fund portfolio managers.*[13]

Similarly, in another study by two leading economists, it was found that 'past performance cannot be used to predict future returns, or to infer the average skill of active managers'.[14] Seeing all these evidences, our regulatory bodies have made it mandatory for the mutual fund companies to tell its investors that past performance is no guarantee of future results. Sad that people miss those warnings.

TWINKLE-TWINKLE LITTLE STAR

Now comes the one parameter which most of the investors usually don't miss to catch. It is the star rating assigned to mutual funds by different rating agencies.

---

[13] Mark M. Carhart, 'On Persistence in Mutual Fund Performance', *The Journal of Finance* (1997).
[14] Jonathan B. Berk, and Richard C. Green, 'Mutual Fund Flows and Performance in Rational Markets', *Journal of Political Economy* (2004).

The first thing to understand about the star rating to mutual funds is that all it does is tell which fund has done good or bad in the past and it doesn't tell anything—not even an iota of information—about the future. So when you invest in a mutual fund based on the star rating, what it essentially means is that you are driving a car looking at the rear-view mirror. And what will happen when you do so? Well, you will hit something. And that is what is being happening to the retail investors all this while.

Second, the star ratings of the fund are heavily based on their most recent performance. These ratings that you see in various Internet portals and in magazines are based on a composite of a fund's record over the previous 3-, 5- and 10-year periods with more weight given to the most recent performance. As a result, the previous two years' performance alone accounts for 35 per cent of the rating of a fund with a 10-year history and 65 per cent for a fund in the business from 3 to 5 years. A clear and heavy bias in favour of recent short-term returns.

Now the question comes how successful are fund choices based on the number of stars awarded for such short-term achievements? The answer is 'not very'. According to a 2014 study by the *Wall Street Journal*, only 14 per cent of the 5-star funds in 2004 still held that rating a decade later. Approximately 36 per cent of those 5-star funds dropped to 1 star, and the remaining 50 per cent dropped to 2 or 3 stars.[15] Yes, fund performance reverts towards the mean, or even below. As John Bogle once commented:

> *The stars produced in the mutual fund field are rarely stars; all too often they are meteors, lighting up the firmament for a brief moment in time and then flaming out, their ashes floating gently to earth.*[16]

---

[15] *The Wall Street Journal*, 'Mutual Funds' Five-Star Curse' (7 September 2014).
[16] John Bogle, *The Little Book of Common-Sense Investing.*

Now observe what happens in the real world. Out of 100 funds, 10 funds do pretty well and, thus, their net asset value (NAV) increase during their upswing and 10 funds do really bad which decrease their NAV. The 10 funds which topped the chart are now overvalued and our rating agencies seeing their past performance assign them 5 star. However, the funds which performed badly are pretty undervalued and adorn the rating of 1 star. And since our not-so-intelligent investors invest based on the star ratings, they pull out their money from the 1-star fund and put them in the 5-star fund.

Our academicians have been studying the flow of money into the funds based on the number of stars on their badge. In one such study, it was found that an amazing 97 per cent of fund inflows went into 4- and 5-star funds, while even 3-star funds experienced outflow.[17] And in a similar study, it was found out that a larger part of overall inflows to mutual funds go to those funds which were upgraded to 4 or 5 stars. Further, the funds which were downgraded to 3 stars and below witnessed the least inflow and maximum outflow from them.[18] So what investors are actually doing is that they are buying high and selling low—a perfect recipe of losing your money.

In the investment parlance, this is known as 'hot money' wherein naïve investors throw in their money into the hot funds glowing brightly because of their superior past performance. This superior past performance is more often than not a sign that the top is near. And even if it may not be the case, then the fact that the fund manager has been loaded with so much money that he can't find the worthwhile investment opportunities for all its new investors to deploy their cash results into a much lower performance than what it had achieved in the past. Guess what, most of the investors are 'hot money' investors chasing the hottest fund available in the market.

---

[17] Christopher Blake, and Matthew Morey, 'Morningstar Ratings and Mutual Fund Performance', *Journal of Financial and Quantitative Analysis* (2000).

[18] Diane Guercio, and Paula Tkac, 'Star Power: The Effect of Morningstar Ratings on Mutual Fund Flows', *Journal of Financial and Quantitative Analysis* 43, no. 4 (2007).

Now don't be tempted to think that investing in 1-star fund could help you achieve superior returns. There may be more than one reason why that fund is at the bottom. It could be the fund is charging too heavy a fees and the end result to investors is very low. It could also be that the fund manager is a lousy guy or maybe he/she doesn't have a good support from his/her stock analysts. It could also be that he/she is betting on something else or hasn't given much time on his/her strategy. Whatever be the reason, the fact that it's a 1-star rated fund doesn't guarantee in any way that it will be a 5-star fund in the next two or three years.

WHO ATE THAT FRUIT?

Another reason why chasing past performance is a bad idea is that when you invest in a good performing funds, it is not you who exactly benefit from your investment. Rather it is the investor which has invested in such funds earlier and it is the fund manager who benefits the most from your action. Confused? Let us see how.

When a fund delivers a superior result, it becomes a star for the media. So it attracts a lot of investors. And as more and more new investors pour in their money, the earlier investors with the fund benefits not once but twice. First, such investors benefitted when the fund delivered a superior result. Second, when the other investors on seeing its results start pouring in their money the fund value increases and the original investors benefit again. And since the AUM of the fund has increased with loads of new money, the fund manager benefits from the higher fees as their fees is directly linked to the asset they manage.

Now let us see what happens to the investors who jumped into the fund after it became a 5-star fund. When you put money into the fund which has gained past success, you purchase the fund at a relatively higher price. Further, your purchase of such funds pushes its level to even higher value which may not be stable and consistent with the fund's portfolio characteristics. And since the AUM of such funds has increased to a higher level and with RTM in action, sooner or later the fund's value will come down and the biggest loser of all this would be the investor who put in their money at the time when the fund had gained the media limelight and paid hefty price to grab their share.

Jonathan Clements, of *The Wall Street Journal*, quips that when an investor says, 'I own last year's best-performing fund', what he usually forgets to add is, 'Unfortunately, I bought it this year'.

THE MARKETING FIRM OR AN INVESTMENT FIRM

By now, you would have realized that our mutual funds interest is highly divergent than those of the end investors. While we investors prefer to earn net positive return, mutual funds focus on increasing its gross return and which, on an average, they fail to achieve. While we investors want our mutual fund to focus on long-term results, they focus on generating short-term superior results. While we want our expenses to be minimized, they focus on maximizing it because that is their primary source of income. While we would like our fund managers to be different, they herd in crowd often following the path taken by their peers and competitors. And while we would like our mutual fund companies to explore avenues of investment opportunities by putting their financial skills to good use, they focus on marketing and promotion, highlight their last year superstars and, at the same time, covering their damp squibs. In short, there is an inherent agency conflict in the investment business and the agent (fund managers) do not always act in the best interest of the principal (the investors).

It is also said that mutual fund companies don't spend as much time in analysing various investment opportunities as much as they spend in marketing and promoting their fund so as to attract as many as gullible and naïve investors. Seeing this malady which has now gripped the entire investment industry, the noted financial journalist and author Jason Zweig in a speech which he delivered in 1997 at an industry forum said:

> This February, two portfolio managers, Suzanne Zak and Doug Platt, left IAI, a fund company based in Minneapolis. As Suzanne Zak told the Wall Street Journal: 'It got to the point where I wanted to get back to the basics instead of being part of a marketing machine'. And Doug Platt, whose father founded IAI, added: 'My father retired over 20 years ago, and the firm's structure and focus are entirely different from what it was then. IAI is basically a marketing company that happens to be selling investments'.[19]

Zweig then went on to ask the participants, who were mostly industry practitioners, if they were primarily a marketing firm or an investment firm. The differences which Zweig quoted during his speech are many such as:

- The marketing firm has a mad scientists' lab to 'incubate' new funds and kill them if they don't work. The investment firm does not.

- The marketing firm hypes the track records of its tiniest funds, even though it knows their returns will shrink as the funds grow. The investment firm does not.

- The marketing firm creates new funds because they will sell, rather than because they are good investments. The investment firm does not.

- The marketing firm pays its portfolio managers on the basis not just of their investment performance but also the assets and cash flow of the funds. The investment firm does not.

---

[19] Jason Zweig, *Putting Investors First* (Washington, DC: The Investment Company Institute, 1997).

- The marketing firm does little or nothing to warn its clients that markets do not always go up, that past performance is almost meaningless, and that the markets are riskiest precisely when they seem to be the safest. The investment firm tells its customers these things over and over and over again.[20]

Now that you know the differences between a marketing firm and an investment firm, I leave it to your good judgement to decide if you are investing with a marketing firm or an investment firm.

LESSONS FOR THE INVESTORS

- Stocks are mean reverting. Today's winners are most likely to be tomorrow's losers and vice versa.

- The past record of the mutual funds is incomplete. Only the best surviving funds have made it to the record book while the laggards have been wiped out of history.

- Persistency in delivering superior results beyond 4 years is yet to be found.

- Stars are good to be looked at and should not be used in your decision-making, especially one regarding investments.

- Mutual fund companies have become more of a marketing firm which markets one of its hero from a pile of nine other zeros.

---

[20] Jason Zweig, *The Difference between an Investment Firm and a Marketing Firm*. Available at https://jasonzweig.com/the-difference-between-an-investment-firm-and-a-marketing-firm/ (accessed on 11 January 2020).

17 The Grand Illusion
What You See Is Not What You Get

While it is bad that investors who chase past performance don't get what they expect to get, it's worse for the investors to realize that what mutual fund reports them about their result is not what they actually get to keep in their pocket. Most of the investors are usually unaware of this fact and feel happy about their mutual fund performance as they rely on the earnings report sent by the mutual fund companies. Sadly, very few investors check their account and calculate how much they have actually received.

In 1954, Darrell Huff wrote a book titled *How to Lie with Statistics* where he showed the countless number of dodges (tricks) which can be used to fool people rather than inform. Today, the mutual fund industry has been able to use a tricky method to calculate, publish and advertise its returns which the investors never get. Now before we see what this trick is, it would be better if we understand the two methods of calculating returns, how they differ from each other and why knowing the difference between the two is important for you.

In the world of finance, usually there are two methods of calculating the return. They are known as *time-weighted return* (TWR) and *money-weighted return* (MWR). TWR is simply the geometric mean of the returns generated by the mutual fund companies. It doesn't consider the money invested in the fund and simply multiplies the return generated by the fund. So if the fund has generated yearly return of X per cent, Y per cent and Z per cent for 3 years then the annualized TWR would be simply $\{(1 + X) \times (1 + Y) \times (1 + Z)\}^{(1/3)} - 1$. *All the mutual fund companies report their return and performance using TWR.*

On the other hand, MWR is what is usually called the internal rate of return (IRR). Its method of calculating the return is not so straightforward as the TWR as it considers the amount of money that was invested in a particular holding period. So a return of 10 per cent with AUM of ₹100 crore and the return of 10 per cent with AUM of ₹5,000 crore is same when we use the TWR because all it does is simply multiply the returns and take the geometric average ignoring the money invested. However, we know from the real world that a 10 per cent return with an AUM of ₹100 crore is much easier to achieve than with AUM of ₹5,000 crore and that is where the MWR comes into importance.

Now don't get bogged down by this IRR (MWR). All the introductory finance course has this concept in the very first chapter. And your MS-Excel can do it for you very easily. All you need to do is input your cash inflows (investment) and the final amount that you got at the end of your investment period and you would have your MWR displayed on your screen. And this MWR is the real return that you would get back into your pocket and not the TWR which the mutual fund companies report.

Now let us consider a typical scenario faced by a mutual fund investor. Assume you invest ₹100 at the beginning of Year 1 and the fund generates a return of 12 per cent. Seeing a good return, you invest another ₹150 into the fund in Year 2. This year, the fund does better and delivers a return of 14 per cent. You feel good and think that you have found the right fund and invest another ₹250 into the fund. However, as happens in almost all the cases, success begets failure. So riding high on the past 2 years' performance and with an increase in the asset size, your fund delivers a negative return of 11 per cent in its third year. Hence, at the end of the 3-year period, your total invested amount of ₹500 (100 + 150 + 250) has come down to ₹488. But when you see your mutual fund performance report card, you see that the fund has generated a positive annualized return of 4.35 per cent. You scratch your head and think how an investment of ₹500 which has produced a final output of ₹488 can claim to generate a return of 4.35 per cent. You understand that you have made a net loss and yet you are being asked to believe that you have earned a positive return. Definitely, what you see is not what you have got. There must be some magic you'd say. But you don't know what the magic is and feel helpless and resign yourself to the false hope being sold by the fund houses.

Now that you know the difference between TWR and MW, you understand that the magic used by the fund houses is nothing but using the TWR approach to calculate its return.

So continuing the earlier example, if you would use the MWR method, you will end up with the result of –1.42 per cent. Now, this looks more reasonable. A loss has to be a negative return. It can't be a positive return. And this is where the investors have to see whether they are actually getting what they are made to see and believe. The computation of the two returns is presented further.

$$\text{TWR:} \{(1 + 12\%) \times (1 + 14\%) \times (1\text{–}11\%)\}^{(1/3)} - 1 = \textbf{4.35\%}$$
$$\text{MWR (X):} \ 100 + 150/(1 + X) + 250/(1 + X)^2$$
$$= 488/(1 + X)^3 => X = \textbf{–1.42\%}$$

All the returns reported in the mutual funds prospectus and annual report is the TWR, and I can very easily tell you that this is not the return what the investors actually get back into their account. The investors receive much less than that. They receive the MWR which is usually much less than the TWR. And how less is this MWR compared to TWR? Well, we don't have such a statistic for the Indian equity market but for the US equity market it has been computed and the figure is worth noting. John Bogle, the founder of Vanguard, says, 'We've compared returns earned by mutual fund investors—money-weighted return—with the returns earned by the fund themselves—the time-weighted return—and the investors seem to lag the fund themselves by three percent per year'.

TWR is like looking at the profile picture of a guy/girl on some dating site and going on the date thinking that you will get what you saw. But more often than not, it's not the case. You don't get what you see. The mutual fund report card is no different.

Now the question comes why mutual fund companies report TWR instead of MWR when it is the later return which the investors receive. Well, I don't know the exact reason, but mutual fund companies claim that it is much easier to compute TWR than to compute MWR and to save time and effort they use TWR. Further, for computing MWR, they would need to track all the cash inflows (when investors put in money) and cash outflows (when investors pull out their money). And since with so many investors putting in and pulling out their money frequently, it's difficult to do so.

Well, I would have bought their idea of difficulty in computing cash inflows and outflows had we been in the pre-computer era. Now, with improvement in computational technologies where we can find the distance between 2 stars as precisely as the distance between two electrons, where we can calculate the daily trading volume of each and every stock and where we can calculate how much foreign money is coming in and going out of our country every day, citing the difficulty in computing cash inflow and outflow from a mutual fund company looks like the excuse given by a grade 5 kid who couldn't score high in the exam saying that the exam was tough. The only reason I can think of why mutual fund companies report TWR and not MWR is because for most of the time TWR is greater than MWR and it is this relationship which helps mutual fund companies to artificially boost their performance luring more and more people to bring in their money.

Now you might ask what the reason is for TWR being greater than MWR. It is because of the simple fact that investors pour in their money mostly after a good performance and pull out their money after funds start failing to deliver. As we saw in Chapter 16, most of the investors new money go to the best performing funds and worst performing funds received the least money. Further, you as an individual investor also invest more when the fund is doing good and stop investing or probably withdraw when the fund seems to lose its touch.

The reality is that whenever the mutual funds report good performance, new money comes in bloating its asset size. And since the bad performance is observed when the fund has a higher AUM, the MWR comes down (since there is a bigger weight [of large amount of money] tied to the bad performance).

In the unusual event of money being pulled out after good performance and poured in after bad performance, MWR would be greater than TWR. But the mutual fund companies know the investors' behaviour and the reality. They know very well that as long as money keeps coming in after good performance, the TWR will always be greater than the MWR and that is why they keep reporting TWR in their performance reports.

So the next time when you see your mutual fund report card, don't believe that. Chances are that your actual return would be much less than the return advertised by the mutual fund. And it would be better if you would open your investment account and see how much money has actually come in there.

INCREASING THE SHARPE RATIO

One of the parameters of measuring the performance of a mutual fund is the Sharpe Ratio (proposed by and named after William F. Sharpe, one of the originators of CAPM). It measures the risk-adjusted excess return earned by a fund and is calculated by subtracting the risk-free return (typically those earned by government bonds/bills) from the fund return and then dividing this excess return by the standard deviation (risk) of the mutual fund's return.

Now, since a typical investor wants a higher return and lower risk, the higher the Sharpe Ratio, the better it is for the investor. This is the reason many investors also look at the Sharpe Ratio of the fund before investing in it.

But just like the returns reported by the mutual funds can be misleading, so can be the Sharpe ratio mentioned in their prospectus. In one of their research papers on *portfolio performance manipulation*, four economists have shown that Sharpe ratio can be easily manipulated by the fund manager using various techniques.[1] The important thing that you should know is that this ratio is not something you could easily rely upon and you should never make your investment decision by just using this ratio.

A HOLE IN THE BOAT

While it is bad that on an average the active mutual funds fail to beat the stock market which they claim to be their main objective—often resulting in suboptimal return—it is worse that investors are paying high fees and commission for the lower return that they are being handed resulting in even much lower return. Moreover, the return that mutual funds report card claims to achieve is not what the investors get as they receive much less than that. And even far worse of all is that whatever little is left over after the feast enjoyed by all the financial intermediaries is then taxed by our government. The poor hapless investor then gapes at the stock market and all the bull run the market witnessed over the past five years and think, 'who took away all the money that I was supposed to get?'

The issue of tax is what Bogle called the black sheep[2] of the mutual fund industry. Just like every family has a problem which they hide

---

[1] Jonathan Ingersoll, Matthew Spiegel, William Goetzmann, and Ivo Welch, 'Portfolio Performance Manipulation and Manipulation-Proof Performance Measures', *The Review of Financial Studies* 20, no. 5 (2007).
[2] 'Black sheep' is an idiom in English language where it refers to a member of a family or group who is regarded as a disgrace to them.

from the outside world, mutual fund industry keeps the taxes out of sight and out of mind from the investors. But investors can't afford to turn a blind eye to this issue. Unfortunately, most of the investors are not aware of this tax issue when they invest in (active) mutual fund. Remember, at the end of the day, you have to pay the taxes on a mutual fund's dividend income and on the capital gains (both long term and short term) distribution generated by the fund's constant churning of the portfolio.

Now the question comes: why do mutual funds do not make its investors aware (hiding would be an appropriate word here) of the high taxes they are liable to pay? It is simply because a fund manager's performance is measured and appraised only on the basis of gross return the fund earns (this return is before the fees and commissions paid to the fund managers and before the tax that would be paid to the government) and they really don't care how much *net* return the investors would get to keep.

The second reason why they keep the tax issue under the ground is that once the investors realize that what they get are the peanuts and not the almonds they would hardly hand over their money to them. Yes, just like our politicians thrive on the illiteracy and unemployment of the masses, the financial industry thrives on the ignorance of the investors as far as money is concerned.

It is important for you to understand that most of the active mutual funds are highly tax inefficient. Why? It is because of the short-term focus of their fund managers, who keep on churning their portfolio on a constant basis in an attempt to beat their benchmark. The very nature, the very fabric of the active mutual fund is to keep looking for a good 'buy' and include that in their portfolio. Similarly, they keep on selling stocks which they consider to be a good 'sell'. This activity of portfolio turnover attracts short-term capital gain which is then passed to the investors to pay. The fund managers register a good gross return (if any) in their name and the investors after paying fees to the fund manager and taxes to the government are left over with peanuts and not the almonds. Charlie Farrell of CBS MarketWatch once observed:

> *So, although their marketing material encourages investors to buy and hold, the managers certainly don't practice what they preach. What they really mean is buy and hold their mutual fund, while they trade your retirement savings like crazy.*[3]

Remember, the age-old wisdom of buy-and-hold strategy means that whatever stocks you own, you hold them for a very long term. Holding your one specific mutual fund does no good to you as your fund manager keeps trading the stocks in the fund portfolio, thereby increasing your trading cost and the tax liability. If you track your mutual fund investment closely, you will think: 'What the heck is this trading cost and capital gain tax that I need to pay. I didn't do any trading. Then why I am suppose to pay them?' Well you definitely didn't do any trading but the person whom you have appointed to take care of your money is trading your money like anything.

While there are no exact figures for the average portfolio turnover in India, it is estimated to be in the range of 90–100 per cent. What this essentially means that every year the typical mutual fund almost changes its entire portfolio. This hyperactive trading of stocks not only entails huge trading and transaction cost, it also attracts a very high capital gain tax for the investors. Unfortunately, it is the end investor who ends up paying all these costs and taxes. Remember, this tax inefficiency for active fund managers will continue as long as they continue their pattern of hyperactive trading and constant churning of their portfolio.

Now you would say, 'Okay. I agree. With active mutual funds, I pay taxes on capital gains and this reduces by overall net return. But is there anyway by which we can save these taxes?'

---

[3] Charlie Farrell, *Buy and Hold, Except Mutual Funds Don't*. CBS News (19 August 2011).

The answer is 'yes'. The index fund serves the purpose and without much ado let us see how.

The very basic premise of index fund is to remain passive, that is, buy and hold. And when you don't actively trade, you don't earn any short-term gain and, hence, avoid paying taxes. Since the index fund doesn't convert paper gains to realized gains, it doesn't attract capital gain tax and by doing so it keeps on deferring the taxes— meaning you keep postponing the taxes. And as taxes are deferred, the money multiplies significantly with each additional year that an investor elects to hold the index fund shares.

However, with the active mutual fund, substantially all gains are realized fairly quickly. And the problem created by the relatively prompt realization of capital gains by funds is that investors must pay taxes on them almost immediately.

Now this tax deferral of index fund doesn't mean that you wouldn't need to pay any taxes. You will probably owe the tax someday when you would cash out your profit, but you don't have to pay it until then. However, this tax deferral by staying passive has three advantages. Let us see one by one.

First, this tax deferral that you get with the index fund can be very much likened to an interest-free loan from the Indian government with the maturity period equal to the number of years of deferral. By postponing the taxes, you get to keep the money with yourself along with the return earned on this money, that is, instead of the government earning return on your tax liability, you get to earn the return on that amount.

Second, if you redeem your index fund shares post your retirement then the tax bracket under which you would fall would have come down drastically as you would not be earning your regular income. Also, this redemption would be taxed at long-term capital gain rate, which is lower than the tax rate of short-term capital gain meaning you would be paying a much lower tax.

Third, if you chose to bequeath your entire investment to your next generation or to your grandkids, then you would never have to pay any tax on your investment gains. In such cases, the original cost basis is stepped up to the market value at the time of death. No wonder generations after generations of the rich family keep on becoming richer and richer as they never pay any taxes on their investment to the government.

LESSONS FOR THE INVESTORS

- Investors don't get back the return as claimed by the mutual fund companies.

- Performance metric of the mutual funds are not difficult to be manipulated.

- Active mutual funds are highly tax inefficient.

18 The Wolf in the Sheep's Skin
Stockbrokers Know Nothing Apart from Selling

Most of the people often confuse stockbroker to be someone who is financially expert and who helps people in their investment decision. And when they approach them or take their advice on selecting a stock or mutual fund, they are basically asking them how they can be robbed in full daylight in front of entire public and that too legally. Now before we see how your stockbroker and the brokerage house is stripping you of your hard-earned money, let us see what the stockbrokers are supposed to do and what they actually do.

Stockbrokers, by definition, are supposed to buy and sell securities on behalf of their clients in a listed market for a fees or commission. Naturally you can't buy shares of ITC Ltd by giving your money to the CFO of the ITC and asking the corresponding shares to be transferred in your name. Similarly, you don't know any person who would like to sell their shares of ITC. So what do you do? You hand over your money to the stockbroker—the likes of ABCD Securities, PQR Direct and XYZ Broking[1]—and then they put your money in the exchange, matching a corresponding seller or use their own pool of shares if they are also active as a market maker and then assign the share of ITC in your name. And then they charge you a fees or commission for doing this transaction on your behalf.

---

[1] While it is tempting to write the full names of different brokerage firms, it would be better not to pick any names in particular. The readers can very well guess who these brokerage firms are by reading the aforementioned hints.

Naturally the more the stockbroker does such transactions—buying and selling of shares—the more money he/she makes and the less he/she does such transactions the lesser is his/her income. So given their business model, it makes sense for the stockbrokers to make people trade—buy and sell shares—as much as possible so that they can earn as much as possible. And guess what, that is what they have been doing since long. They make people trade unnecessarily. And how do they do it? It is by providing the public—the investment advisory services which they claim to be *free of cost*.

Now why you should worry about the investment advisory services of the stockbrokers? It is because apart from the art of impeccable selling where they can sell anything to anybody, they know nothing about the stock market and security analysis. The typical stockbroker that you talk to would have an undergrad degree and he/she would have cleared two very simple multiple-choice question exams called the NISM Series VIII and NISM Series IX exams. These exams are so simple that even a grade 10 guy can simply cram up the handbook in 3 hours and pass the exams with flying colours. Remember, there are no higher educational requirements or some specialized courses in finance or economics mandatory to become a stockbroker in India. Just pass that exam by mugging up the study material on your way to the exam hall and you come out with a license to become a stockbroker.

Remember your stockbroker knows nothing about security analysis—either fundamental or technical. He wouldn't have heard of Gordon growth equation or EMH all his/her life and he/she definitely wouldn't know the human biases and the irrational decisions that we all take. But he/she knows one thing for sure. His/her livelihood depends on your trading activity. The moment you follow the buy-and-hold strategy, his/her income stream stops, and he/she will start persuading you by all means to sell your existing holdings and buy new ones. The very stock that he/she would advise you to sell citing some research and report; he/she would advise another client of his/her to buy the same stock citing another research and report, and thereby earn his/her commission. Further, while you seek to minimize turnover, fees and commissions, it's in your broker's best interest to maximize these expenses. And that is the reason why you should be worried when your broker comes to you with ideas on new stocks and funds. An old broker phrase expresses this objective perfectly, 'My job is to slowly transfer the client's assets to my own name'.

And, most importantly, your stockbroker owes no fiduciary duty to you. And what does this 'fiduciary' mean? It simply means putting the interest of their clients ahead of theirs. So with no fiduciary obligation for their clients, the stockbrokers have really no interest in putting the interest of their clients ahead of theirs. Doctors and lawyers owe their clients fiduciary responsibility. Not stockbrokers. And they are bang on this. As you will see in subsequent paragraphs, the stockbrokers leave no stones unturned to strip their clients off their wealth. And the best part of all these is that they do it right in front of the eyes of their clients at the pretext of helping them. The only sad part is that the investors don't get to know that they are getting naked.

In the following pages, we'll see the legal and unfriendly practices of the brokerage industry and how its interest and yours are diametrically opposite.

YOUR BROKER IS NOT YOUR BUDDY

By now, you would have got an idea what and whom you are addressing to when you meet or speak to a stockbroker. As we already saw in the earlier chapters that your investment return, on average, will be the market return minus your expenses. And it doesn't take much effort to realize that your broker has an incentive to keep those expenses—the nearly exclusive source of his/her income—as high as possible. And if you have any doubt on this, then just look at what brokers do and don't recommend to their clients. The stock they asked you to buy last month is a 'sell' recommendation now and the mutual fund which often carries a very high cost is always in their recommendation list. And to top it all, I haven't seen any stockbroker recommending index fund to their clients till date. Michael LeBoeuf, who is an author and professor, once observed: 'I helped put two children through Harvard—my broker's children'.

THE AGENT AND THE PRINCIPLE

There is one more important player in the entire investment process. He is called the 'market maker'. This guy maintains a pool of stocks and, thus, provides liquidity in the market. So when you place a buy order with your stockbroker, the stockbroker reaches out to the market maker and the market maker sells that stock to you via your broker. In this way, the stockbroker doesn't need to find a separate individual who would be willing to sell the stock. Further, this market marker quotes two prices for the stock. The 'bid' (lower) price at which it buys stocks from the stockbroker and the 'ask' (higher) price at which it sells stocks to them. The difference between the two is called the 'spread'. Thus, every time the investor buys, and later sells a stock, he/she loses the spread between the bid and ask price. The spread goes to the market maker, who at all times maintains an inventory of stocks to allow for smooth trading.

In many cases, the broker acts as an 'agent', meaning that he/she and his/her company are not the market makers. Instead of earning the spread, the broker earns the commission from the investor for every transaction he/she executes. But frequently the broker acts as 'principal', meaning his/her company is, in fact, the market maker. In this case, they do collect the spread and are not allowed to charge the additional commission from the investors.

Now comes the twist which most of the people are not aware of. The commission which the broker earns just for executing the trade is small compared to the spread earned for being the market maker. And when you place a buy order with your stockbroker, you will never find out whether the stock your broker purchased was acquired from another of the firm's client at a much lower price or was it from a market maker. If the purchase is from its own client meaning the stockbroker is acting as the 'principal', you will be told that there is no brokerage commission and you become happy that your broker is such a nice guy.

But the catch is that when your broker is acting as the 'principal'— the market maker—he/she usually can't hold the entire universe of stocks as an inventory, neither could he/she easily find clients who would have all the stocks. He/she will usually have access to some small set of stocks when he/she is acting as the 'principal'. And since it is in his/her interest to earn the spread than the commission, he/she will always recommend you buy stocks which he/she has in his/her own pool of stocks. Needless to say, the stock recommendation that you receive from your stockbroker is highly biased and serves only one purpose—to help them earn as much spread as possible and if they are unable to earn the spread they will make sure that they get to keep their commission intact.

Also, many brokerage firms buy some of the not-so-successful IPOs at a heavy discount and unload those toxic wastes to naïve investors citing some beautifully crafted equity research reports. And brokers who can dispose of such shares to unsuspecting clients are rewarded with bonuses and prizes which, many a times, are exotic foreign vacations. Now, the question comes: are you buying stocks for your future or did you just buy a ticket to New Zealand for your stockbroker?

THE INVESTMENT NEWSLETTER

Of all the services, whether free or paid, provided by the stockbrokers, the worst of all is the investment newsletter and their stock recommendations. Also known as the investment insights and by other fancy names, these newsletters claim to provide some kind of foresight to the investors so that they can buy those recommended stock before it goes on to become a multi-bagger.

Have you ever thought how your stockbroker comes up with his/her recommendations? Do you think that he/she carefully analyses the market, reading through the annual reports of each and every stock, looking over each company's fundamentals, industry trends and the performance of the overall economy? No. The typical stockbroker can't do that because they know about security analysis as much as your car salesman knows about mechanical engineering. Yes, stockbrokers are not the go-to finance guys but the run-away-from salesmen. So how come they come up with their recommendations?

Usually your stockbroker receives the list of recommendations from his/her company's headquarter where all the security analysts are busy preparing various research reports. These analysts then send their recommendations simultaneously to thousands of brokers spread across the country. Two–three days later, you are presented with the hot tip from your broker. It is not that these reports are always bad. The problem is that you, as a small retail investor, are last in the line of information flow. The large institutional players—mutual funds, insurance companies, pension funds—have received the news long before you got to know the hot tip and the price of the stock has already been bid up by the time your broker phones you with his/her recommendations or sends an e-mail with his/her tips. And when you act on those recommendations, you lose because the food that your broker presented on your plate was cold and stale.

Second, in the world of investments, no one knows for sure where the market is going to head tomorrow or in a week's time or probably after a month or year. And, most importantly, no one knows which stock will do better tomorrow and which stock will underperform. But your stockbrokers won't accept this fact as it will put him/her in an awkward position. So what does he/she do? He/she recommends stocks and with this he/she kills two birds with a single stone. First, it gives you an impression that he/she is an expert of his/her field and knows everything about the market. Second, it induces you to act on his/her advice and you start buying/selling on his/her recommendation, thereby generating commission and spread income for him/her and his/her firm.

THE INSIDER TRADING

Stockbrokers are like the gatekeepers of the stock exchange and no stocks could be bought or sold without them. This gives them an advantage which no other player in this entire game of stock investing has. And when the stockbroker has any kind of advantage, they exploit them. Let us see how.

When an investor places a buy/sell order of a particular stock, the stockbroker is the first person to know this and before executing such orders he/she can inform any other person and/or institute who then, in turn, can take advantage of such trade orders. A team of economists has found evidence that brokers routinely leak confidential information about large stock trades to their best and most lucrative clients.[2] And these lucrative clients then reward the brokers in cash or kind. So when a savvy active investor submits a trading order through a brokerage firm, for example, the brokers may exploit this information by telling their favourite clients all about it. Those clients can then imitate that investor's strategy, thus earning higher returns themselves—to the detriment of that investor and the rest of the market, which was not privy to the leak. Professor Di Maggio from MIT who is one of the economists in the aforementioned study says, 'If I'm the broker, then I know an order, and I know how this will impact the price; what I can do is use this information to generate more and more commissions from my best clients'.

[2] Marco Maggio, Francesso Franzoni, Amir Kermani, and Carlo Sommavilla, 'The Relevance of Broker Networks for Information Diffusion in the Stock Market' (Harvard Business School Finance Working Paper, Boston, MA, 2016).

Now understand why the brokers leaking information to their best and the biggest clients are detrimental to the retail individual investors like you and me. When the brokers leak information about the trade they execute, they deliberately execute these orders slowly, while the big and wealthy clients of the brokers who have been informed of these orders take advantage of this period and by the time your order is executed you don't receive the price which you initially had expected for. It is very much similar to high frequency trading (HFT), though here your brokers are working against you.

In the same study, the researchers observe one more critical point about the business of fund management. They say:

> Our findings highlight that an important source of returns for fund managers in the stock market is not their superior skill or investment acumen. Rather, some managers appear to free-ride on the information provided by stockbrokers about the best ideas of other investors, which in turn is acquired thanks to the brokers' ability to observe order flow before the rest of the market.

This again proves the point that fund managers if ever earn a superior return, then it is not by any skill or expertise; it's by chance or probably by getting a tip from one of their many friendly brokers working in some big brokerage firms.

DIRECT VERSUS REGULAR

The financial intermediaries have always worked hard to make the life of common investors harder so that people like you and me give up the hope and put our money in the hands of these intermediaries who then eat a huge chunk of our money in the forms of various fees and commissions. The investment in the mutual fund was no exception. The stockbrokers and their close friends—the distributors—worked their way up so that common investors couldn't invest in mutual fund directly and had to go through them. So when the typical mutual funds cost the investors 2–3 per cent of their invested capital, the stockbroker and distributor took another 1 per cent just for taking your money and passing it to the mutual fund companies. No wonder when the stock market delivered an average return of 15 per cent, the typical mutual fund investors were handed over just another 11 per cent as the intermediaries ate their share of the pie. Mutual fund companies were also happy with this set-up as the stockbrokers and distributors helped them bring in new customers every day. This method of investing in mutual fund is typically called the 'regular' plan.

SEBI on seeing such a horrendous act of these intermediaries ordered the mutual fund companies to open a direct channel where the common investors can place their money in the mutual funds without going through the stockbrokers and distributors. This 'direct' plan would help the investors save the upfront fees paid to the stockbrokers and distributors. But since these direct plans cut down the income stream of these brokers and distributors, they hardly recommend them to the investors. They try through all the possible means to keep the investors ignorant of such a route and if someone asks about it then they will tell why it is such a bad option to go through the direct route of mutual fund investment. They will say if you chose the direct route, then you wouldn't get any recommendations, insights and newsletters, and you wouldn't get the experts look into your portfolio and suggest which stocks and mutual fund you should invest. I sometimes wonder how someone can be so arrogant and can go to any length to deceive people just to fill up their pockets.

My one piece of advice: if you ever decide to invest in an active mutual fund (though that's not what I would recommend), then never go for the 'regular' plan. Always go for the 'direct' plan and save your fees which you are unnecessarily paying to stockbrokers and distributors.

THE BUTCHER AND THE DIETICIAN

Given the very nature of their job and the advantageous position they occupy in the investment process, it should not surprise you that the result is systematic abuse of the common investors. From an insider's perspective, the brokerages appear geared almost entirely to excessive trading and the resultant fees, commissions and spreads they earn. Almost every stockbroker is given a target of collecting a minimum of 2 per cent in fees and commissions—overt or covert—on their client's assets; otherwise, they are out of job.

The most shocking aspect of the brokerage business is that brokers almost never actually calculate the investment results of their clients, let alone reflect on methods for improving them. If you have a close friend who is a stockbroker then ask him/her, how often does he/she think of improving the client's return. Chances are that he/she would say, 'Are you mad? Most of the time I think of saving my job first and if I succeed then I look for getting that bonus. Improving clients' return is not my forte'.

Remember brokers do undergo rigorous training, sometimes lasting months—not in security analysis but in sales techniques. All brokerage houses spend an enormous amount of money on teaching their trainees and registered reps what they really need to know—how to approach clients, pitch ideas and close sales. They aren't taught about the relationship between risk and return, and why trading is injurious to clients' wealth. But they are told that if they didn't fill their sales quota, they better look outside. However, sometimes these brokers are given some basic lessons on stocks and bonds, but again the purpose of these sessions is geared towards keeping them just one step ahead of their clients so that they can impress them and close the sales deal.

Once I had a chance to watch a video titled 'The Butcher vs. the Dietician'.[3] In a two and half minute animated film made by Elliot

---

[3] Available at https://www.youtube.com/watch?v<hig>=</hig>Dg5RRMAc1GY (accessed on 14 January 2020).

Weissbluth, the founder of HighTower Advisors, Weissbluth says that when you walk into a butcher shop, you will always be encouraged to buy meat. Ask any of the butcher what you should have for dinner, and the answer will always be 'Meat!' The butcher doesn't care whether a fish would be good for you or probably you should eat vegetables. But if you meet him/her and ask him/her what you should have, he/she would say 'Meat'. However, when you go to a dietician, he/she will advise you to eat what's best for your health. He/she will look at your health report and suggest what's best for your body. He/she has no interest in selling you meat if fish or vegetables is better for you. Needless to say, the typical stockbroker doesn't look like a dietician. He/she looks more like a butcher always eager to sell you 'meat'. Worse, most of the time those are rotten meat.

LESSONS FOR THE INVESTORS

- Interest of stockbrokers are highly divergent from those of the investors.

- Stockbrokers are more of an excellent salesman than a security analyst.

- When it comes to advising clients, brokers often act as butchers selling their own meat.

19

Smitten by the Hype and the Beauty
Media Houses Blare Unnecessary Horns

Some of you might be thinking what media houses are doing here when we are talking about the likes of security analysts, fund managers and stockbrokers. Do they play a role in how we invest and where we invest? Do they provide any kind of service to the investors? And does their interest align with those of the investors? Well, these are some of the questions that we would answer in this chapter.

A SYMBIOTIC RELATIONSHIP

Now, not many people know the relationship between the media houses and the fund companies and brokerage firms. The reality is that there exists a symbiotic relationship between them, though it is subtle, complex and, most importantly, very powerful. The media houses rely on the fund companies and brokerage firms to come out with some star performers so that they can highlight them and sell it to their viewers. Similarly, the fund companies and brokerage firms rely on the media so that they can market and promote their best mutual funds and trading strategies to the investors. Without the media, the people will not get to know which funds are doing good, which fund managers got the fund-manager-of-the-year award and which brokerage houses are helping their clients reap profit by providing them with high-content research reports free of cost. Similarly, our media houses need content to sell on their business news channel. And who can provide a better content than the mutual fund companies and brokerage firms with all their star fund managers and experts views on where the market is likely to be headed tomorrow and day after tomorrow?

Now why this relationship between our trios is important for the common investors? It is because unless you don't read any newspaper or magazine, don't watch any television, don't listen to radio, don't browse the Internet and have no friends, that is, in short, unless you are leading a hermit life—you are very much likely to be influenced by the world of business journalism in one way or the other. And the more you get influenced, the more its impact will be on your pocket; not positively but negatively. Let us see how!

SELLING SENSATION IS PROFITABLE THAN TALKING SENSE

Business news channels sell sensation. They talk how the market has been doing recently, which all stocks have gone up, which all stocks are moving down, which sectors are seeing some reforms and how the new government policy might impact the business in general. And to add to the aura of their show and to increase their authenticity, they run a flashing image of the market movement graphs and tickers of the various stocks and funds in the background.

Understand that the bread and butter of the financial journalist is the 'successful' fund manager, trader or newsletter writer. Every month, they come up with a new fund which has done the best in the market and show why investors should invest in those funds. Now having read this far, you would understand that there is a flaw in this type of journalism. The maths tells us that in a group of hundred there will always be one who has done the best, and the laws of probabilities tells us that the one who has done the best this month will not get to wear the winning crown the next month.

We have already seen how there is no persistence on the performance of mutual funds. So we can very easily say that all successful market timers are simply lucky coin flippers and almost all successful fund managers are fortunate and not skilled. But our media houses are there not to tell the truth but to maintain their symbiotic relationship. Afterall, crores of rupees as advertisement income would stop flowing into their account.

The noted personal finance columnist of *Newsweek* and author of multiple books Jane Bryant Quinn calls this style of journalism 'financial pornography'—alluring, seductive, but utterly lacking in value.

Now, if the viewership of these business news channels dips, they lose huge amount of advertisement commissions from mutual fund companies and brokerage house. So to keep their viewers engaged, they keep on teasing them with some experts' views and opinions and how their experts' views can help the investors reap extraordinary profits. In the book *The Bogleheads' Guide to Investing*, the authors say:

> ...the investment media churn out massive amounts of what has become known as investment pornography. Unlike valuable information, investment pornography is designed to hold your attention, get you excited about beating the market, and get you to buy products or information, with the hope of getting rich. When you stop and think about it, calling it investment pornography is actually somewhat flattering. Real pornographers deliver what they promise. Investment pornographers are more like the hooker who takes the customer's money, sits on the side of the bed, telling them how good it's going to be, and then leaves. It may be exciting, but its ultimately unfulfilling.[1]

---

[1] Mel Lindauer, Taylor Larimore, and Michael LeBoeuf, *The Bogleheads' Guide to Investing*.

THE GHOST OF 24×7 REPORTING

With 24×7 model of reporting, our media houses faced a major roadblock. They didn't have much content which they could air all day long. And since they have a target to attract and hold audience, they can't keep telling the investor one single message—ignore the market volatility and invest in index fund—all the time. So they resort to selling investment strategies of different fund managers which have worked in the past but has no guarantee if it will work in the future. And the very fact that they are disclosing such strategies to the entire world, it has a very good chance of delivering a below par return.

WOULD YOU DIG YOUR OWN GRAVE?

Imagine for some time that God Almighty comes one morning to you and because of all your noble deeds he wants to reward you. Being an investment enthusiast, you ask him to give you a foresight for 1 year about the stock market. So he agrees and tells you which all stocks will go up in the next year, which all stocks will go down, which sector will do good, how the interest rate will move throughout the year, on which dates the market will dip, on which dates it will have a bull run and what would be the major government decisions which would have an impact on the stock market for the next one year.

So with this superpower at your disposal, would you:

- Appear for an interview on a TV news channel telling people how the stock market will behave, what all stocks will go up and what all stocks will go down?

- Write, publish and sell an investment newsletter telling people what's going to happen?

- Call a business magazine editor and tell him/her the name of five stocks which all the investors should own for the next year so that he/she can run a cover story on you and those stocks in his/her next issue of the magazine?

- Go to a radio channel and tell the listeners about your superpower and how your superpower will help them become super rich?

- Start an investment course telling people how to invest, where to invest and when to invest?

- Keep your mouth shut, mortgage your house, borrow to your hilt and make a fortune?

Well, if you would do anything except for the last one, you would have distributed your entire wealth to the public and would have foregone the chance of becoming the richest person on earth.

LESSONS FOR THE INVESTORS

- Switch off your idiot box.

- If you want to learn more, read the books mentioned in the references in this book.

- If you want to learn even more, read the research papers mentioned in the references.

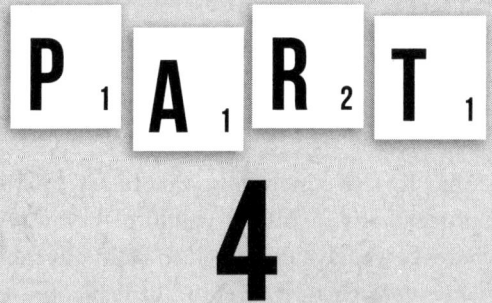

PART

4

THE SOLUTION

20 The Triumph of Indexing
In Simplicity, We Win

We have come to the concluding chapter of this book now. So before we proceed any further, it would be better if we did a little recap of whatever we have discussed so far about the mutual funds and the business of investing. Here's a little recap:

- Most of the actively managed mutual fund underperform their benchmark (they fail to become an average).

- Even though fund managers may be highly educated, their qualification and skills are of no use to end investors as they fail to deliver any superior return to the investors on a consistent basis. Further, even if there are some skills which pass the test of time then reward of those skills is earned by the manager himself/herself and end investors earn no special benefit of those skills.

- Active mutual funds fleece its customers by charging them umpteen number of different fees (both overt and hidden).

- Past performance has no correlation with the future results in any way as any superior return is more likely because of luck or chance.

- Investors get a much lesser return than those advertised by the mutual fund companies.

- Active mutual funds are typically highly tax inefficient making its investors to pay more and more in taxes.

- Stockbrokers' income depends on how much you trade and the more you trade the more you lose.

Now with so many imperfections in the typical investment process, it shouldn't surprise you that why so many investors get less than what they deserve, and why so few people chose to invest in stock market. All the drum beatings by the mutual fund companies and brokerage houses of how they are working hard to encourage investors to enter the equity market is a lie and nothing less than a false propaganda to promote themselves. They aren't doing their duty of 'financial inclusion' which they should be doing. In fact, they are doing the job of 'financial exclusion' very well making the investors run away from the stock market by charging huge fees, commissions and spreads from their customers and delivering them a suboptimal result. But not anymore. It's time the investors get to know the power of being a passive investor and how index fund can solve all the problems associated with the active mutual fund. And it's time to earn your fair share of stock market return which no one should ideally take away from you.

HORSE OF A DIFFERENT COLOUR

All through our life we have been taught, trained and preached to be the best in whatever we do because only the best ones get the best things of the life. For example, the following life principles are some of the common goals shared by most of the people who like to get something different and something better in their life.

- *Don't settle for average*: You have to be in the top in your studies and in your work. Only the best students get the best college/job and only the best employees get the bonus and promotion.

- *Listen to your heart*: When in doubt, always listen to your heart for it knows what's good for you.

- *If you don't know how to do something, ask an expert:* Learn from the expert what it takes to achieve what you have always wanted to achieve. And, if possible, hire the expert to do your job. That will save you a lot of time and you wouldn't need to reinvent the wheel.

- *If there is a problem, then try to find the solution*: You need to take action to overcome your problem. Sitting idle will not do any help. You have to be an initiator and proactive in dealing with problems.

- *You get what you pay for*: Good things always come at a good price. And at a lower price, you will get the goods or services you want which would be at best a mediocre or mostly below par.

- *History repeats itself*: The best predictor of future performance is past performance. A bright student who scored 95 per cent in his/her last exam is very much likely to repeat his/her feat and top the class next year as well. Similarly, a top performing employee of the last year is likely to be the star performer this year as well.

Now, all these principles work well in the real life. But when it comes to investments, applying these principles will make you poor and that is what is happening to most of the investors. Most of the people think that only by being active, regularly checking their portfolio, adjusting them frequently, trading at every possible signal, investing in top performing mutual funds and seeking advice from the experts, they would be able to beat everyone and earn superior returns. Guess what, we don't have much of the success stories to share who follows the aforementioned philosophy.

It may seem to be counter-intuitive, but the reality is that when it comes to investment you can be above average just by targeting to be an average. Although it sometimes pays to hire an expert, but in the world of investments there are no experts—accessible to common investors—who can help you in anything apart from motivating you to save and invest. Further, trying to fix a perceived investment problem by taking action is usually a recipe for even poorer returns. And paying a higher fees and commission to your mutual fund manager doesn't yield in better returns; rather it decreases your return by the amount of fees that you pay. Finally, using yesterday's performance to pick tomorrow's high performing stocks or funds is yet another loser's game. Investing has a whole new set of rules, and if you want to be successful in your investment journey, then you need to play by these new rules.

So is there a solution to our investment woes? Is there a way in which we can play this investment game according to its own rules and not those of other fields? And is there an approach which can help us earn our fair share of stock market return without much fuss?

The answer is yes. And probably by now, you know the solution. Invest in the entire stock market by investing in an index fund of your choice and live your life pursuing other better things than regularly watching those stock market tickers while you earn a better return than all those hyperactive investors.

INDEX INVESTING—A PASSIVE APPROACH TO A BETTER LIFE

Let us see why indexing works and why it makes sense to remain a passive investor trying to be just average in this game of stock market investing.

LOW COST

Index funds outperform nearly 70 per cent of all actively managed mutual funds in a given year and as the investment horizon lengthens, this win ratio extends easily in the excess of 90 per cent. And they do so for one simple reason: rock bottom cost. In a random market, we don't know what future return will be. However, we do know that an investor who keeps his/her costs low will earn a higher return than one who does not. That's the indexer edge.

The cost of investing in an active mutual fund is typically in the range of 2.5–3 per cent as lot of your invested money goes to pay the salaries, bonuses and vacations for the stock analysts and fund managers. By contrast, managing an index fund is very cheap and easy. Nobody has to decide which stocks to buy or sell and when to buy or sell. The passive manager simply replicates the index and keeps the stock in his/her portfolio as long as it is in the index. As a result, the cost of investing in an index fund is as cheap as 0.2–0.5 per cent. So the investor is able to save at least 2 per cent every year and this 2 per cent when compounded over a period of 30 years nearly doubles the retirement corpus people would have at the end of their investment period.

Remember, when you pay less to the intermediaries, you get more to keep with yourself. Successful investing is all about minimizing the share of the returns earned by our corporations that is consumed by Dalal Street (where the brokers and fund managers live) and maximizing the share of returns that is delivered to the *Main Street* (where the investors live).

NO FALSE PROMISES

Almost all the active mutual funds are in the business with only one single agenda and only one single promise to their investors that they would beat the market, that is, their return would be higher than the return delivered by the stock market (or their benchmark). However, the numbers show that no mutual fund has done so in the past consistently and given the market efficiency and stiff competition among the different mutual funds, none can do so in the future as well. So the belief with which the common investors invest in mutual funds are often broken.

Index fund, by its very nature, doesn't make any false promises. It simply claims that it will deliver its investors the stock market return and they are always bang on this.[1] The index funds never

---

[1] Sometimes, because of the tracking error, the index fund return is slightly lower than the stock market return, but such instances are few and the difference in the return is also small.

claim to deliver any superior result. Neither they claim that they would beat the market. They just claim that whatever the stock market as a whole will give, they will pass it on to you and they do that effortlessly without much drum beating and expensive advertisement.

TAX EFFICIENT

Most mutual fund performance data that you get to see are pre-tax, and nearly all mutual fund managers are compensated on pre-tax returns. Taxes incurred in the manager's buying and selling of securities within the portfolio is passed on to the fund shareholders—the end investors. Accordingly, mutual fund managers have little reason to minimize shareholder taxes in their pursuit of higher returns.

Broad market index fund, by contrast, have very little turnover. And since these index funds convert paper profits into realized gains less frequently, passive investors pay less tax each year to the government. Burton Malkiel in his book *A Random Walk Down Wall Street* says:

> *Index funds are … tax friendly, allowing investors to defer the realization of capital gains or avoid them completely if the shares are later bequeathed. To the extent that the long-run uptrend in stock prices continues, switching from security to security involves realizing capital gains that are subject to tax. Taxes are a crucially important financial consideration because the earlier realization of capital gains will substantially reduce net returns. Index funds do not trade from security to security and, thus, they tend to avoid capital gains taxes.*

HIGHER DIVERSIFICATION AND LESS RISK

The fastest way to become rich in the stock market is to own the Infosys before everyone else bought it and the fastest way to lose all your money is to own the next Satyam. The only problem is that identifying them in advance is impossible. The good thing, however, is that investment is not about picking individual stocks and you don't need to worry about developing such stock picking abilities. The best possible solution for an individual investor is to diversify his/her portfolio and own as many stocks as possible at the lowest cost. And the index fund does exactly that.

Remember when you own over 200 stocks in a single fund, you greatly eliminate all the unnecessary risk which is not compensated by the stock market. All the individual stock risk, all the sector-specific risk and all the risk of fund manager selection is eliminated. Only stock market risk remains, and it is this risk which you are compensated for.

NO NEED TO SEARCH FOR TOP PERFORMING STOCKS OR FUNDS

One of the main reasons why individual investors shy away from investing in the stock market is that there are too many stocks and mutual funds to choose from and they often get confused in selecting which stock or fund they should proceed with. There are more than 5,000 listed companies on the Indian stock exchange. And there are more than 2,500 mutual fund schemes available for the retail investors. Second, even if he/she decides to invest, he/she has to search which stock to choose or which mutual fund he/she should invest in and hand over his/her hard-earned money to the fund manager.

Index fund, on the other hand, eliminates all these stock/fund selection problems. You don't have to search for any right stocks/funds. You don't need to analyse any past performance. You don't have to see which particular stocks are doing good and you don't have to analyse which sector is having an edge presently.

In the book *The Bogleheads' Guide to Investing,* the authors Mel Lindauer, Taylor Larimore and Michael LeBoeuf have put it very beautifully. They say:

> *In school, it usually takes a lot of work to earn an A, less work to earn a B, and so on. In investing, if you spend lots of time and effort studying the market, or pay someone to manage your investments, you have less than a 20 percent chance of being an A investor. However, if you know nothing about investing, spend minimal time on your investments, and buy index funds, you have a 100 percent chance of being a B investor. In a world where most investors get a D or worse, B is beautiful.*

The beauty of the index fund, then, lies not only in its low expenses but in its elimination of all those tempting fund choices that promise so much and deliver so little. Focusing on the long term, doing one's best to ignore the short-term noise of the stock market and eschewing the hot funds of the day, the index fund can be held through thick and thin for an investment lifetime. The winning formula for success in investing is then owning the entire stock market through an index fund, and then doing nothing. Just stay the course.

NO DEPENDENCE ON SUPERSTAR FUND MANAGERS

Most of the active mutual fund companies hire the best of the fund managers available in the market by offering them the best of the salaries and bonuses. Most of the time, their pay package is in excess of ₹50 lakh per annum and some even earn in crores. Now, the performance of a mutual fund depends on the stock picking abilities of its fund managers.

However, we have already seen that no fund manager can claim to have such an expertise using which they can deliver superior results to the investors on a consistent basis. Any returns better than that of their respective index can be easily ascribed to mere luck or chance. And in case some of the managers have such an expertise, then the benefits of such expertise are not earned by the investors but the manager himself/herself.

Index fund, by contrast, doesn't require any superstar fund manager as you don't need any expertise to create an index fund. Index fund already has the best fund manager of the town and that too at zero cost—the market. All you have to do is see the list of stocks present in the index and pick them in your portfolio. And this can be done by writing a very simple computer program, and executing that program requires no special skill for which you would have to pay salaries in excess of crores to any of fund managers.

NO NEED TO HIRE A FINANCIAL ADVISOR

Most of the financial advisors recommend creating portfolios consisting of 10–15 asset classes—large cap, mid cap, small gap, growth fund, dividend fund, value fund, hybrid fund and debt fund. You name it and they have one such product. The only reason for such complexity is to generate fees for themselves and justify their existence. Keeping things simple would raise question on the work and service they provide. And that is why no financial advisor, broker or any wealth manager would recommend you to invest in index fund. Because if you had to invest in index fund, then why on earth you would even visit them. Investing in index fund is so simple that you don't require any of their advices and/or services. Just go to an AMC website, pick an index fund of your choice—Sensex, Nifty, BSE 100, BSE 200, Nifty 500—and invest your money. That's all. And repeat this process every month or whenever you would like to invest.

ONLY INDEX FUND CAN OUTLIVE YOUR INVESTMENT HORIZON

If you are a long-term investor who would like to invest and forget (an ideal strategy for long-term wealth creation), then you can't rely on your typical active mutual fund. It is because you never know when your fund will stop attracting new investors, and seeing no growth in the fund's AUM its manager will either kill this fund or merge with a one which is doing relatively better at that moment.

With an index fund, you can relax and go to sleep because an index fund will be there as long as the stock market is there.

HELP YOU FORGET ALL YOUR HUMAN BIASES

One of the best advantages of investing in index funds is that you don't need to take care of all the human biases and irrational decisions that we often take. If we choose to invest in an index fund, then we don't need to think of all our human biases and irrationalities. We can simply forget all the overconfidence, disposition effect, prospect theory, information cascade and herd mentality as investing in index fund is a no-brainer exercise.

A SURE SHOT GUARANTEE TO BEAT INFLATION

While index funds have multiple benefits, which have been discussed by professionals and academicians alike in various literature, they have one special benefit which not many people have discussed so far. It is that the index fund beats inflation on a consistent basis.

Inflation means that cost of the goods and services that you purchase and consume is increasing every year. So, with inflation, the price of wheat flour, rice, toothpaste, cements, and clothes, etc., increases every year and you feel a pinch in your pocket whenever you have to pay a higher price of salt or oil. And where does this increased money from your pocket goes? It goes to the company and ultimately to the shareholders of that company which manufactures those products. And what will happen if you are one of the shareholders of those companies? Your monies come back to your own pocket. So if you own a little piece of those companies that make those products, you are virtually guaranteed to stay ahead of inflation and you would get a little of the money back which those companies have been getting off from you for years.

And guess what? Index funds help us achieve this. When you invest in an index fund that purchase shares in top 500 companies of India, you virtually own a share of stocks in companies that make everything from tires to toothpastes, flour to processed food and cement to coke. And a part of the rupee that you spend on purchasing these products comes back to you when you own shares on such companies. This is one area where index funds score over direct investing into stocks and actively managed mutual funds because it is practically impossible (and not advisable also) for an individual investor to hold so many stocks on his/her own. Further, none of the actively mutual fund would hold as many as 200 or 500 stocks.

LET YOU PURSUE OTHER THINGS IN LIFE

Let's be frank here. We don't want to spend countless hours studying, analysing and watching all the short-term market trends being shown on TVs and printed in other medias. It doesn't matter how much we study or analyse; we simply cannot beat the market. The best of the fund managers is not able to do so then how can we think of ourselves achieving that feat. It is only when we accept this simple fact that we cannot beat the market consistently and accept the stock market return as our fair share of return (which is much better than the return earned by most of the active investors) we would set our sail towards growth, happiness, richness and contentment.

Moreover, investing in index fund allows us to pursue other important things in our life. Instead of watching those dumb head speaking the latest ups and downs of the market, we can spend time with our family and friends. Instead of reading those market timing newsletters, we can read something worthy which will broaden our horizon and improve our perspectives. Instead of trying to become a stock market expert, we can spend time in becoming an expert of our chosen field. And instead of having a sleepless night pondering over how our portfolios are doing, we can have a nice and peaceful sleep.

WHY PEOPLE DON'T INDEX?

Now the question comes: if indexing works so well, then why do so few investors take advantage of it? Why can't people simply accept that they can't beat the market and try to get their fair share of stock market return? The reasons for such an unreasonable action (of investing in stocks and active mutual funds) of the individual investors are manifold. Few of them which I think can explain such irrational decision are listed further.

IGNORANCE

Index fund has been in existence since 1975 and its asset size has been growing like anything. Vanguard which has championed the cause of index fund and passive investing had tough time initially when it started with this idea. However, as the common people started realizing its benefits, many of them started to switch from active fund to index fund. Vanguard is now the world's second largest mutual fund company after BlackRock and its AUM is now over $5.1 trillion. To give you a perspective, the GDP of India is just $2.3 trillion which is less than half of the Vanguard's AUM. Just imagine, a single company asset is more than double the size of our entire economy and if you think that all these people who have migrated to index fund are fools then you would need to think again. Many of my finance professors at UCLA Anderson School of Management told us in the class that a major part of their portfolio was invested in an index fund and if you think that all these economists need lessons from your stockbrokers and fund managers so that they should also start trying to beat the market, then you need to get out from your deep-seated belief and accept the reality.

In India, the mutual funds promoted by private companies started as late as the 1990s and these private companies definitely wanted to earn as much for themselves as they possible could. And seeing the growth and popularity of index fund in the developed market, they feared that if they taught the investors about such a simple product, they would lose their high fees and commission. So what did they do? They kept the entire investing community ignorant. Worse, they started writing articles, blogs and newsletters that why index fund is a bad choice for the investors and why they should stay away from them.

IT'S BORING

All through our life, we have been told that investment has to be thrilling, full of excitement and, most importantly, it should have its own entertainment quotient. And if any such financial product lacks any of these elements, then it isn't an investment and if you choose these then you are a big loser.

It has been proven in multiple studies that gambling is the second most enjoyable human activity (no activity can replace the first one when it comes to fun and enjoyment, and I hope I don't need to tell you what exactly it is).[2] People love to bet and get easy money. Why else do people throng to casinos and indulge in all sort of illegal betting when they know that, on average, they'll return with a lighter wallet?

The reality is that excitement and entertainment are two of the deadliest investment traits. If your investment portfolio has either of these two elements, then you are going wrong with your investments. Paul Samuelson, the noted and acclaimed professor of MIT, once observed: 'Investing should be more like watching

---

[2] One of my professors at UCLA once said that he had an opportunity to fly an aeroplane (not commercial one though) and he said we should try it too (there's a private aerodrome in Los Angeles where you can do so by paying the requisite fees). He added, 'you would love it and it would be the second-best experience for you all—the first one will still be having sex as you are young'.

paint dry or watching grass grow. If you want excitement, take $800 and go to Las Vegas'.

DEVOID THE CHANCE TO BECOME SUPER RICH

One of the biggest disadvantages of index fund is that it can't make you super rich by way of providing extraordinary returns. But wait, getting super rich is not and should never be the purpose of your investment. The purpose of your investment should be to get a return on your money which is fairly over and above the inflation rate. Though we may dream to get very high returns, those extraordinary returns are not a thing of the reality and sooner we accept this fact the better it is for us. Except for few exceptionally talented investors, we don't get to see anyone who has made millions and billions simply by way of investing. However, we do see many promoters and owners of businesses who are millionaires. Remember, it is hard to become a multimillionaire just by investing money, but it is much easier if you hone your primary professional skill and work towards it to progress well in your career. All the super rich people that we hear about have become rich only by their primary professional skills. Be it a doctor, a lawyer, an engineer, a businessman, an actor or an athlete. Think about Mukesh Ambani, Ratan Tata, Sunil Mittal, Azim Premji, Shah Rukh Khan, Mahendra Dhoni, Ram Jethmalani, Narayan Murthy, Naresh Trehan and the likes. All these people have worked hard in their chosen profession and it is their primary skill set which has helped them accumulate wealth. But you would say, 'what about Rakesh Jhunjhunwala?' Well, there is only one Jhunjhunwala but there are hundreds and thousands of business owners who have more wealth than Jhunjhunwala. The reality is that Jhunjhunwala is more an exception than a general rule.

Now don't get confused that investment can't make you rich. It definitely will make you rich. If your present wealth is, say, ₹50 lakh, then by regular investment you can grow your wealth to reach to the level of ₹5 crore or even to ₹10 crore over the next 20 years depending how much you save and invest every month. But if you think that you can increase your wealth from ₹50 lakh to ₹50 crore simply by investing, then it is nothing less than a daydreaming. However, if you start a business of your own and become successful, then chances of you accumulating wealth in excess of ₹50 crore is very high.

Words of Wisdom

It's the paradox of investing today: aiming for the average is your best shot to finish above average.

—Charles D Ellis, Author, Investor and Professor

Despite the superior returns generated by passively managed funds, financial publications are dominated by forecasts from so called gurus and the latest hot fund managers. I believe that there is a simple explanation for the misinformation: It's just not in the interests of the Wall Street establishment or the financial press to inform investors of the failures of active managers.

—Larry Swedroe, Author

An index fund dooms you to mediocrity? Absolutely not: It virtually guarantees you superior performance.

—William Bernstein, Author

Most investors, both institutional and individual, will find that the best way to own common stocks is through an index fund that charges minimal fees. Those following this path are sure to beat the net results (after fees and expenses) delivered by the great majority of investment professionals.

—Warren Buffett, Chairman of Berkshire Hathaway

If you buy—and then hold—a total stock market index fund, it is mathematically certain that you will outperform the vast majority of all other investors in the long run. Graham praised index funds as the best choice for individual investors, as does Warren Buffett.

—Jason Zweig, Senior Writer and Columnist

I am a huge, huge, huge fan of index funds. They are the investor's best friends and Wall Street's worst nightmare.

—Jonathan Clements, Author and Columnist

So much attention is paid to which funds are at the head of the pack today that most people lose sight of the fact that, over longer time periods, index funds beat the vast majority of their actively managed peers.

—Paul Farrell, Author and Columnist

There is a crucially important difference about playing the game of investing compared to virtually any other activity. Most of us have no chance of being as good as the average in any pursuit where others practice and hone skills for many, many hours. But we can be as good as the average investor in the stock market with no practice at all.

—Jeremy Siegel, Professor of Finance at Wharton School and Author of *Stocks for the Long Run*

Index fund operates with minimal expenses and with no advisory fees, with tiny portfolio turnover, and with high tax efficiency.

—John Bogle, Former Chairman, Vanguard Group

The fund industry's dirty little secret: Most actively managed funds never do as well as their benchmark.

—Arthur Levitt, Former Chairman of Securities Exchange Commission

You should switch all your investments in stocks to index funds as soon as possible, after giving proper consideration to any tax consequences.

—Chandan Sengupta, Author

You will never see an S&P index fund leading the best performing charts in the Wall Street Journal. But—and this is the point—your fund's returns will almost certainly beat those of the majority of actively managed funds over a period of five years or more. And you will

never see an S&P index fund at the bottom of the Wall Street Journal performance charts, either.

—Douglas A. Sease, Author

Index funds have regularly produced rates of return exceeding those of active managers by close to 2 percentage points. Active management as a whole cannot achieve gross returns exceeding the market as a whole and therefore, they must, on average, underperform the indexes by the amount of these expense and transaction costs.

—Burton Malkiel, Professor at Princeton University and Author of *A Random Walk Down Wall Street*

About the Author

Abhishek Kumar is a financial consultant with one of the world's leading valuation firm at its San Francisco office where he looks after the valuation of derivatives and other complex securities. Earlier he worked as a corporate banker for nearly six years where he helped clients raise debt to fund their business operations and capital investments.

A proponent of MPT and a believer of passive investing school of thought, Abhishek is a critic of conventional ways of managing money which he says have been designed not to help the investors but the financial institutions and the intermediaries which reap benefits by exploiting the ignorance of people. His earlier books *Master Your Money, Master Your Life* and *The Richest Engineer* have been well received.

Abhishek has earned a Master of Financial Engineering from the University of California, Los Angeles, an MBA from Indian Institute of Management Kozhikode and a BTech in Electronics Engineering from Indian Institute of Technology (BHU) Varanasi.